VIGILANTE!

VIGILANTE!

RON FAREBROTHER
WITH
MARTIN SHORT

BLAKE'S
TRUE
CRIME
LIBRARY

Published by Blake Publishing Ltd,
3 Bramber Court, 2 Bramber Road,
London W14 9PB, England

First published in paperback 2000

ISBN 1 85782 347 8

British Library Cataloguing-in-Publication Data:

A catalogue record for this book is
available from the British Library.

Typeset by t2

Printed in Finland by WSOY

1 3 5 7 9 10 8 6 4 2

For Dean, Simon and Debbie

CONTENTS

Dear Reader

Meet Ron Farebrother. His history is a murky one; his trade is a dangerous one. His story will shock and amaze you.

Ron is the terror of every criminal on the streets today, and the secret to his success as a modern-day vigilante is that he was once one of their number. In an earlier incarnation, Ron was the Ambassador — the mysterious figure that linked the US mob with their UK counterparts.

Now the tables have been turned. In this book you will read incredible stories of how Ron brought to justice the husband who tried to take out a contract on his wife for the insurance money; and how he exposed the sinister grave-robber who was so shameless, he took Ron on one of his dastardly expeditions. You will find a catalogue of crimes — told by the one man who has been on both sides of the fence — that almost defy belief.

Adam Parfitt
Editor
Blake's True Crime Library

Who saved Lenny McLean's life? Ron Farebrother. Who was offered £5,000 to put a bullet in Lenny's head but instead went straight to the 'Guv'nor' himself and warned him about the contract? Ron Farebrother. And who put both Lenny and 'Pretty Boy' Roy Shaw against each other on television for the first time, slugging it out in the ring? Ron Farebrother.

When Muhammad Ali couldn't bear the crush and mayhem of five-star hotels, who had 'the Greatest' sleeping at his home? Who cracked jokes with Frank Sinatra? Who fronted as the London crime syndicate's Ambassador to the Mafia in Hollywood? Who faced death himself when he represented those same gangsters to US fight mogul Don King? And who had a wife who became the most wanted woman in America? Ron Farebrother every time.

But now this former robber, fraudster and jailbird, once feared throughout London as 'Ron the Gun', has gone straight for almost ten years and established himself in a wholly different career. Today to police, press and even the underworld he is the 'Vigilante', the man you turn to when things need straightening out, when someone's stepped outside the bounds of acceptable behaviour and deserves massive public exposure. People like the businessman who wants his wife murdered so he can pocket a vast insurance pay-out, or the woman who wants her ex-husband crippled for life. People like the computer expert with a House of Commons pass who's a paedophile and video-porn peddler, and the thug selling sub-machine guns on the street. People like the tomb-robber looting children's graves, and the serial woman bigamist who marries illegal immigrants just so they can wangle British nationality. The Vigilante has exposed them all.

'I go where the press and the police can't go,' says Ron. 'I can step over the line to gather information when reporters and detectives daren't get directly involved. But when I've set up the operation, in go the tabloids and splash these dirty bastards all over the front page. That's how they get so many great results. If the police want to jump on the bandwagon and lock up the offenders, that's fine with me.'

Law-abiding folk may find Ron's self-justification repellent but we live in an age when most people believe crime is relentlessly increasing, however much politicians toy with the statistics. Entire communities feel helpless as homes are burgled, cars are stolen, drugs proliferate — not just on council estates but in private schools — and even four-wheel driving mothers have Rolexes snatched from their wrists. Meanwhile the police are viewed no longer as thief-takers first and foremost, but as pen-pushers, social workers and front-line targets for allegations of racism (true or false).

The police themselves feel 'cabined, cribbed, confined' — restricted by rules and regulations brought in to combat the all-pervasive corruption of major detective squads in Scotland Yard and other big city forces in the 1960s, 70s and 80s. Detectives are no longer allowed to fraternise with villains, they cannot mix and mingle in criminal clubs and dives, and their relationships with informers are under constant scrutiny. With so many detectives now assigned to 'rubber-heeling' — investigating fellow officers — it is no wonder that few big criminals get captured. 'These days we spend more time trying to catch each other than trying to catch crooks,' one disillusioned inspector recently told me. 'That's why the Vigilante and the newspapers who hire him now do the job we ought to be doing.'

Another veteran Scotland Yard detective justified the Vigilante's role in far more positive terms. 'Ron is better than any undercover cop, he's worth a hundred phone-taps, a thousand public appeals. He's done more for law and order than the last five Home Secretaries. For sure, he has been a serious villain, an ingenious con-man, and he was once even described on police files as a liar, but, as the old saying goes, it takes a thief to catch a thief.'

There is always the risk that entrapping offenders with the help of intermediaries such as Ron Farebrother may involve agent-provocateurism, verging on coercion and duress. Defence lawyers and civil libertarians are rightly ever watchful when the police use low-lifes to gather evidence, and yet some of the finest investigative journalism in defence of liberty has required a descent into the gutter: W. T. Stead buying a little girl from her mother to prove the evil and prevalence of child prostitution in Victorian England; in recent years, the work of both newspaper and television journalists in exposing police corruption in Scotland Yard. It's a dirty job, but somebody's got to do it. These days that somebody is often Ron Farebrother.

Former Detective Sergeant Roger Hull knows Ron better than any other police officer: Ron is a very strong character. That's what can make him so difficult to deal with. I was lucky that I got on with him, but, even so, we had our ups and downs. Sometimes I used to think he was telling me the most extraordinary lies but 99 per cent of the time it turned out to be the truth. The other 1 per cent we just couldn't prove, but I never caught him lying even when he came out with the most horrendous stories — like that one about the dreadful man who wanted Ron to kill his wife for the insurance and was stupid enough to hand Ron a signed cheque for £30,000 in advance. If you were a fiction writer and you put that in a book, you'd be a laughing stock, yet here was Ron, in real life, telling me it was all true — and it was!

Ron is hard to handle. You cannot tell him what to do. He's a law unto himself. This means that whatever you do with him, you've got to stick strictly to the rules of the system, so every job that Ron ever gave me went on paper. Technically he was usually a participator in the crime he was helping to expose, so we had to get authority right from the top of the Yard or the South East Regional Crime Squad before any job went ahead. That was why, when some defence lawyers and journalists later tried to make trouble for us, we had no problems at all, because everything about our involvement with Ron was in an official docket. In high-profile policing like ours, you have to play it correctly, right down the middle — and we did. With someone like Ron you cannot afford to make any mistakes.

Only one person has ever got the better of Ron over a long period: his bigamous ex-wife and partner-in-crime, Sylvia Barnes. Is she now the most wanted woman in America, the notorious 'Chameleon', suspected of chopping off another woman's head and hands? Is she dead or alive? Is she still in the United States or back in England? And will she ever turn up on his doorstep and shoot him like she did before?

Read on and make up your own mind. And then ask yourself, if you have anything bad to hide, would you want the Vigilante on your case?

TAKING OUT INSURANCE

September 1991.

The phone rang.

'Yeah. Hallo, Martin.'

No need to ask who was on the other end. I knew only one man who began a conversation with 'Yeah'.

'Hallo, Ron.'

'You'll never believe what's happened. I can't talk about it on the phone. You'd better come round.'

'Ah, I'm in the middle of something, Ron. Is it worth my trouble?'

'Oh yes, it's worth your trouble. Trouble's what it's all about.'

I had been seeing Ronald Farebrother for three years, on and off. More off than on. The off bits were when he was locked up in jail and when he disappeared to America for a year and a half. He had now been back from the States for five months, ducking and diving, looking for some way to earn a living, legitimate or otherwise.

As my living comes partly from reporting on crime, no call from Ron was ever a complete waste of time.

'Right, Ron. I'll see you in an hour.'

When I reached his high-rise flat in Kilburn, Ron was in a thinking-out-loud mood. With a perpetual cigarette in one hand and a glass of vodka in the other, he talked through a proposition.

'I've had a call from Alan, who's a bit of a gangster himself. So I had a meet with him and his mate Pete. They told me about this guy who wants his wife killed and they've asked me if I'd do it. There's a lot of money involved. Thirty grand. All to come out of life-insurance policies he's taken out on his wife. £560,000 worth. I don't like the sound of it. The guy's an amateur, some businessman. He's not one of us. Besides, what kind of a bastard wants to kill a woman?'

'So what are you going to do about it? You've got to go to the police, surely?'

'It's not that easy. They haven't told me who the guy is yet. If I go to the police they'll want to know who's approached me. I can't tell them it's Alan. If I do, I'll have half London's underworld on my back for the rest of my life. Which won't be long in those circumstances.'

'But why has Alan approached you? Can't he find a hitman nearer home? And why does he think you're a killer? Are you a killer? What about that guy Smith you once told me about? Whatever happened to him?'

'I never said I did anything to him. All I know is that I was acting as his minder and bodyguard. Then he upset me. Then he disappeared. To this day I don't know what happened to him. On my daughter's life.'

'OK, so why does Alan think you're the man for the job?'

'It's just my reputation. In his circle they think I'm a killer. See, I've got this nickname: Ron the Gun. Now, of course, they don't expect me to go around saying I've killed anybody in particular. No one who's connected is going to be that dumb. Imagine a professional hitman saying "Yeah, I did Johnny J or Alfie K!" No, once you've got a name for this sort of thing, propositions do come up from time to time. But that doesn't mean I've ever done anything to deserve it.'

'You did have that charge back in 1987. I've dug it out. It's on your record: possessing a firearm.'

'Yeah, I was found not guilty.'

'But the cops did find a firearm in your office, and they did order it's destruction. Then back in 1982 there was the three years you got for possessing a handgun during a burglary in Finchley.'

'Yeah, but that was an imitation firearm, not the real thing. But the conviction did increase my street cred. Anyhow, that was then, this is now: there's a geezer who wants his wife killed. I'm not going to do the job, and I'm not going to the police neither.'

Ron paused, to take a puff and a drink. He was looking straight ahead. 'But I'm skint and you're a TV producer.'

Silence.

So it's down to me, I thought, whether this woman lives or dies? Yes, it's like this: if I don't get Ron some money from a TV show or a newspaper pretty damn quick, she could be killed — not by Ron, I'm sure, but by anyone else Alan gets to do the job. Hitmen aren't hard to find: there are dozens of guys in London bursting to kill for a few hundred quid. Christ! They may have found someone already! So am I now to play both detective and God with a woman's life on the line and a gangster in the middle? That's stretching the hack's function a bit: Things they don't teach you at journalism school . . .

But if Ron won't go to the cops, I can't either. I can't tell them what he's told me. Not yet, anyway. I've only his word for this tall tale, and they won't believe him. They hate him. He has a long criminal past; they think he's still at it, and he's upset some individual detectives so badly they'd charge him on the slightest excuse. Anyway, how do I know he's telling the truth? I've no name for the would-be killer or his wife, and I can't go and ask Alan.

Still . . . there may be a way through.

'Ron, this is a great story. Maybe I can persuade a documentary series to fund some undercover filming, but I doubt it. They might like to do the story, but they'd be scared stiff of it going wrong. What if we all sit on the information while we're filming, then the husband hires someone else to murder the wife? Imagine the headline: REPORTERS LUST FOR GLORY LEFT HITMAN FREE TO KILL. Oh, and by the way, the TV folk won't want to pay you either.'

'In that case, forget it.'

Ron's big worry wasn't bad publicity or

journalistic ethics. It was how to pay the rent.

'There's another problem. TV documentary slots are scheduled months ahead. There's no chance of getting an instant slot for a film about a death plot unless its a royal death plot! So, if you find out this man's mother lives in a large house at the end of the Mall, we might be in with a chance.'

'Na, this fella lives in Surrey.'

'But I have to say, if you find out exactly who he is, where he lives and when he wants his wife killed, you've got to tell the police. Then, as soon as they've got hard evidence, they'll arrest him and charge him straight away. That means any TV show must wait till he goes on trial — a year at least — and they still won't pay you, because the defence would claim you're saying all this just to make money! You're a tainted witness.'

'Yeah, but that's where you're wrong, cos I won't be a witness. I'm not getting in any witness box. If I do, everyone will say I'm a grass. And I'm no grass.'

'Well, Ron, in this case you've no choice. You will be a grass. But a grass for a good cause. You've said yourself that this man isn't "one of us" — not one of the chaps, the brothers — so the underworld can hardly be upset if you save the life of a straight lady. Anyhow, even if you say you're never getting in the box, the TV company can't take your word for it. You might be subpoenaed by the defence. I'll ask around, but I don't see how they'll ever pay you a penny.'

Ron lit another cigarette and poured another vodka. 'You'd like a beer. I'll get a can from the fridge. This needs more thinking through.'

Before he went through to the kitchen, I said, 'There's another angle. If it goes any further you've got to tell the police, otherwise you're committing an offence yourself: at the least failing to report an intended crime; at the worst accessory to murder.'

I looked out of the 11th floor window, over the main railway line from Euston to Birmingham and on up the West Coast to Scotland. It was raining and miserable. I could see a thousand dwellings: blocks of council flats just a hundred yards from million-pound houses on the fringes of St John's Wood. All human life is there. People in desperate straits, not knowing where the next penny's coming from, close by folk with more money than they know how to spend. It's not surprising that some of the people in the flats try to equalise the system by robbing the rich. What is surprising is that so few do it. Most live within the law the odd fiddle here and there, sure, but they don't go round robbing and killing. Yet here we are, calmly discussing if anyone will pay Ron to stop a woman getting killed.

Suddenly, as Ron handed me the beer, an idea came to me. 'That's it! "All human life is here." The old sales slogan of the *News of the World*. That's the place for the story. They're sure to find some way of paying you — and they've got more friends in the police than I have.'

I had a feeling Ron was already way ahead of me. 'Look, Martin, you try and set something up with TV, meantime I'll get Alan to introduce me to this guy. Then we'll see where we stand.'

A few days later Ron reported back.

'Yeah, so I met this man, and his name is

Malcolm Stanfield. He has to be about 60 to 64. And over coffee and biscuits, would you believe, he outlines this plan he wants carried out: he wants me to murder his wife, who he's been married to for 28 years and who's the mother of his three grown-up children!

'My first reaction is, this is a joke, this is a set-up. Maybe Alan and his friends are having a laugh at my expense. Or its some kind of test: they're seeing what I'll do when I'm asked to kill a total stranger. So I say to Stanfield, "Whatever your wife has done, you don't murder the mother of your children, even if you hate her guts."

'But then he goes into real long details about why he wants her murdered, which is unbelievable even for me, and I think I've heard everything. Nobody can shock me, or that's what I thought.

'He really does want her killed for £560,000-worth of insurance, but it has to be in a lane close to where they live. He's already thought all this out down to the last detail. He's going to tell her to park the car in a lane not far from this pub where he'll meet her for lunch at one. He'll say she can't park at the pub itself because it doesn't have a car park. But come one o'clock, while she's walking down this very narrow lane, he wants her run down by a lorry!

'The next thing that comes out of his mouth is so unbelievable, I know he's one evil, evil bastard. He says, "But make sure you hit her full-on and she ends up dead, not a cripple, because I don't want her in a wheelchair for the rest of her life."

'By the time he's finished telling me all this, I know what I'm going to say: "I don't know where you're getting this sort of crap from — I don't know why you're talking to me about it — but forget it. You are not going to murder your wife."

'Then this slimy, evil bastard sits back in the chair and gives a smirk, a knowing grin: "So, OK, you're not going to do the contract? "No, and Im going to stop you doing it as well."

'Stanfield leans on the table and says, "I am a successful businessman. I've been married for 28 years. She doesn't know anything about it. We're not having any rows. It's just pure insurance. If you don't do it, I'll find somebody else."

'Then I stop him. "Excuse me. If you even think about trying to go ahead on this with someone else, I'll let your wife know you're trying to bump her off. That way, she'll fuck off and leave you straight away."

'He says, "If my wife or even the police come to me about this, I would be in hysterics. I'd be laughing ha, ha, ha. Even if they could prove I met you, who would they believe? Me, a businessman, wealthy, no criminal record, or you, a criminal with known links to organised crime. You'd be laughed out of the police station."

'Then I say, "No, I wouldn't go to the police anyway." He says, "That's why we picked you. We know you'll tell the police sod all. Anyway, let's pack in this meeting. I take it you're not doing the job. And I'm not worried who you tell, because I don't give a shit."

'Well, my first reaction is to put the guy in hospital there and then. But then I'm thinking, how would beating him up prove anything? He'll just tell his wife he was mugged, or that I'm a thug who suddenly leaped on him. Obviously, if you look at the size of him, then look at the size of me, I'd be branded the bully. So I have to think quickly. I have to retrieve the situation and play for time to think how to stop this bastard getting someone else to murder his wife. So I tell him, "Hold on, I'll take the job, but I won't do it myself."

'So he says, "I don't care who you get to do it. You've got a reputation for organising things. Organise this!"

'And with that, he takes a photograph out of the inside pocket of his jacket and puts it in front of me on the table. So here I am looking at a photo of his wife, knowing that if I don't stop him, one way or the other, she'll very soon be dead. So I take the photo, and I say, I'll give you a call in two or three days.'

I was shocked by Ron's account. Shocked not only at the crime this Stanfield was proposing but also that he could be so dumb as to tell a criminal stranger so much at their first meeting. I also could not puzzle out how Ron had managed to retrieve Stanfield's trust after saying so forcefully that he would have nothing to do with the hit.

But what about Ron's underworld friends who had offered him the job?

'They know my feelings, and they understand. They're saying, "Just walk away. Walk away and forget it. Don't have anything to do with him. He's a shit." So I told them, "Its easy enough for you to say walk away, but he's just going to find some low-life who'll take this job on without blinking. Are we going to allow that?"

'Ron, these guys obviously will allow that.

They're the people who got you the job in the first place. They don't give a damn about this woman. All they've been seeing is the £30,000 Stanfield's offering you, and presumably a big cut for themselves. I bet they're looking for another guy to do the job even now. So if you squeal on this deal, that'll hurt their pockets — and it won't do their reputation any good either.'

'So, Martin,' said Ron, puffing on a cigarette, you'd better see what you can come up with.'

'Well. Hawking a real-life murder plot round the television networks isn't easy. I've already talked about it with ITV, but they're not interested. Sky don't do anything undercover. And the other folk I know are scared stiff of keeping this kind of stuff from the police. No, you'll be better off with the *News of the World*. The best reporters there recognize good stories in a flash, which other journalists couldn't grasp in a month of Sundays. They've got their own ways of working, of course, but that shouldn't worry you. They'll pay well, and they'll protect you from avenging cops. I'd love to handle the story myself but I'm freelance: I don't have the clout or the cash. I'll just watch this space instead.'

'Fair enough,' Ron said, 'because you know I can't give this story away, and I've got to have protection. But there's another thought running through my mind, really nagging me: what if this is all a set-up by the cops? Some of them hate my guts so much they'd willingly frame me with conspiracy to murder, just to lock me up and throw away the key.'

'Are you saying Alan's an informer? An entrapment merchant?'

'Na. What if Stanfield's working for the police? What if he's an agent provocateur? Christ, the cops have been gunning for Alan's dad for 20 years and never got a case together against him. What if some special gang-busting squad has made him a prime target?'

'Yeah, I see that — but you're not Alan's dad.

'No, but what if Stanfield's been put up to this, to ensnare whichever friend of the family is game for a hit? Then the cops'll leap straight on the hitman. Boom! "Conspiracy to murder. Ten years! Take him down." '

'That still doesn't nail Alan's dad.'

'Nope, but they won't charge the hitman straight away. They'll try and turn him. They'll say, "We won't lock you up if you do the business on the old man", set him up with guns or drugs, call him London Gangland's Mr Big, frame him over prostitution. Any mud that's fit to stick. Then hand the case over to some silky-tongued QC who'll talk an Old Bailey jury into burying him. That kind of thing's never failed yet.'

'So?'

'So that's why I need someone like the *News of the World* to cover me. Scotland Yard can't arrest Rupert Murdoch as well, can they?

And that's how it happened. Ron went to work with the *News of the World*, while I just had to sit back and watch an astonishing story unfold.

That Friday night Ron rang up the newspaper and laid out the story to a reporter to whom he had never spoken before: Gary Jones. At first Jones was sceptical and rightly so. As the newspaper itself would later explain, an anonymous Ron told Jones he had been offered money to kill someone, and if the paper didn't pay him for the story, he just might go ahead.

Jones replied, 'It's Friday night, mate, and I'm still in the office. I think I might just shoot somebody myself.' When the caller refused to give his name, Jones told him to call back when he was willing to identify himself. Ron thought about it and quickly rang back announcing who he was. The pair agreed to meet, and, over lunch, Ron told Jones as much of the story as he himself knew at the time.

If the story were ever going to make it into Britain's most voracious scandal sheet, Jones had to secure evidence that would convince not just himself but also the newspaper's lawyers that it was 100 per cent true. Ron Farebrother would have to be wired up with a tape recorder and meet the murderous Malcolm Stanfield again while, close by, Jones and a photographer, Edward Henty, would monitor the meeting.

So a few days later, at one in the afternoon, the newspaper watched as Ron met Stanfield outside East Croydon railway station. The would-be wife-killer drove up in his Jaguar XJS and took Ron off to the Selsdon Park Hotel, renowned as the place where Conservative Party leaders had gathered 21 years earlier, to shape the future of not only the party but also (it turned out) the nation. Selsdon Man would become the template for the new Tory: the self-made entrepreneur rather than the grandee, the idle aristocratic beneficiary of inherited wealth. Fine-honed by Margaret Thatcher during the late 1970s and

1980s, the ethics of small business consumed the entire country.

In a way Stanfield was the very image of Selsdon Man: he had built himself up into a substantial businessman and was determined to stay that way by whatever means.

And now Stanfield laid out his latest money-spinning scheme with Thatcherite bluntness. As for Ron, exercising a cunning that an undercover cop would need months of training to acquire, he drew Stanfield on to repeat from scratch almost everything he had told him at their previous meeting.

Stanfield: I've been told you're the one to take care of this.

Farebrother: What do you want done?

Stanfield: I want my wife taken out.

Farebrother: What do you mean, you want her taken out for a meal or something?

Stanfield: What I mean is, taken out permanently — dead.

Again and again Farebrother told Stanfield to drop the idea. He said that, even if the lady had been sleeping around, it wasn't right to kill her. Whatever your wife's done, whether she's been unfaithful or not, you don't bump her off.

Stanfield replied, 'She's never been unfaithful. It's not that.' He was the one who'd been sleeping around, not his wife. 'There's another woman in my life, but that's got nothing to do it. I want it done for the insurance money. The premiums are costing me a fortune, so the sooner you do it the better.'

Stanfield was in deep trouble, it turned out. He had lost over £100,000 in the property game, and he owed £127,000 to a builder who was now suing him. With Selsdon Man, the prospect of bankruptcy concentrates the mind wonderfully. Now, like a ruthless entrepreneur, Stanfield was determined to get the job done quickly. He plucked a sheet of the hotel's headed notepaper and drew a map, showing how his wife, Lorraine, would have to walk several hundred yards to a pub along a wooded lane without a pavement.

The pub was the Bell at Outwood in Surrey. Stanfield told Ron, 'I'll get her to park some distance away so she has to cross this narrow country lane. Then along would come a lorry, with the hitman at the wheel, ready to fell her in what would appear to be a hit-and-run. It's got to look like an accident, so that I can get the cash straight away ... Make sure it's a big truck, the bigger the better. And make sure that you hit her full on. I don't want her knocked off the road.'

By sketching in his own hand the layout of the place where the awful deed was to be done, Stanfield showed an astonishing forensic disregard for self-preservation. But this was only the beginning. He proceeded to hand Ron a recent photo of himself and his wife at another couple's wedding reception. He even wrote out and signed a cheque for £30,000 in his own name. When he gave it to Ron, Stanfield's sole caution was to say it was not to be cashed until after the insurance firm had paid out the £560,000. Throughout the meeting his only sign of nerves was when he spelt his wife's name wrongly on the sheet of paper: not as Lorraine but as Lorrian. A Freudian cross with the word lorry?

Then, in as matter-of-fact a way as the meeting had begun, the pair downed their drinks, and Stanfield drove Ron back to East Croydon station.

The encounter had gone so smoothly, so neatly confirming Ron's previous account, it occurred to Gary Jones that this Stanfield character might be working in league with Farebrother, so they could both make money out of the *News of the World*.

Whether or not Stanfield really did want his wife killed, or if perhaps he and Ron were merely blagging the paper, the reporter decided to speak to an officer in the South East Regional Crime Squad (SERCS), a team of detectives selected from all the different police forces in south-east England. When a SERCS detective first talked the tale through with Jones and Farebrother, he also found it hard to swallow. The least dangerous way to test the truth of it was to insinuate an undercover cop into the plot. This would also be the best way to win over a jury in any future trial. For sure, you could not present Ron Farebrother in court as a witness of truth. Besides, he had vowed never to testify — even in this case — for fear of being branded a grass, an informer.

George had been an undercover cop in the Metropolitan Police for ten years. Through instinct and experience he had a sceptical frame of mind. Yet when he went with Ron to meet Stanfield for the first time, he was quickly convinced that this was no mere conspiracy to trick a newspaper out of a bundle of cash: it really was one man's scheme to murder his wife.

Ron introduced George as the man to drive the hit-and-run lorry. Stanfield instantly accepted him without the slightest suspicion and without putting him through any probation test. He said, 'I want a complete termination job, I don't want a hospital job. I want it completely zappo — the sooner the better,' and he then went straight into a scheme for George to take a close look at Lorraine when he took her to central London's Theatre Royal in Drury Lane to see Miss Saigon. As the couple dallied at a prearranged spot, George and covert surveillance photographers recorded Stanfield coldly setting up his wife for execution.

As soon as George phoned him to say he was sure to recognize her if he saw her again, Stanfield fixed the day of the murder just a few days ahead: on Saturday, 5 October.

That morning he told Lorraine to meet him at the Bell at half past noon when he would also have some cash for her to settle a few bills. But why should she leave the car half a mile away? Not because the pub had no car park (as he had told Ron) — it had a large one — but because, he said, he did not want his lunchtime companion, a businessman, to know he had a flash motor. Then as sweet Lorraine walked down the lane, along would come George to squash her as flat as a pancake.

But where would her loving Malcolm be at the instant she was done to death? He would be playing golf! At the Royal Ashdown Forest club!

That morning, Stanfield planted a ritual kiss on Lorraine's cheek and told her he would see her at the Bell. But at the hour of her execution, he was heading for the 14th hole, which, as it happened, was a difficult 200-yard par three.

He wasn't much of a golfer. He had a 28 handicap, and yet he played the hole with astonishing composure. He was unaware that a stray golfer nearby, apparently looking for lost balls, was another undercover cop, keeping a close eye on him. This officer later reported that he displayed no emotion at any point, an extraordinary achievement in a game where even the slightest tremor of nerves can have a disastrous and instantly detectable effect on your play.

Lorraine herself still knew nothing. She had not been told of the plot lest she blurt out something to Stanfield. The police had no idea how she would react so, while ensuring she was at no risk whatever, they never spoke to her. Yet from the moment she parked her car at the spot her husband had dictated, then stepped out with an umbrella into the rain, she was being watched by detectives who monitored her every move.

And just in case Stanfield had told someone else to be there to make sure everything went off as planned, the police arranged for an open-back Leyland truck to drive along the lane in her direction, seemingly straight towards Lorraine. Instinctively she edged out of the way, an action that another detective in the cab beside Killer George caught on video as the lorry roared to within a few feet. No one else was in sight. Just as Stanfield had predicted, there was not a soul around to witness anything that might have happened.

Of course, when Lorraine reached the pub her husband was not there. He was still at the Royal Ashdown, completing his round. As his playing partner Ron Haworth later recalled, 'I'd never have guessed in a million years that Malcolm wanted his wife dead. There wasn't the slightest clue. His game didn't change at all. He showed no emotion. He was laughing and joking. In the clubhouse afterwards he even said, "I've got to go home to win a few brownie points with the missus." '

Stanfield then drove home. A few minutes later there was a ring at the door. It was the police. His first words were, 'Lorraine? Is everything all right? She should be here.'

The officers did not reply. Instead they asked him to go with them to Reigate Police Station. Their dead-pan unresponsiveness drove even ice-cool Malcolm to lose control. 'Is it something awful?' he blurted out.

A wise-cracking cop responded, 'Well, if you think being arrested on a murder charge is awful, yes.'

By now Lorraine had been approached by two other detectives outside the Bell. Only now did she learn of her husband's plot to kill her, but she would not believe them. It was not until she heard it from his own mouth in the police station that she changed her mind. 'It is true,' he told her. 'It was the only way to solve my problems. I'm a shit. Get a divorce.'

On 22 April 1992 at the Old Bailey, Malcolm Stanfield pleaded guilty to plotting to kill his wife. He was jailed for nine years. The *News of the World* claimed the credit, which the South East Regional Crime Squad seemed to concede. Detective Inspector Des Cooke issued a statement saying, 'When we were first informed about this murder plot, we believed it was almost too bizarre to be true. I'd like to thank your paper for its assistance in bringing Stanfield to justice. Your evidence was presented to us in a most professional manner.'

On 26 April, the first Sunday after Stanfield was sent down, the paper splashed its story under the banner headline: NEWS OF THE WORLD SAVES WIFE FROM HIT AND RUN KILLER, with a subtitle: Wives Read This! It Will Make You Shiver.

'I'm still in a state of shock,' Lorraine Stanfield was quoted as saying after the trial. 'I can't think why, after 28 years of marriage, he should think these awful things and callously plan to kill me. I'm so relieved to think I'm alive when I wake up in the morning. I could so easily have been killed and lost the love of my children and grandchildren. To have lived with someone so long, then to discover he wanted you murdered is like having lived a farce of a marriage.'

And 49-year-old Lorraine expressed her gratitude to the newspaper: 'I'm so lucky that I'm here to tell my story. I wouldn't be here if it wasn't for you. I am now changing my birthday to October 6, the day after my husband intended me to die.'

She was now figuring to sell the marital home to settle Stanfield's debts. 'I didn't realise he was in such a mess,' she said, 'but, even so, that's no reason to have me murdered. I want to put this behind me, but I don't think life will ever be the same. Friends and family have rallied round, but I still can't sort things out in my mind. Perhaps I never will. I can only thank the *News of the World* for helping me in my hour of need.'

The person who deserved most of the thanks — Ron Farebrother — got no public credit at all. Instead he was portrayed as a rather unwilling party to

Stanfield's downfall. Crime reporter Gary Jones wrote him up in unflattering terms:

'We heard that a cousin of Costa del Crime fugitive Ronnie Knight had been offered cash for a made-to-measure murder. When we tracked down Knight's hard-man cousin, bit-part actor Ron Farebrother, he agreed to co-operate with us.'

The story made it seem as if another underworld figure had informed on Ron. The truth was that Ron had informed on himself. The deception was necessary, he felt, to protect his reputation as a staunch member of the criminal fraternity. The Fraternal Union of Gangland Hitmen would have taken a very dim view of a member who had not only turned down a lucrative assignment, but also screwed up the job for anyone else! The awful truth is that, if Stanfield had shopped around, he could have found a dozen hitmen who would have done the job for a mere £300, not £30,000 and he would have run a far smaller risk of betrayal.

The *News of the World* had come up trumps for Ron. The deal it had reached with the Regional Crime Squad meant that no police pressure came on him to reveal the gangland figures who had first lined him up to kill Mrs Stanfield. The paper also paid him well — far better than I could have arranged. The police gave him a modest £500 reward, but the life insurers came up with nothing. Yet if Lorraine really had been killed, they would have paid out exactly £560,000. For saving them that loss, Ron might have received a 10 per cent reward, but he did not get a penny. However, if he had said nothing, let Lorraine get killed by others and only then come forward to reveal the fraud, the

insurers would probably have paid him the full
£56,000.

Soon after Stanfield had been arrested and
charged, I found Ron in extraordinary good spirits.
He felt he had been reborn. After years as a low-life
he was now redeemed. I was wondering whether he
was going to claim he had found God as well, but he
spared me that. Instead he started to write a memoir,
in which he congratulated himself on bringing a
nightmare on Stanfield and a blessing on Lorraine.
The experience, he claimed, had wrought a 'major
reversal of my outlook on life.

'After all these years of learning in the
environment I was in, I had something inside me
which I am pleased to say I had: I had principles. Well,
not so much principles, as I had this one principle:
how can any man blatantly murder his wife for
money — or for any reason?

'Fate? Being at the right place at the right time.
Well, I was, because in a very big way, I did save Mrs
Stanfield from being murdered. But how I did it still
amazes me — especially me. In league with Old Bill!

'What was the alternative?

'Silly things go through your mind, like taking
him out — killing Stanfield himself, not his wife. I am
not saying I would have done that. I am just saying it
could have happened. He could have had an accident.
But then his wife and children would have been in
mourning, and they would have been feeling sorry for
that arsehole. No, he had to get what he had coming
to him.

'It occurred to me one morning, sitting here over
a cup of coffee. Could it work? Could a professional

criminal and a professional detective work together to get the evidence? How can I trust the police and how can the police trust me? That was the scenario I gave to the crime reporter, who then told his connection at the Yard, and it worked.

'The beautiful part is that two professionals did get together. A very strange situation. To me George looked like a hardened villain. In fact he looked like a professional hitman, extremely professional. Against all my childhood training as a criminal, we got on very well. He admired me just as much as I admired him.

'Now, if anyone reading this thinks what I did is called being an informer or a grass, I would like to tell you one thing. I made the right choice. If you think I'm a grass, I could not give a shit! I saved this woman's life, and I would do it again tomorrow.

'So that is the beginning of my new life. It is amazing each day as I get older. I am quite content away from the criminal element. I still speak to them occasionally on the phone. But my attitude has changed towards the police — the professional ones. Sure, there is scum in the police, too, but the majority of them are doing the right thing.

'As for me, until I reach my goal, I will still be Ron Farebrother, and I will do what I think is good for me, whether it is the right way or the wrong way of the law. So everybody is confused now. The police are confused. The criminals are confused.

'Where is Ron Farebrother going from here? I know.

'Take care. There is a lot more to come — a lot more.'

As I read through this first chapter of his draft memoir, alongside Ron in his flat, I felt I was watching a transplant operation, even a sex change. He seemed to be saying Ron the Crim was about to become Ron the Vigilante. After years on the wrong side of the law, he was about to cross over. Except that in the world of cops and robbers, it is not always easy to spot what's wrong and what's right. Things are rarely so black and white as in the Stanfield case. They are usually shades of grey.

A DOG'S LIFE

It was back in August 1988 when a friend in the feature-film industry asked me if I would be prepared to meet Ronald Farebrother. He explained that, until a few months before, Ron had been running a cab company out of Elstree Film Studios in Borehamwood. Now he was in deep trouble and wanted a journalist to cover his case to see fair play.

According to my friend, Ron was claiming he had been stitched up on charges of conspiring to cash bank drafts worth £2.2 million. One of these — worth a whole million by itself — he had tried to pass in a bank in Borehamwood. The police had got wind of the transaction, and Ron was arrested and charged. And yet, despite the huge sum involved, he had been given bail. My friend explained that Ron's wife was a respected member of the community — until this happened she was due to become a magistrate so when

Ron came up with sureties worth £100,000 he could scarcely be locked up, especially as the offence seemed to be a non-violent, white-collar affair. What neither the police nor Mrs Farebrother knew then was that Ron was running round with another woman who was far from respectable. Indeed, she seems to have had distinct criminal tendencies.

So early one evening I found myself in Hampstead's celebrated Bull and Bush pub, listening to this suave stranger protesting his innocence. He was not alone. He had brought along his tall, busty girlfriend, Sylvia, who had an instant gushing appeal. She spoke with a rural burr. West Country? Norfolk? It was difficult to tell, now that it was partly buried in the suburban tones of outer north London. Whatever, I confess it was not her accent that really caught my attention. It was her Junoesque figure that I tried to ignore, as I could also see that Ron, despite his superficial charm, was a street-fighting man. Indeed, his blue eyes had a steely glaze that, whether induced by booze, brawn or bravura, compelled me to dedicate my entire attention to him.

The bank-draft case was difficult to grasp, especially as Ron did not offer many details, though he seemed confident he had worked out a plausible defence. But before getting immersed in that affair, I needed to know far more about Ron himself. Who exactly was he? Where did he come from? How bad was his record? Only when I was armed with that kind of knowledge could I begin to assess his likely guilt or innocence over the £1 million job.

After several vodkas for him, and a few pints for me, Ron thrust a load of papers on the bank case in my hands, along with the complete first shot at his memoirs. I said goodbye to him and Sylvia, then went home to study the literature. I put the legal bumf aside and read the autobiography. It was poignant but punchy.

My mother was the best. My father — he left when I was four. He cleared off to America. I was glad. I had three older brothers. I learnt from their mistakes and found out at a very early age what life was all about. Streetwise? I invented it! Survival? I fought for it!

By the age of five, I knew all about fighting from my brothers. I put it into practice at school. I was eight when I had my first brush with the law. The police were always raiding our house because my eldest brother, Fred, was a tearaway. He had been sent to Borstal (a young offenders' prison) for 18 months and was very well known to the police. One night he could see them creeping round the back of the house, flashing a torch. He realised they were going to raid the house looking for guns so he came in our bedroom, woke me and my third brother, Lawrence, and put a gun under Lawrence's pillow and a big bag of bullets in mine. He then took the bulb out of our light.

When the police came in, they tried to look in our room but Fred said, 'You aren't going in that room. I've got two kid brothers in there, and one of them's got asthma.' That was meant to be me, but I didn't have asthma at all! I had to pretend I was asleep. I had to push my head into that pillow with all those big heavy army bullets sticking in my head. They arrested Fred anyway, but they never found that gun or those bullets.

From that early age I knew that I was part of a

family that the police look at. The heartbreak I put my mother through. At the age of nine, I saw her in a juvenile court pleading yet again for one of her own sons. I was shocked at the time. It was me.

Over the next year and a half I watched Fred and Lawrence and their associates. I was learning a lot from them about crime but doing disastrously at school, St Mary's Roman Catholic. I still have a school report for July 1958. English: Until he learns to read there is no prospect of progress. Arithmetic: 26 per cent. Within the bounds of his very limited ability, he has produced some satisfactory work. History: 1 out of 20. Geography: 2 out of 20. Nature: 0 out of 10. Conduct: satisfactory. Progress: nil. There will be no progress in any of these subjects until he can read. Position in class: 42 out of 43. I often wonder what happened to the poor bastard who was 43rd.

What I would call my early manhood came two weeks before my 11th birthday when the authorities tried and almost succeeded in taking me away.

I was in trouble because one day I felt like going for a swim in the local pool. But I needed to go home quick to get 2s 6d from my Mum for admission to the pool, so I borrowed someone else's bike. When I got back to the pool with the bike I was arrested because I hadn't asked to borrow it. Whoever's bike it was had called the cops, and they were hovering around when I showed up, riding the evidence! Caught red-handed! When this offence was added to everything else I'd been caught doing, I was considered ripe for being put into care.

To get me out of this mess, my mother borrowed a lot of money and rushed — I mean rushed — to the

American Embassy to send me to my father so he could look after me. I had not seen him for six years, but my mother felt that, to keep me out of childrens' homes and a life of crime here, she had no alternative but to send me over there.

I will never forget the day I asked my family, 'Why are you sending me away?' They looked so sad but said nothing. So I found out myself what it was all about, and, at the airport, I told my mother and brothers, 'Don't you dare cry when I walk away.' I could see they were all very upset. As I was led off, I shouted to them, 'I'll be back to look after you lot.' Now the tears were coming from my eyes, but I didn't let them see.

The plane journey was all new to me — one of the stewardesses taking care of me and making a fuss — I really enjoyed it. When I arrived at San Francisco I was the last one to leave the plane. My only baggage was a holdall.

As we were going through US Customs, the stewardess said I had to put a label on, and she held my hand, which I thought was rather strange. Coming out into the reception area, I did not know what to expect. Then suddenly I was being given a huge hug by my father, whom I did not recognize. The stewardess then gave me a goodbye kiss and a big smile.

We went to my father's car. I noticed a packet of Rolos on the top of the dashboard. Then I remembered that he used to buy me Rolos when I was three or four back in England. But this time the sunshine was so hot, they had all melted.

What happened next, I shall never forget. My father had always been known to me and my brothers as the Old Man especially during all the years since he had left home. We didn't mean any harm by it. It was just an expression, quite a friendly one, really. So now, when he asked me about the family, I told him everyone was fine. I said, 'They're always talking about the Old Man.'

His hand left the steering wheel and caught me across the mouth. He said, 'I'm your father, not the Old Man!' I took a tissue from the glove compartment and noticed blood on my lip.

It took three hours to drive from San Francisco to my father's house in Ukiah. By the time we had arrived, I had made up my mind I would not be staying.

The next day was just a formality, meeting Elsie, my father's so-called wife — my stepmother. She constantly let me know that she was to be my new mother — at least, that's what she thought!

After about two weeks she started coming into my bedroom, first thing in the morning, to squeeze her spots in front of the large mirror — the only one in the house. I couldn't take this so I asked, 'Could you do that somewhere else?' I will never forget what she said to me: 'Fuck off back to England where you belong and don't come back. You'll never be anything.' I knew then it was time to start making my way back to my roots, back to London, where I knew I could survive.

I left the house the next morning at eight. I realized I would not be able to fly home, so instead I was planning to get back to San Francisco, sneak aboard the *Queen Mary* or the *Queen Elizabeth* and sail back to England. I had no idea that they only docked into New York on the Atlantic coast. I was on the Pacific, 3000 miles away!

Going out of Ukiah town, I knew I had to keep off the roads to avoid getting captured by the wicked witch. I used the hills and mountains. By five in the afternoon I was well away from Ukiah. I felt good and enthusiastic because I was making my way back home.

I remember seeing a house and knocking on the door. I had it in mind that if anyone was in, I would pretend I needed water. I reckoned that with an English accent I could have got away with it. But nobody was there, so I went inside and took food and a carton of milk. I left a note saying thank you.

From the mountains I kept watching the road, because I knew it would lead me to the boat that would take me to England. That first night was quite terrible for me — I was very scared. While I was trying to get to sleep, I saw baby deer coming down the mountains for water. But the following morning, I felt fine again, on my own walking home — or running most of the time because that made me feel even better.

I wanted to phone my mother to tell her I was coming back. But as night fell again, I had to find another house to sleep in. This time it was a log cabin. The people were away so I broke a window with a chunk of wood and was able to get inside. I spent the night there, sleeping on the couch. Then I put on the television. I was surprised to see a story about the police and the highway patrol searching for an English boy. Then up came a photograph. It was me!

Next morning I felt even happier because I was sure I was nearing San Francisco. It took me three days to get there. Seeing the Golden Gate was like seeing London Bridge. But I knew I had to be careful: people were looking for me.

I found a bus station. I asked for a bus to take me to the docks. The ticket girl said one would be leaving soon. She asked for $3. I handed her a 10-bob note, which my mother had given me at the airport. No, I wasn't very streetwise then, was I! Well, you can imagine what happened next: they had found the English boy!

The police were very good to me. They wanted to know why I had run away from my father. But, being brought up the way I was, I did not tell them: even if you hate someone, you never grass.

Then I told one particular policeman, 'I almost made it!' He smiled, gave me a big hug and said, 'I wish I had a boy like you, but you're 3000 miles away. The boat sails from New York, not San Francisco.'

Just 24 hours later I was back with my father. It was strange but he did not take my (for him) embarrassing escapade out on me. Things were softened by the arrival, a few hours later, of my second eldest brother, Albert, who was serving in the US Airforce at the time. He had taken time off just to come and see me. He also had a fiancée in Ukiah, who later became his wife. Their being around helped me to settle down for a while.

Then a new experience came into my life — my first sexual encounter! Near our house lived a girl who was about 16 or 17. One day she asked if I would like some American comics. Of course, I said yes, so I went over, and she asked me a lot about England and whether I liked America. I told her I loved America, but England was my home.

She remarked how hot it was that day. She gave me some lemonade and said she would not be long.

Then she called out that she was sorting out the magazines in her room. When I went in, I saw her leaning under the bed, wearing just her bra and pants. She pulled out a pile of comics and carried them back into the living room. She asked if I found her good looking, and I said she had a nice smile. Then she sat on the couch beside me and said, 'Have you ever had sex?' I will never forget how much my knees and legs shook. And she seduced me.

Later I returned home with the comics.

The next day I went back for some more.

By now I was getting into a regular routine. Going to school and, of course, fighting. Even at the age of 11, I had become a well-known fighter in the town.

Then I had another blow-up with my father's wife. She told me to pack my bags and, this time, to make sure I made it to New York.

As I walked out, I decided I couldn't go through the mountains again, especially as I had a suitcase. So instead, on this very hot day, I made it the three miles to Mrs Corner, a relative of my brother's fiancée.

As I reached her house, I collapsed and fainted. When I woke up, several days later, it turned out that I was suffering from severe sunstroke. I stayed with Mrs Corner for 14 months. She was so kind, I came to think of her as my second mother. The police seemed to think I should be put in care, but she kept me out of any such institution.

My father accepted the situation. Once a week he came and handed me a $20 bill through his car window. This was to give to Mrs Corner for my keep. I was just beginning to feel settled in my new way of life when I had another shock. The next time my father came to see me, it wasn't to give me another $20 bill. It was to give me two tickets: one for a plane from San Francisco to New York, the other for a boat from New York to Southampton.

Mrs Corner, who I loved, took me to San Francisco to get the plane, but my father like the fool he always was messed up the dates, and I arrived in New York a day too soon. I was taken into custody for another 24 hours, but this time a policeman took me to his house.

Next day, feeling on top of the world and sure that I would take charge when I got back home, I boarded the boat to Southampton. The trip was straightforward except for one thing. I shared a cabin with two men. The fat one in the bunk above me was very drunk that first night. By the morning I had had enough, so I told him that if I had to put up with any more farting from him, he would not be looking too good in the morning.

I knew he got the point because the following day he reported me to the captain. For the rest of the journey I shared a cabin with one of the crew.

Arriving at Southampton and seeing my mother there was a big occasion for me. I had been away for two and a half years, and I had changed dramatically. When I got home I saw my two brothers again, Lawrence and Fred. They were pleased to see me — at least I think they were.

After two weeks I was back in school where I was the instant success I had always been: I was expelled within half an hour. This was because I would not say I had been to a Catholic school while I was in America.

There was a very good reason for this: I had not been to a Catholic school in America, and I did not see why I should tell a lie. When I got home, my mother was not happy. She had to go to the school and explain everything to Sister Catherine, so back I had to go too.

Now I may not have been particularly good at reading, writing and spelling, but I already knew about life. Too much perhaps. I was expelled for the last time when I was 14. My crime was hitting a teacher over a remark he had made about my brothers.

Leaving school was no problem. I quickly drifted into older company — 18 and 19 year olds — and into their bad habits too.

At this point I had a strange life-changing experience. Not as spectacular as Saul getting struck blind on the road to Damascus but something similar. It was in 1962 when I came out of a pub in December and found the snow coming down. I was sure this boded for a really good Christmas, when suddenly I saw a car skid across the road and just miss a little puppy. I grabbed hold of the puppy and took him home. He had lumps of ice and snow stuck to his fur, so I bathed him, wrapped him in a blanket, took him to bed and cuddled him. The next morning, I knew that my mother would go mad if she saw him, so, as he was just a little bundle of fluff, I kept him in my bedroom for two days.

Eventually I had to let my mother know because the puppy kept messing on the floor. When I told her, she was pretty relaxed about it and allowed me to keep him. I called him Toby, and we became very close. Wherever I went, Toby went. He turned out to be one hell of a clever little dog. He never had a lead or collar: he would simply follow me. He lived and breathed for me.

One day I saw an advertisement in the local paper for a film company that was auditioning dogs for a part. Toby and I went along just to see what was going on. As we were watching, up comes some guy who asks if I want to enter my dog. I told him we had just come to watch, and, anyhow, Toby was much brighter than all the rest. I said, 'I'll show you what my dog can do.'

I then told him to do a few tricks, which I thought were quite normal, like telling him to go to the third car along the street and sit on its roof. The film people thought that was amazing. Then I told him to crawl on his belly and only to stop when I told him so. Amazing again, they said, and they gave him the part.

He went on to have a brilliant career, getting lots of parts in TV and films. He even got the part of the dog in *No Hiding Place*. Obviously I had to take him to the shoot in the mornings, so they sent along a car to pick up Toby and his chaperon — which was me.

Well, as you might guess, Toby proved to be my ticket into another side of life altogether, the world of film and television. It sounds superficial I know, but these people really are a lovely crowd, and I learned more in my first year with Toby mixing with those people than I did in most of my childhood. I was only 15.

Within two years Toby had become such a big star — to everyone's surprise but mine — that he was earning a fortune: so much I was able to fund a pop group. Toby even appeared on the David Frost

Programme, nominated as the highest-paid dog, and probably the most intelligent, in the world.

I started getting offers myself then, especially when I invested more of Toby's earnings in acting lessons for me at the Corona Drama School. I also spread the money around a bit. Some of my less fortunate friends had become active in the thieving game, and so I invested some cash in the quality goods they were offering. It was obvious that they were stolen, or else they had fallen off the back of a very high-class lorry.

At 19 I married Anne, a girl I had been going out with a couple of years. And my best man — yes, you've guessed it — was Toby. After all, he was my best mate.

Even so, I did feel I shouldn't just ponce off my dog. I felt driven to do some part-time work myself, not for money but self-respect. I should put my toughness to the test and show I was still one of the chaps, so I became a bouncer. When my reputation with my fists was added to my reflected glory with Toby, I became a well-known character in my neck of north London.

Eventually, of course, Toby had to be retired. He was earning so much money, I did not want everyone to think I was incapable of earning my own living. But the only other game I knew was crime, and that was what I now drifted into. Being me, of course, with my inflated ego, I wasn't interested in becoming just a run-of-the-mill villain. I had to be the best.

I was captured and taken to court over several serious offences, but I managed to stay out of prison. By the time I was 23 I had a lovely large house, I was partner in a club, and I was one of the biggest 'receivers' — buyers of stolen goods in north London. I also financed a lot of other crime. I had a reputation.

I now climbed into the top market of the criminal world. I went through what I call a probationary period. I did not like people telling me to prove myself, but prove myself I did — in a very big way and in a very short time. A crime boss nicknamed me the Ambassador because I could, and did, carry out anything that I said I would do, anywhere he sent me.

Then things started to go wrong. I had risen too fast. I had drifted away from crime and the streets where my real strength had been, into the make-believe world of paper gangsters, where you really think you're a Mister Big.

I will never forget my experience of being badly hurt. I had gone into a pub and two men came into the bar. They stuck out like sore thumbs, even in the circle I was mixing with. Then another two men came in. One asked me for a light. Straight away, I knew something was wrong. I was injured quite severely with coshes and iron bars. I had to have stitches on the inside of my eye to hold it together; my eye was completely closed, and my nose was broken, but I discharged myself from hospital that night and went back the next day to the pub to take my revenge.

After again getting heavily involved with the top of the criminal world, around the early eighties I had another brush with the law that resulted in me getting a three-year prison sentence at the Old Bailey.

When I came out of jail I had another shock. My wife met me at the station. I knew we had lost our beautiful house, as the judge had said it was paid for with the proceeds of ill-gotten gains. That's the biggest loophole in the law I know of. Coming home to find that my wife and three lovely children were living in a squalid flat is something I will never forgive myself for.

A lot of things happened that are now water under the bridge. After 20 years of marriage, Anne divorced me. She is still a lovely lady, and I respect her. Even though I have remarried, I owe her for the decency of being my wife for so long and putting up with me throughout our time together. My children are lovely. I love them all.

Humph! This memoir told me some things but not enough. The stories about Ron's pre-teen years were touching, poignant and probably true. The tales about Toby were a little sentimental but easily verified. The family stuff was fair enough. What perplexed me were the paragraphs about life as a rising young gangster. They were written with a bit too much swagger. Not a run-of-the-mill villain. 'I had to be the best . . . I had a reputation . . . the top market in the criminal world . . . the Ambassador . . . I had risen too fast.'

If Ron had grown this big, why was he talking to me in a north London pub? And who was the mystery crime boss who had elevated him to Ambassador status? Why hadn't this godfather hired London's top criminal solicitor to save him from what seemed certain jail for years to come? Or had Ron tried the £2.2 million bank fraud on his own? Was Mr Big vexed because the Ambassador had tried to represent himself, not his country?

Ron was unlikely to tell me these things before he went on trial for the bank job, but I had to find out. I would get hold of his criminal record.

CATCH A FALLING STAR

When I saw Ron Farebrother's criminal record, it confirmed that, with his showbiz career on hold after Toby's retirement, he had drifted into low-level thieving. In 1966, when he was 19, he was convicted of taking and driving away a car without the owner's consent, without insurance, and of stealing some of its contents. He was fined a total of £15. The record did not reveal who the owner was — perhaps to save red faces among the boys in blue.

You remember those old Black Marias, big enough to carry a dozen cops and just as many prisoners? Well, I was standing outside a pub in West Hendon, with my mate Bruce Blackman, when this Black Maria pulled up, and all the cops jumped out and ran into this pub. So I walked over and saw they'd left the keys in it, so I said to Bruce, 'Come on, let's have a laugh,' and I jumped in and drove the Black Maria off. I went all the way to Audley Road, where I lived, flashing the light and ringing the bell, and I parked it right outside my house. Well, of course, I got nicked. So when we came up in court I said I had got carried away because at the time I was learning a part for a TV drama called *Juvenile Delinquents*. The magistrate just burst out laughing and fined me £5 for each offence. The police driver didn't look too happy.

So, right from the start of his criminal career, Ron was displaying two characteristics that he has never lost: an impish sense of humour and an irritating knack of humiliating the police. A year later he was done for obtaining petrol and oil on false pretences. He asked for ten other cases to be taken into consideration and was fined another £15. In 1970 he acquired a car on hire-purchase but sold it on for £150 without paying off his debt or telling the purchaser. He was fined £40.

Petty stuff. No hint of an emerging Mr Big. But then I recalled that all the grand Mafia bosses in America — even Al Capone, Lucky Luciano and Meyer Lansky — had juvenile records that made them look like street punks. Thats how they all started. From little acorns mighty oak trees grow.

Despite these early, undistinguished brushes with the law, Ron had managed to get some acting work even without his dog. In 1967 a local newspaper gave this glowing report of his talents.

RON BREAKS LEG FOR ARTS SAKE

He arrives at work. Stands around. Does a bit of skiing. Chats with his fellow workers some of them in the surtax bracket he hopes to squeeze into one day and then breaks a leg.

But, as his colleagues will often remind him, its all for the sake of art. And the art is acting.

Only just 20 years old, and, ignoring the smarmy publicists scroll so often pushed down a journalists throat until he chokes a story, young Ronald Farebrother of Audley Road, Hendon, really IS on the way up.

As Mill Hill boxer Terry Downes once remarked, Ron's a natural, even with the gloves off.

It was his way of saying that Ron (he has now changed his name to Ron Cane) is landing pukka jobs in the precarious celluloid world.

Breathless stuff. The article went on to recount how Ron has just finished six weeks shooting, the last four at ABPC studios in Borehamwood for *The Double Man*, a film starring Britt Ekland and Yul Brynner. In one scene Ron had to pretend to break a leg skiing and spent two weeks hobbling about on the set wearing a knee-length plastercast.

This newspaper story was not a fantasy, for when *The Double Man* was duly released in 1967, Ron really was in it. A publicity still shows the lad from Hendon, complete with plastercast, standing right up close to Britt Ekland and Yul Brynner. He was playing the toyboy of British actress Moira Lister, in her day almost as glamorous as Britt Ekland.

Ron went on to take small parts in other features including *Salt and Pepper*, *Hostile Witness* and *Robbery*, produced by Stanley Baker. He picked up television roles in *Z Cars*, *Softly Softly* and, in 1968, *Year of the Sex*

Olympics. In 1972 he was cast as the third police constable in *Budgie*, the series starring Adam Faith as a Soho chancer. When Ron read the script he realised he was really playing an undercover detective. The role fitted him like a glove (down to the skill perhaps of director Mike Newell, who would later direct *Four Weddings and a Funeral*), but when the series was broadcast, Ron's appearance provoked derision and howls of laughter among the real-life detectives of north London who were arresting the tearaway on a regular basis. Later Ron would think this casting must have been an omen — a hint that one day he would work with the police — but usually he was type-cast: '99 per cent of the time I was a baddie.'

Where art ends and real life begins was already a conundrum to Ron. In March 1976 he made his first appearance in the columns of the *Sun*. He was clearly visible in a photo showing unlicensed fighter 'Pretty Boy' Shaw (who did not look pretty) struggling with one of his seconds. The occasion was a rough-house match in Harlow, Essex, which, as the newspaper put it, began as a grudge fight but ended in a riot with terrified women and children fleeing for safety. The fight was between Ron's brother, Fred Farebrother, an ex-professional boxer, and 'Iron Man' Joey Lazar. Fred had found the going too tough, so he quit early with a bleeding mouth and nose and a suspected broken rib.

Then, in the reporter's words, the BIG fight started. Fists flew as rival supporters rushed the ring. Pow! One of Fred's seconds was cut over the eye as an angry haymaker smacked into his face. Zap! The fighting rival fans tried to climb into the ring and the punch-up spilled into the crowd. 'Pretty Boy' Shaw was in the crowd and allegedly had a go at Fred's second. The punters were angry because they had forked out £2 each, but the fight lasted only six rounds. They must have wanted Fred, past his best at 39, to go on till he dropped (the tradition in rough-house fights). With women and children trapped by the mayhem and police arriving to break up the battle, the show was abruptly terminated.

Afterwards Fred Farebrother, a game boy, claimed his rib had been broken not by Joey Lazar but by world light-heavyweight champ John Conteh with whom he had been sparring a few days earlier. Undaunted, Fred challenged Joey to a return fight — even though Joey claimed to have been unbeaten in 150 unlicensed slogs.

But what of Fred's little brother, Ron? Well, it was Ron who had tipped off the reporter about the fight and thereby got his picture in the paper. Just 21 months later he was back in the *News of the World* in his own right. It was a self-serving piece on how TV actor Ron had recently visited the USA where 28-year-old Susan Bell fell for him in a big way. This Susan was now offering to buy Ron off his wife Anne for $20,000.

On her side Anne already knew about Susan because, she said, Ron always told her about the women he met on his trips. Anne had reason to remember Susan in particular because she had been sending Ron letters and calling him ever since he came home. Then at 6.30 one Sunday morning the phone started ringing. Anne got up, went downstairs and picked it up, only to find Susan on the other end. After the usual small talk, Susan said, 'I like your husband so much, I think he's wonderful,' and then offered Anne $20,000 to leave Ron. Anne asked if this was a joke but Susan replied she was very serious. Anne would get a $10,000 down payment as soon as she signed a separation agreement, and a further $10,000 when the divorce was completed.

At this point Ron took hold of the phone and asked Susan if she was drunk. She just said she was sending Ron and Anne some Christmas presents and asked for a photo of Ron in the nude. The article ended with a line saying he would be back in America in April 1978 to appear in a film, but this time Anne would be going with him to keep him away from such temptresses.

Ron never did make that film (or any other) in America, but he continued to tip off newspapers and television programmes with hot stories — not all about himself. His big scoop came in 1978 when he discovered the whereabouts of Joyce McKinney, the lubricous, bubbly blonde at the centre of the Mormon sex in chains affair. Ms McKinney, 27, had come all the way to England in pursuit of Kirk Anderson, a clean-cut Mormon missionary who had suffered the misfortune of crossing her path back in the USA. Like hundreds of other young adherents of the faith, Kirk was dispatched to Britain to proselytize, but Joyce tracked him down, only to find him steadfast in his resolve to spurn her marital manifesto. She then adopted plan B. In league with another American, Keith May, she kidnapped Kirk, chained him down in a house in Edgware and forced him to make love to her.

It wasn't long before the police tracked down the kidnappers, raided the house, released the upstanding but horizontal Anderson and returned him to the upright. McKinney and May were charged with kidnapping, but while awaiting trial at the Old Bailey they were given bail. They now rented a flat in Hendon, close by a corner shop run by none other than Ron Farebrother. She used to pop in for cigarettes or sweets, and I used to talk to her. Then she did a runner she fled back to America which I knew about before the police did.

At this point Ron spotted a splendid business opportunity: he could set up an interview with McKinney for the BBC. 'She had disappeared, but I knew where her mother lived. So I rang the BBC and persuaded them I really could find her. Then I went to South Carolina, with a reporter, we found her Mum in a shack and told her we wanted to speak to Joyce. Then Joyce turned up in a hotel, we did the interview, and it ran on TV over two nights. The BBC even gave me a researcher's credit.'

Ron's appetite for setting up events for the media was now ravenous. Within hours he was at it again, this time in Los Angeles, negotiating a £2000, six-page feature in *Men Only* magazine. This was to consist entirely of nude pictures of the fiery McKinney, now exposed as a former bondage hostess. The photos were taken, but the deal fell through when she was arrested by the FBI and charged with travelling on a forged passport. Tried in July 1979, she was ordered to enter a mental home for treatment for her obsessive condition. The British never asked for her back. She would have wrought havoc in Holloway.

By now Ron was having more success as a newspaper tipster than as an actor. Despite parts in *The Sweeney* and *Minder*, he wasn't making a living out of either the small or the big screen. He found the pickings far easier playing himself. He set up an afternoon drinker, paying £100 to Finchley football club to keep its two bars open after the pubs had closed. 'For six years this proved unbelievably profitable,' says Ron. He went on to set up a nightclub, also in Finchley. Both these premises were legal, but Ron was never far from villainy. Indeed by his mid-30s his acting career had been superseded by a career not in pubs, clubs or even journalism, but in crime.

On 15 April 1982 at ten in the evening Ron and two other men smashed the glass of a front door in Ballard's Lane, Finchley. They broke into the premises but disturbed the occupier who called the police. The trio ran away, but Ron was soon captured and found to be equipped with the tools of the burglar's trade: a pair of bolt-cutters, a jemmy and a truncheon. He also had some stolen credit cards. Worst of all, he had an imitation firearm, though no one confronting him that night would have known it was just an imitation. In 1983 he was tried at the Old Bailey and jailed for three years. Despite his criminal associations, he had never been jailed before. At 36 the experience came as shock.

'I've spent my first night in Wandsworth, and it's my first morning, and I'm standing in the queue for breakfast. I see the guy in front getting only one sausage, so when it's my turn I ask for another sausage, but the con serving me says, "Only one sausage." Then I move on, and I ask for a second egg, but this time the server (another convict) says, "Help yourself." Then I ask the next guy for another piece of fried bread: "Help yourself."

'Then he stands back — and behind all these prisoners serving the food are a line of warders — screws. Then as I come to the end of the line, and I'm looking for somewhere to sit, one screw blows a whistle, and everyone backs away from me. I'm still wondering what all this is about, when out come the coshes, and the screws steam into me, beating me up and giving me a big cut over my eye. They don't ask questions. So I'm chucked in solitary for three hours, then I'm brought before the governor. And he says, "Started already, eh, Farebrother?" "Started what?" I ask. Then one of the screws says, "You don't know, do you?" "Know what?" "You're only allowed one of anything!"

'And that's what I'd got a good hiding for. And as I was going out of the room, they had a good laugh because they all thought I'd done it on purpose — to take the piss. They must have thought I was a regular con, so I had to know the drill already.'

Ron soon settled in. He even distinguished himself by being found guilty of causing a riot and getting transferred to a high-security jail on the Isle of Wight. On the outside, meantime, he enjoyed a little luck. He had appealed over his sentence, which was halved to 18 months. He was released on 6 July 1984, but while he was inside, both his drinking club and his nightclub had been shut down. Now he had no even semi-legitimate way of earning a living. Even so, he managed to stay out of trouble for a year, until one night he smashed the window of a house in Manor Way, Borehamwood. He was promptly arrested, according to the charge sheet for either intending to destroy the property of the occupier, Mrs New, or being reckless as to whether such property would be destroyed. He was fined £50, with £25 costs and ordered to pay £124 compensation. The supervising officer recorded that Ron was violent and complains always about the police.

Six months later he was caught driving while disqualified and fined £300 with £150 costs. At Borehamwood Police Station the supervising officer noted his truculent manner and recorded that he will complain given the opportunity or not. The Police National Computer (PNC) had displayed a warning signal for Ron. This described him as 'Violent'. When asked to indicate any warning signal that was evident but not shown on PNC, the supervising officer typed 'Liar'.

If that were how Ron was behaving with the police at this time, no wonder his wife Anne couldn't put up with him at home. 'I had been married to Anne for 19 years. We had three lovely children, and we had enjoyed lots of good times, but, with all my villainy, we'd also been having lots of rows and fights. When I came out of jail, I went straight back to criminal bits and pieces, ducking and diving. Not surprisingly, she'd had enough. The marriage was over.'

But, in a twist of undeserved good fortune, something went right for Ron. Just when everything looked lost, something — or rather someone — turned up to save him from tumbling into the abyss.

I hadn't given up hope of some legitimate work, so, picking up the threads of my old life as an actor, I went down to Elstree Studios and sniffed around for any job I could find. There I got talking to a woman running a firm called King and Country Car Hire, which had its own office within the studios. Her name was Pat Sherman, her husband had recently died, and she had just bought the business.

As I talked to her, it was clear that everyone was thieving from her. For instance, she had a problem in Spain. She'd been ripped off for 38 grand over a villa she wanted to sell. She had given power of attorney to an agent over there, so he could act on her behalf. Some time later he said he had a buyer and sent over some papers for her to sign, but she didn't have them read properly. Then one day she rang up her villa, and a Scottish couple answered the phone. They said they had bought the place. It was theirs! And suddenly she realised that this agent had sold the villa without telling Pat, and pocketed the money.

So, without telling Pat, I made a call to Spain to someone a bit heavy who went to see this guy. And the cheque was brought over by hand within 48 hours. The collector refused to accept any commission. I found this extraordinary, but apparently I was thought to be a person worthy of respect in the underworld. Maybe I'd done someone a similar favour along the way. So Pat was overjoyed. That way I helped her quite a bit.

Soon I got to know Pat pretty well. I was divorced within six months of meeting her, but by then I'd already moved into her house. It was one wing of a wonderful mansion called Frogmore House. What's more, I'd taken over the day-to-day responsibilities of running King and Country Car Hire. It was doing good business, and for once I was doing a straight job well. Pat and I did a deal: if I shook off all the hangers-on at Elstree — all the parasitical drivers from other firms that were taking her business — and if I reclaimed the debts and put the company back on its feet, I would get 50 per cent of the shares. Which is what happened.

At Elstree Film Studios — also known as Borehamwood Studios — international stars would often walk into Ron's office after a day's filming to ask for a limousine home.

I didn't normally open up King's Cars on a Saturday, unless filming had been specially scheduled, but this particular Saturday I was in there doing the books, when in walked Michael Caine. I was completely thrown because I wasn't expecting any customers, least of all Michael Caine. He'd been dropped off earlier for a wardrobe fitting, and now he wanted a car home. So I said, 'You'll have to wait about 20 minutes,' but it turned out he waited half an hour. He was all right about it, though, and spent some of the time looking at all the photos of different stars on the walls of my office. Anyway, I told him I'd put the car on the account, and when it came I thought that was that.

A couple of hours later my chauffeur returned after dropping him off and said, 'Oh, Michael Caine sent this back for you.' And what Caine had done was take the band off his cigar and say, 'Give this to Ron and say thanks very much for the car.'

The cheeky bastard! I didn't know if he was taking the piss or what. So Monday morning came, and when Caine turned up I said, 'Have I upset you, by giving you the wrong car or something?'

Now he thought I was having a go at him, which I wasn't, but I did wonder if he'd had a go at me. See, in other circumstances, and in the circles I'd mixed in all my life, that could have led to a stand-up fight. Especially as half the guys in these twilight zones suffer from appalling inferiority complexes. And Caine himself, who came from a similar background in south London, should have known that. Luckily I recognised he meant no harm before I did something I might have regretted.

Sometimes I was asked to do special jobs. I looked after Lauren Bacall when she was filming at Borehamwood. She just wanted a bodyguard, so I did it as a freebie. She lived in a dream world of gangsters, as if she were still with Humphrey Bogart. She loved it! Then in July 1985 David Bowie was working at Elstree, on the Jim Henson film, *Labyrinth*, when along came the Live Aid concert at Wembley for famine relief in Ethiopia. He had his own security, but, because he was at Elstree, he wanted me to look after him. So I did Live Aid with Bowie. That was the big one. It ended up a three-day party. Something else! I had my own bus back behind the stage, parked beside Elton John. Elton — typical mad bastard he was then — was frying up hot dogs and hamburgers with grass in them, before going out front to perform to over a billion people. And there they all were: Paul Young, Mick Jagger, Bowie and Elton John. After the show we went to Brown's nightclub and then on to Elton John's mansion near Watford.

Such diverting jobs were a bonus. Most of the time Ron was building up the firm's bread-and-butter turnover. Business was looking up partly because there were two studios at Elstree: the main film studios, where King's was based, and the old ATV Studios a couple of streets away. When Ron started with King's there was almost nothing in production in the ATV Studios, but then they were taken over by the BBC. In no time they were being used to produce *EastEnders*, soon to become the most successful soap in BBC television history.

Before *EastEnders* they weren't doing anything there. When it started we were ideally placed to get all the car work, like taking the actors home, because we were right on the spot. With the exception of Wendy Richards the cast was unknown, complete nothings, nobodies to the general public: even actors who would soon become household names like Leslie Grantham, Anita Dobson and Letitia Dean. They were all relative youngsters then, so Julia Smith, the creator and first producer of *EastEnders*, told me, 'Make sure they get home, and they don't go clubbing.'

EastEnders was a fantastic success. It took off almost immediately. Then about three months later I started noticing the difference in the attitudes of the actors, most of all, Dirty Den: Leslie Grantham.

A typical example. When I sent the cars over every Wednesday and Thursday night, my drivers all knew precisely who they were picking up. I used to go across with a list and make sure everything was all right.

So this particular Thursday night when I went over, I found all my drivers waiting, and I saw each of the artistes get into the right car. Then I saw Leslie Grantham go over to one driver, and I heard him say, 'Were you all right last night?' Now straight away I knew this particular driver shouldn't have driven Grantham last night, because my manager was meant to have done that job himself.

So I interrupted and said, 'What happened last night?', and my driver said, 'No, no, nothing. We had a bit of a bang and had to get away quick.' Then it all became clear: my drivers had switched bleeding tickets, this particular guy, Tommie, had then gone clubbing with Leslie Grantham and had some kind of shunt. So I said to Tommie, politely and calmly, 'Don't ever swap tickets again or you're out of a job.' And he said, 'All right Ron.'

At this point Grantham in his wisdom — whatever you want to call it — or Jack the Lad fucking shit he was trying to pull — raised his voice and said, 'If you want to have a go at anyone, have a go at me. I'm the one who took him out.' So I said, very quietly, 'Well, now you're talking like that, don't raise your voice to me,' and Julia Smith, Wendy Richards, everyone heard this — so Grantham continued, 'Well, if you want trouble, you don't know who you're fucking around with!'

I said, 'OK, then, I'm sorry.'

Whack! I banged him. He went down like a ton of shit. And I said, 'And you don't know who you're fucking around with, you little cunt.'

And Julia was in the back there. She was holding her little dog, Roly, on a lead (in fact it was a bloody great poodle), and he was barking. I swear she put her thumbs up and mouthed, 'Thank you, Ron! About time he was put in his place,' but I may be wrong.

And after that Dirty Den was as good as gold with me. Funny thing is, I could have ended up alongside him in *EastEnders* myself. It had been going for a year, when Julia jokingly told me, right in front of the scriptwriter, Tony Holland, 'You would make an excellent wayward brother for Dirty Den.' I said, 'What? "Dirty Den and Randy Ron?" Yeah, all right, Julia! You couldn't afford me!'

I'll give all the actors their due — I thank them now for sticking up for me when the BBC tried to take the *EastEnders* car work off King's. Until that moment the BBC had recognised Elstree Studios as a location, which meant the artistes were entitled to cars booked local to the Studios. But suddenly someone at BBC headquarters in west London turned round and said to the artistes, 'Right! Now you get all your cars booked from here.' I was amazed when the whole cast threatened to strike unless they were allowed to keep on using King's Cars.

Mind you, I had previously got a little memo out to

each of them, saying, 'Do us a favour: they're trying to take the contract away from me.' So they all made their threat to strike, and Julia told the BBC bureaucracy they preferred my cars. That secured my monopoly of *EastEnders* work — for the time being at least.

I'm not sure I wholly deserved their loyalty because sometimes I really took the piss out of them. There was one occasion — a Royal Variety Show, I believe — when the whole cast of *EastEnders* was called up to the West End. As usual, I was supplying all the cars, but then Julia Smith turned round and said, 'Now, nobody must have a better car than the others or they'll all start moaning "Im not getting in that car", and all that nonsense.' So I said, 'They'll all have the same cars, don't worry about it. We'll number each car, so that when they come out they'll see the number 2 in the window, and they'll know it's theirs.' She told me this would be at five o'clock so I thought I'd give her a treat because she was, after all, the godmother of the whole thing: I got her a white Rolls-Royce.

But suddenly, late in the day, she rings me up and says, 'Darling, I don't want to panic you but we need an extra car: for Roly the Dog!' I said, 'No!' 'Yes, seriously. The dog's got to have it's own car, 'cos none of the actors will let it get in their cars in case it spoils their clothes.'

So I thought about it, and I said, 'I've got the ideal car. Hes going in car number 1.' And I sent the white Roller over for the fucking dog, while all the others were getting in saloons. Up rolled number 1, and I went out and said, 'Come on, in you get, boy, that's yours!'

Julia Smith had a big smile on her face. She said it just knocked everybody's ego on the cast. They could not compete with that — especially when the dog turned up outside the Palladium or wherever in the white Roller.

I'm making light of it, but the media pressure on the cast was huge. It's probably even bigger today. Wendy Richards, Anna Wing, Letitia Dean: they all stayed at my place some Wednesdays and Thursdays, the rehearsal and recording days. That was after the novelty wore off of staying at the local Hilton Hotel, where you always had pressmen sitting there and taking photos.

Leslie Grantham had a very hard time from the tabloids. His criminal record was worse than mine. He had been convicted of a murder in Germany, so he'd spent 11 years in jail before he became an actor. When this first came out, he was getting a lot of bad publicity, so I told him, 'Let it ride.' I told him I should know because I'd also been an actor, and I'd been in all sorts of trouble with the law.

After we'd got over our little disagreement, he used to come over to the office lunchtimes to have a chat. He and that other *EastEnders* star Peter Dean never got on, they hated each other, they were like schoolboys. Peter used to come over too, but naturally not when Leslie was around. They'd both slag each other off.

Letitia Dean was a lovely girl, with lovely parents, a great Dad. I met him a couple of times — he came into the studios to speak to me. He asked if I'd keep an eye on his daughter, not to go wild and chaperone her, but just make sure she was looked after, sit down and chat to her. Then there was Adam Woodyatt: I told him to get rid of his silly fucking bike. And lovely old Anna Wing — Loo Beale. I also did Wendy Richards a favour or two. She was having problems with her boyfriend. He was a bit of a drunken bully, so she wanted an outsider to come in and have a quiet word with him. He had to be spoken to, and he was spoken to. Then he left.

I did a lot of services like that, but I can't go into the details of what they were or who they were for. Let's just say that King's became quite well known for easing *EastEnders* actors' personal difficulties, but I could never invoice them for that.

One client Ron did invoice was the Ministry of Defence establishment round the corner from the studios in Borehamwood. 'I was doing all their stuff. Taking their VIPs and generals around, carrying their top secret documents. That was a big contract I had with them, my biggest, so I didn't rely solely on the studios. I had it well sewn up with the Ministry too.' Clearly, Ron was one servant of the Crown who was not positively vetted. If only the Ministry had known who his real masters were at that time. But then, outwardly, he was now the employee of a pillar of local society: Pat Sherman.

'Pat was a highly respected woman. She was so respected, she was going to be appointed a magistrate. The only thing she had to do was pass some final test or exam, and she would be sitting "on the bench" as a JP at Watford. But three weeks before that was due to happen, I was back in big trouble over an unfortunate incident.'

It was unfortunate for several people, firstly for the owner of a house a few miles away that was petrol-bombed in July 1986. The police put Ron down as a suspect. At dawn on 10 July he was arrested on suspicion of causing criminal damage and taken to Watford Police Station.

'Obviously they thought I had something to do with it, but I wasn't saying anything. One of my drivers was having trouble with a bloke who was threatening his daughter and her mother. He was a big lump. So someone went round and got him in the bath, then his car got smashed up, his driveway was wrecked, and then someone went back at one in the morning and fire-bombed the top and bottom of his house. See, we knew he was the sort of guy who would come back on us, so someone had to go back first, to give him the message not to bother. Of course, when the police asked me, I said, "No comment." '

Soon Ron was on the verge of a far worse charge: attempted murder, and there was more to come. In a simultaneous raid on his firm, King and Country Car Hire, Elstree Studios, the police had searched Ron's desk. In one drawer they found a 7.65 mm Mauser automatic pistol and ammunition clip. Illegal possession of a firearm is manifestly a serious offence, but for Ron it was doubly serious because to possess a firearm within five years of leaving prison is a further crime in itself. Ron was held in Watford Police Station for six weeks (the prisons were full up at the time), during which he was put on an identification parade for the bombing. If picked out, it would be attempted murder.

'First the wife came right up to me and said, "No, he's definitely not here." Then the guy walked in and said, "No, he's not here," and that was it. So you see, they got the message.'

This did not mean Ron was out of trouble — he still faced the gun charge — but, appearing at St Albans Crown Court in May 1987, he played a faultless defence. He testified that drivers under his control often had to collect props needed for films like *Raiders of the Lost Ark* and *Superman IV*. He said he had seen the gun lying around in an outer office a few months earlier, but when the police found it in his drawer, 'My first reaction was shock. I said it was probably a prop from a film set, it was not mine. I also pointed out that other people had access to my desk drawers, which were always full of junk.'

The jury believed Ron and found him not guilty. The judge even awarded him costs, but he also ordered the Mauser to be destroyed. As it had been found only yards from the Albert Square set, it was inevitable that Ron should announce he was going to celebrate with a right old *EastEnders* knees-up.

'Though I was cleared, the affair completely scuppered Pat's hopes of becoming a magistrate. I was already living with her so she felt she had no choice but to withdraw before her name went up on the list of new beaks. She could hardly avoid this because she would have been sitting as a magistrate in the very same court in Watford where I first came up on the gun charge!

'You would think Pat would have had enough of me by now, but no. Despite all the trouble I was causing her, she wanted to marry me. The first I knew about her scheme was on a Thursday when she told me, "By the way, you haven't forgotten, this Saturday you're getting married." Forgotten? It had been arranged completely behind my back! So I said, "Pat, this has to be a windup. Yes?" But no. So I phoned up the kids and told them about it.

'Luckily my mate Bill Goodman had got back from holiday a day early so he became my best man. But when we got to the Register Office, the registrar gave every appearance of being — well, in my terms — a raving poofter. He was camping it up, just like Kenneth Williams. The only thing missing was make-up. The next wedding group were in the same room, queuing up behind us. So he started:

' "Today we have two lovely couples getting married!," in that kind of voice, sounding like a right queen. "Do you, Ronald Patrick Farebrother, take Patricia Sherman to be your lawful wedded wife?"

'So by now I was pretty far gone and I said, "Hold on," and I took out a coin, and I said to him, "If it comes down tails, we're on!" I flipped it up, and the guy was shocked. "This is a solemn occasion. A marriage." So I blew him a kiss, and I said, "Don't worry, darling, it's tails! Go for it!" And he looked at Pat, and she smiled and said, "Carry on!" and that was it. And the kids and everybody couldn't believe it especially the people behind us who wanted to get married as well. The other groom and his friends were crying with laughter, they thought it was a Carry On film. I've even got a photo with Bill Goodman holding up the wedding certificate and two fingers as well. Believe it or not, even Pat thought it was a joke.'

Some other folk did not find Ron so funny. All the time he was working at King's Cars, one policeman was keeping a very close eye on him: the chief of Borehamwood CID, Detective Inspector Morse. Yes, Morse really was his name, though unlike his fictional namesake, his first name was no secret. It was Dennis.

Dennis Morse saw himself as Ron Farebrother's nemesis. To him Ron was a grave danger to society, a major villain who delighted in giving local cops the runaround. It therefore became Morse's personal mission to lock Ron up, preferably for a very long time. Today Ron recalls the inspector's relentless harassment almost with affection.

Morse used to take a perverse pleasure in phoning me up

as soon as I walked in my office. He knew when to call because Borehamwood Police Station was only 200 yards from the studios, so he often saw me as I walked in each morning from my car.

He was a real character. He used to ring up and say, in his singsong voice, 'G'mornin, Mr Farebrother. I see you're just arrivin' into work.'

I'd say, 'What do you want, Morsey?', and he'd hang up. Then he'd come down to the studios and knock on my window: 'Mornin, Mr Farebrother! Just thought I'd pop down for a cup of coffee, wiv a respectable businessman like yourself!' I used to take it as a joke. Surely the police had something better to do than piddle around like this. And this was no footslogging constable, this was a DI! I could not believe Morse was in charge of the local fucking CID, but this was the farthest outpost of the Metropolitan Police, so it was never going to be filled with Scotland Yard's finest.

One day Morse rang up and said, 'I like to see you come out of your office, Mr Farebrother. Had a nice game of pool and a few drinks? Next time I come round, can I have a bit more vodka?' That's when I said, 'Get on with your fucking TV series, Morse, and leave me alone.'

He was a character, Morsey. He used to ask favours. Well, they all asked for favours, the Old Bill. He said, 'I've got my sister-in-law coming over from Australia. It'd be nice if she could be picked up from Heathrow in a nice little limo, wouldn't it?' I said, 'Free of charge, as usual, Morsey?'

One day he wanted to play a trick on a sergeant. This guy was a custody officer who had served at Borehamwood for donkey's years. He was retiring, these were his final days, so Morsey asked if I knew anyone in special effects. He wanted a rotting corpse.

So I said, 'For you, Morsey, anything! I'll have a look and call you back.' I went to the special effects area, saw some old dummy corpse they had lying around, and it really looked as if it had only just snuffed it. So I rang him back to say I'd bring it over to the station myself. I came in the back way — I knew my way around the place as Morse had brought me in the back way often enough in handcuffs — and meantime they had got rid of the custody officer. He was having his lunch break, and this was his last day. Then they took one of the live prisoners out of his cell, put him somewhere else and replaced him with this fucking corpse, covered up with a blanket.

Then, as Morsey told me later, they get the uniform inspector to come in and do the usual check on the condition of the prisoners, before giving the custody officer a rousing send-off. The inspector opens each cell in turn and confirms everything is all right. But when he gets to the end cell he asks, 'How long has this gentleman been in here?' And the custody officer says, 'He's been in here overnight.' So when they open up the door, the inspector says, 'I think he's been in here a bit longer than that! The man's fucking dead!'

Of course, when the custody officer looks in, he panics, because all he sees is this dead body, caked in blood. Worst thing that can happen to a custody officer, especially on his last day! Then roars of laughter from everyone else: 'Don't worry, pal, it's a joke!'

Performing such favours for the police gained Ron no immunity. Still perpetually surveilled by the steely-eyed Morse, never knowing when he was going to be arrested again, he carried on unbowed. Far from retreating into his shell, he aggressively sought publicity. In October 1987 a local paper carried an article by Anna Avino headlined TOUGH GUY RON'S GOT A NEW ROLE.

Tucked away in a corner of Cannon Film Studios in Elstree is a small office. Amid the battered furniture and scruffy decor sits Ron Farebrother looking every bit the smart company director despite his surroundings.

At once it is obvious he is in control of the proceedings, and in this case, that means playing chauffeur to the stars and providing them with protection against any eventuality.

The piece went on for an entire page eulogising Ron and his staff. He remarked that his minders-for-hire weren't blokes with broken noses and cauliflower ears. They must be polite and diplomatic, be able to fit into any situation and know how to spot trouble before it starts. The piece ended with an optimistic prediction:

Although he has led a chequered life and dabbled in a variety of enterprises he says he is now settled and happy and would not want to do anything else with his time. But he is still only 40, so who knows?

What the reporter did not know — and nor did anyone at Elstree Film Studios — was that Ron was already doing a lot more with his time. He wasn't just the boss of a car firm with a few minor convictions. He was heavily involved in international organised crime. He was a front man for one of the strongest factions in London's underworld. He was nothing less than this British mob's roving ambassador to the Mafia in America.

AMBASSADOR TO THE MOB

Ron's behaviour towards the police in the mid-1980s — violent, complains always, will complain given the opportunity or not — as inscribed on his arrest sheets reflected far more than the anti-authority attitude he had worn like a medal of honour ever since his tempestuous infancy. It stemmed from his mounting irritation at the local coppers' habit of treating him with the disrespect due to a low-grade neighbourhood villain when his real status in London gangland was soaring year by year.

Of course, Ron could not brag to the Plods of Borehamwood about his connections, but the truth was that he now belonged to one of Britain's most enduring underworld firms. This outfit owed its 30-year survival largely to the fact that its godfathers lived lives of outward respectability. Ron's arrest record for petty crime and his volatile temper jarred with this strategy. Indeed, his freelance antics could have embarrassed the clan, except that no one high up in British law enforcement seems to have known that Ron was part of it.

He had first come to the clan's notice through the boxing game in the 1970s while minding his brother Fred, sparring partner to world champions Terry Downes and John Conteh. The presiding genius in this circle was the leading sports and show business ticket agent, Alex Steene. From his offices in Panton Street in the heart of London's West End, Steene ran a flourishing legitimate business through which he sold tickets for fights licensed by the British Boxing Board of Control (and fought under the Marquess of Queensberry's Rules) as well as maintaining an interest in the unlicensed version of the sport.

From as far back as the 1960s Alex Steene had powerful allies in both the overworld and the underworld. He was a staunch friend of the Kray brothers. He was happy to be photographed in their company. He posed for press photographs with Ronnie Kray, the notorious former East End gang boss, at Ronnie's wedding party in Broadmoor in 1985. Much later, in 1995, he would turn out, proudly and unashamedly, as a pallbearer at Ronnie's spectacular funeral, unmistakable with his shock of flowing silver hair and ever present dark glasses. Far from concealing his underworld associations, for 30 years Alex Steene had advertised them — without any obvious adverse effect on his business activities.

Steene's partner in some of these activities was Joey Pyle, another friend of the Krays but with his own fearsome underworld reputation (merited or not). For much of the 1970s and 1980s both men found themselves playing a considerable role in Ron Farebrother's life, or so Ron claims.

Ron says he first made an impression on 'the Alex Steene set' over a boxing match between the two giants of the unlicensed version of the sport. For weeks beforehand Steene was bursting to get publicity for the fight so Ron hit on the idea of exploiting his huge credit with the BBC over the Joyce McKinney interview, to perform a big favour for the bizarre impresario.

I told this BBC producer all about the unlicensed fight game and how it had never been covered on television. I said there was this huge grudge match coming up between Lenny McLean and Roy Shaw, which the 'Guv'nor' was desperate to win because 'Pretty Boy' had licked him last time. I had an 'in' with Steene because my brother Fred was also fighting that night, lower down the bill. My other lever was that Roy Shaw was in Steene's own stable and he was always looking to boost the profile even of this rather nasty side of his sporting interests.

The *Tonight* programme jumped at the idea, so I took the film crew down to Sinatra's Club in South Croydon where the show was being put on. Maybe Steene thought the BBC would portray the fight as just as well regulated as a licensed contest: with doctors in attendance, a strict referee, each round no longer than three minutes (but any number of rounds) and a bucket passed round for donations to charity. It turned out to be nothing of the sort.

When Roy Shaw paraded into the ring I took one

look at him and realised he wasn't himself. That wasn't the Roy Shaw I knew. He didn't know where he was and I knew he wasn't going to do himself justice. Most nights he could have given Lenny a real good hiding, like he had at their previous meeting, but this time he was out of it. He looked as if he'd taken too many vitamins. The fight was a walk-over. Lenny was all over him but don't have any doubt about it: Lenny was just a big bully. There was nothing noble about the 'Noble Art' when he was in the ring. He knocked Roy to the ground but, instead of walking away till Roy had recovered — like he'd have to do under Queensberry Rules — he put the boot in. He was kicking Roy in the face time after time and roaring like a gorilla, 'Who's the fucking Guv'nor now?!!!'.

The BBC cameraman was shaking like a leaf, especially when I steered him into the ring to shoot close-ups of all this brutality. Through his lens Lenny looked just like King Kong but without King Kong's gentle touch. When the programme went out, the Steene camp might have realised it was a disaster for the unlicensed game, especially as Steene's man Shaw had been schmeissed to smithereens. But instead Steene loved it. He thought it was a triumph. Getting the fight on TV really impressed him and it also seemed to impress Joe Pyle.

Through the Steene connection I got to know Roy Shaw pretty well. He ran his own unlicensed fight nights in an ex-servicemen's club in Dagenham for five or six years. I used to go there quite often because Roy always put on a good show. Don't get the idea that his fighters were prime hunks of British manhood: toned, muscled, in perfect condition. Most were either fat old slobs or average local lads willing to get in the ring and earn a few quid. Many looked as if they had never stepped in a ring before.

Roy was ruthless with them. He'd be standing at the ringside giving hell to anyone who didn't deliver. If some guy got knocked over and hit the canvas, he'd be yelling in his ear, 'Come on you cunt, you're not staying down there! Get up or you're not getting paid!'. Then the guy would mumble, 'I've had enough', and Roy would shout back, 'You! Fuck off! You get up. You fucking challenged him!'.

A lot of bouts were challenges. One time a twenty-stone greengrocer from Essex told Roy he wanted to fight a trader he had some grudge against. When he got in the ring all the punters burst out laughing, "Look at the state of him," and inevitably he was being punched to pulp. Then his corner threw in the towel but, instead of letting the guy retire, Roy threw the towel back and bellowed, "You said you wanted to fight him! Now get back out there!".

Of course, Roy's tirades were all part of the show. The punters loved to hear him giving some poor tub of lard a good bollocking.'

Another man Ron met at this time was young Frankie Warren, today Britain's leading licensed boxing promoter.

It helped that Lenny McLean was a friend of his. That's how I met them both. I'd show up at unlicensed fight venues all over the place, not just Dagenham, but Romford, and all the way to Leeds. And somehow I ended up driving Alex Steene to these dos. And Joe Pyle too. I had to take Alex to a lot of charity functions, often for one of his favourite causes, the Ex-

Boxers Association which Roy always supported.

One ex-boxer who benefited from Steene's goodwill was Joe Erskine, the Welshman who had become British heavyweight champion in 1956, only to lose the title in 1958. He retired in 1964 and like many headline fighters before him, he gambled his winnings away and was left almost destitute.

And so it was that on Sunday, 29 April 1979 at the Club Double Diamond in Caerphilly, the worlds of showbusiness and boxing joined together to pay tribute to Joe Erskine. Topping a star-studded bill were the comedian Jimmy Tarbuck and the singer Frankie Vaughan. According to the souvenir programme, the show's sponsor was Alex Steene, and on the front cover was a heart-warming photo of Joe Erskine, Frankie Vaughan and Alex Steene in a beaming triple embrace.

One page of the programme was sponsored by none other than Ron Farebrother whose bold features gazed out from beneath an uncharacteristic mop of curled hair. Never one to undersell himself, Ron wished Joe Erskine a successful evening on behalf of the entire cast of his forthcoming television series, *Minder*. This quotation may mystify *Minder* addicts who would swear that the stars of this long-running comedy drama were George Cole and Dennis Waterman. Ron's fleeting appearance in one episode may have passed by even his own most ardent fans.

The Caerphilly show, to which many good people gave their unstinting efforts without charge, was by way of an apology for the embarrassing aftermath of a far bigger fund-raiser for Joe Erskine in London three months earlier. The occasion had been graced by the biggest draw in boxing, no-one less than Muhammad Ali, the charismatic ex-world champion, who had flown the Atlantic to help out his old adversary. Ron Farebrother claims that using Alex Steene as his calling card, he had set up the great man's trip,

'I had gone to America to see Muhammad Ali's secretary and arrange to get him over here to do a benefit night for Joe Erskine for no fee whatever. The connection was Alex Steene. Naturally I was with Ali when he was picked up at Heathrow, and I arranged the security for his appearance at the Rainbow Theatre in Finsbury Park on 14 January 1979.

'That evening we used two white Rolls-Royces to pick him up from the Hilton Hotel, Park Lane. It was horrendous. Everyone was trying to get to him, the press and the punters. We had to bring him down in the service elevator.

'At the Rainbow we hit other problems. The theatre had its own security for the premises alone, so I took care of the artistes' security — a different ballgame altogether. I'd told the Rainbow people how I wanted Ali to come in through some back door but, whatever I wanted, Ali insisted on coming in the main entrance. Of course, I had to say OK, even though this increased my headaches. Now he's a well-loved man, and hundreds of people wanted to be near him. So I decided I should stand way in front of him on a raised area. This meant that, as he's coming towards me, I can look down at the crowd following him and see everybody's face. And about 15 people back from Ali I could see this white guy going, "Ali! Ali! Ali!"

'Now what struck me was that he was wearing a dirty old raincoat — a sort of flasher mack — so on the walkie-talkie radio I called up the staff and said, "Get hold of that guy!" He was getting nearer and nearer to Ali's back, but these security guys on the ground beside him could see fuck all. So I go forward to take this guy myself, and when he was only two people back from Ali, I grabbed him by both his arms so he couldn't do anything.

'This was just to calm him down, but when we opened up his mack we found he had a carving knife. If we hadn't stopped him, he would have stabbed Ali, maybe killed him.

'Now right there in the Rainbow lobby was a fountain, so I decked him, and he went down in that. I broke my finger. Then we found out later that this guy was a mental patient.

'Ali thanked me, so did his secretary, and later that night I got a programme, the only one of its kind, signed by both Muhammad Ali and Henry Cooper, and dedicated to Ron and Anne — my wife then and the mother of my kids. This was a bit special, but it followed on from a private meeting between those two fighters with only me in the room with them.

'Henry said, "I hear you've just had a narrow escape out there," and Ali replied, "Yeah, but it was no problem because Ron here sorted it all out."

'Once we'd done the show, to get over the security problems and away from the Hilton, we drove him and his secretary to my place, and they stayed with us for the night and most of the next day. He loved it over there. You wouldn't believe it. There was this huge personality — the most famous sportsman in the world at that time — and he was sleeping in this three-bedroom chalet bungalow in Well End with me, my wife and kids.

'As for the show itself, that turned out to be a disaster. There were lots of stars on the bill, Tom O'Connor and Frankie Vaughan, but the money went missing. We were gobsmacked that anyone would actually fuck off with all the cash. The git that did it was someone else on the show. Now the shit hit the fan. The friends of Joe Erskine all thought we'd taken the money, but none of us had it. We were really pissed off. That's why we put on another show quick in Caerphilly. But we couldn't get Ali for that.'

Ron says Muhammad Ali remained under his protection during several more visits to London over the next three years — all arranged through Alex Steene. According to Ron, Steene has always been very generous, using his big-name connections to help all sorts of old boxers, broke and down on their luck. And through ex-prisoner charities, he has helped a lot of villains too.

'There'd be complimentary seats at top fights for these people. I'd arrange that they'd have no hassle getting in. The promoters all knew me by now, I'd arrive early and make sure the seats were there for "the chaps". When I showed up it was clear I was representing Alex Steene and Joey Pyle.'

Ron claims he earned Steene's affection through showing blind loyalty: being prepared to take on any task the Office, run by Joey Pyle, asked him to perform.

There was one occasion when Ron's loyalty was put to the sternest test. It was early in April 1979 when the Office asked him to go to Uganda and meet the notorious bullying tyrant, President Idi Amin, on their behalf. During Amin's eight-year rule thousands of people had disappeared, so Ron had a reasonable fear that he might join them. 'They thought I was going to back out, but I didn't.' That impressed them.

'The Office wanted me to go to Uganda with a certain blonde woman Amin had here in England. I think she was a stripper. She used to be his girlfriend, and my job was to protect her. I was going to keep her company, and, if anything went wrong, I was going to be the fall guy.

'They also wanted to do business in Uganda: supply toiletries, maybe — and I was going as their spokesman. I was told to follow certain rules in Amin's presence — when to bow, that sort of thing — but this lady was going to do the talking. She was already supplying him with home comforts from old England — toilet rolls and the like — but I think the Office had bigger deals in mind.

'Before I went to Uganda I had to go to Harley Street to have injections against malaria and other tropical diseases. One of these jabs didn't take. My arm came up like a balloon so we couldn't fly on the day we were booked, but I was still determined to go, so we were booked on the next flight. I was sitting at home with my suitcase packed in front of me and my ticket in my hand, when suddenly it came on the TV news: PRESIDENT AMIN OVERTHROWN.

'Then it hit me. If we had gone on the day we'd planned, I'd have been right in the thick of it. I'd probably have been arrested as a crony of the disgraced dictator. I could have been locked up or worse. That proved my loyalty to the Office.'

This wasn't the Office's only African venture.

Another leading underworld character, former south London gangland boss Charlie Richardson, had picked himself up after spending 18 years in jail and built up a portfolio of African interests, notably in mining. Through such entrepreneurial endeavours, Richardson had made great strides to become a legitimate businessman.

This, of course, was what Richardson had always claimed to be, before coming to grief in the notorious gangland torture trial of 1967. Throughout his ups and downs Charlie Richardson had remained a close friend of Joe Pyle's, and the pair would often meet to co-ordinate their ventures. In tow would be Ron Farebrother. 'We used to hold meetings quite frequently at the Russell Hotel [in London's Bloomsbury]. There'd be Joe, and Charlie, of course, along with Alex Steene and me and one or two others. There'd be discussions of different ventures — straight business, mining and the like — in different African countries. I'd turn up over breakfast to make sure everything was all right. I'd be chatting to Charlie as a friend of a friend. Representing the interests of our corner.'

By the early 1980s, Ron claims, he had so impressed Joey Pyle that he was being entrusted with the ultimate responsibility: representing the Office in America. This wasn't just on trips to get a fairly easygoing guy like Muhammad Ali to do charity shows but to front for them in active business negotiations. According to Ron, they even called him the Ambassador. Between 1984 and 1989 he flew to the USA on Office business two or three times every year. One of his early missions was to offer a peace treaty to stop a war before it had even begun. His Excellency was despatched to meet a very important person, by then arguably the most powerful character in all world boxing.

'They sent me over to see Don King. I was paid about a grand to deliver a letter: to make sure he opened it (and no one else did) and to make sure I got an answer. I didn't know what was in the letter, and I didn't bother to ask. I got there, phoned this number and said I had to bring the letter over. The guy said, "I'll pick it up," and I said, "No, I've got to deliver it myself direct to Don King. Stick it right in his hand."

'So they came to my hotel and picked me up. I was searched to make sure I wasn't carrying a weapon, then ushered in to see King. I handed him the letter, and he read it. Then he handed it to a really heavy-looking guy who turned out to be his secretary. King said, "Do you mind if my secretary reads this?" I said, "No, by all means," and the secretary guy pored over it.

'Don King asked, "Do you know the contents of the letter?" and I lied and said, "Yes, I do. All I need from you is a yes or no answer."

'At this point King handed me the letter, and I glanced at it for the first time. It was all to do with boxing. It said that if any US boxers come to England, they — the Office — want the same respect in England as Don King demands in America. In other words, if you take a boxer to America, King supplies all the minders. You always have to employ local security from Don King. We — the Office — were demanding the return deal here in Britain.

'Then his secretary said, "We'll kill him now."

' "Well, what a turn-up!" I thought. "Kill him now!" Does this guy mean it or is it just his sense of humour?"

'Whether or not he meant it, I knew the main thing was not to show fear. In a flash I decided I had to pretend to ignore the remark. I just repeated, "I want your answer yes or no in 24 hours."

'I certainly did not take "Kill him now" as a joke. I took it seriously. That would have been one way of answering London: Kill the messenger, meaning a bit more than No. More like Fuck you!

'At this point Don King was just smiling, in his normal way. He turned and walked out of the office. I turned, too, to leave. That was the first time in my life that I felt my back get warm. I visualised bullets going into it. But they didn't get fired so I quickly left King's place, got back to my hotel and rang up the Office. I said, "Right. I've delivered the letter. I'm packing my case and coming straight back. Then, as soon as I put the phone down on London, another call came through. It was Don King's office, and the answer was, "Yes, I'm sure we can do business."

'Strange to say, these people hadn't had any contact with King before. I don't think he'd ever been to Britain at that time. It was only later that I found he had a conviction for kicking a man to death and had done five years in jail. So I don't suppose knocking me off would have given him any sleepless nights.'

Back in London, with Alex Steene around, life was never dull.

'Alex is accident prone. We used to have these meetings, attended by a select few, maybe eight of us, and Alex would say, "Right, gentlemen, the meeting's open' and with a grand sweep of his hands he'd knock the phone off the table on to the floor.

'And then there'd be a guy called Micky, Joe Pyle and me killing ourselves with laughter. Mick used to make me crack up all the time. Steene would say, "We've got a very important man from America whom we'd like to welcome. He's very close to King, very close to Ali, he's come over here, and we'll be setting up our joint business." Meantime Mick would look at the American and whisper to me, "Look at his socks!" And I would look down and see he had on odd socks — a bright red one and a bright green one! So while Alex was being all formal and polite, we were giggling like schoolkids. These Americans would often be over here, and it was our job to take care of them, entertain them, and to find them female company.'

By the mid-1980s Greg Steene, Alex Steene's son, had become a leading boxing promoter and manager. This didn't do Alex's ticket business any harm, especially when Greg started managing a black light-heavyweight fighter called Dennis Andries, who became world champion in 1986. In March 1987 Andries was due to defend his title against Thomas 'Hitman' Hearns in Detroit. Sent along to mind him was Ron Farebrother.

'Detroit is like the capital city of the world of boxing. They've even got a statue of a gloved fist in the main street. When it came to the night of the fight, I walked Dennis out, and we stood there in the ring, while they played the national anthems, first the American (because Hearns was the challenger), then the British.'

'Now this girl who sang "The Star-Spangled

Banner" was absolutely brilliant. She had an organ playing, and the flags were flying, and after we'd finished "God Save The Queen", she came across, and I held the rope up for her so she could leave the ring. And I was so impressed with her that I said, "Excuse me, love, but you are going to go really far. You've got a great voice."

'There was this particular bloke standing by her, and he said, in his American drawl, "What do you mean, go furr?" I said, "No, far, as in a long long way, cos she's a really good singer. She's going to go places."And he looked at me as if I was fucking mad.

'Then Dennis Andries fell back on his seat laughing — this was just minutes before beginning a world-title fight and he was crying with laughter in the corner. And he turned round and said, "Aretha Franklin, you stupid bastard! That's Aretha Franklin." And I said, "Oh, bloody hell!"'

Dennis Andries lost the fight and his world title, but he would later win back the title twice — a unique achievement for a British fighter. He and Ron stayed friendly. Dennis used to go and see Ron in his office at Elstree on Saturday afternoons, just for a chat. Eventually he left the Steene fold and became his own manager, but the Andries-Hearns fight had demonstrated the link between the Office and Don King, whose organisation supplied most of the fight guards, the T-shirts, dressing gowns and the merchandising. This provoked something of a row with the Andries camp, which felt aggrieved at the small purse.

In the USA, boxing and showbusiness are closely intertwined, so Steene and Pyle's links with that world came in handy for Ron and his car-hire operation, especially when the biggest star of all showed up at Elstree, someone even Ron could not fail to recognise.

'Frank Sinatra was over here on a visit. Of course, he's a powerful man, and he had his own corner, his own security, wherever he went, for obvious reasons. Despite that, his head minder — his secretary — would still call on the resident facilities in London. So he would contact me and say, "We need three or four of your people to help out my people," and that's how the contact was made. The thinking was that we would know the "faces" over here — who to keep an eye on, who to avoid — and what particular local security Sinatra would need. And Sinatra, obviously, needed 24-hour security when he was here.

'He also needed cars. So when he turned up at Elstree Film Studios one day, it was obviously a job for King's Cars. So I had lined up a brand-new limousine, a black stretch Granada with just 79 miles on the clock. Tinted windows. It looked beautiful.

'Sinatra was arriving from the hotel at two in the afternoon, so I turned round and said, "We'll take him back from the studios to the hotel, then later, when we take him on to clubland, we'll take on the security from then." So the car's supposed to be arriving at three, after Sinatra's had lunch with Andrew Mitchell, the managing director of Cannon Studios. I made sure I was there, too, having lunch at a different table with Alex Steene and Joe Pyle.

'As he was leaving, I could see out of the window my beautiful limousine, especially for Sinatra. So I walked out, I was briefly introduced by his secretary, and I said, "Nice meeting you" and "Goodbye". Then

I walked round the limousine and said, "Here's your car, sir."

'And as I opened the back door, it fell off. It literally fell off in my fucking hand! The whole door just dropped down on the ground. And he smiled, and he said, "OK, this is a good joke, Ron, I appreciate your sense of humour, but I have got to get to town."

'And I just grinned and made out, "Yeah. Sorry about that." So to the day he died I guess he thought I played a practical joke on him, but it wasn't. The bolts hadn't been put in the hinges! The driver had checked his own door, he knew the engine was all right, it was nice and clean, but nobody had ever opened that back left-hand door. So it just fell. And so I said, "There's your other car, sir." Luckily, I had another stretch limo there. And so he got in, still smiling and waving, as if to say, "You silly cunt." '

Whatever Sinatra's view of Farebrother, Ol' Blue Eyes may have recognised his type. In America he had spent years hanging around wiseguys — Lucky Luciano, Joe Fischetti, Sam Giancana, Carlo Gambino, Paul Castellano — so taking rides in Ron Farebrother's motors should have made him feel at home.

For the guys with whom Ron was now associating, just to be in the presence of Frank Sinatra — let alone to lay on a limo for him — was like touching the ermine of a royal prince. The Mafiosi he had known — even just the ones he'd been photographed with — amounted to a roll-call of the greatest names in the history of organized crime in America. And these were just the kind of people whom Ron was now doing business with in California.

When the Ambassador was fronting for the Office

in America in the 1980s, his destination was usually Los Angeles. His mob connection was a man called Ronnie Lorenzo who ran Splash, one of the most exclusive restaurants on the Coast, located in Malibu, right on the beach near Point Dume. Lorenzo did not just manage Splash in name. When diners entered the restaurant, he often greeted them himself. In July 1987 the *Los Angeles Times* summed the place up in glowing terms: Splash, at 6800 Westwood Beach Road, is trendy and expensive even by Malibu standards. Its parking lot at night is usually filled with high-priced cars and limousines. Secluded and casually elegant, Splash is a favourite with the movie set.'

Citing a financial report, the *LA Times* went on to state that Lorenzo, aged 41, ran Splash with all of 26 employees, but its declared sales constituted a mere $635,000 — scarcely impressive if the prices were that high.

That was the best news in the *LA Times* for Lorenzo. The worst was that Los Angeles Police Chief Daryl Gates had just accused the chic eatery of being a front for laundering drug money. The Los Angeles Police Department (LAPD) had begun its money-laundering probe in March 1987 after Lorenzo was arrested on a fugitive warrant from New Jersey.

Splash was associated with another operation branded a drug-money laundry by the LAPD. This was Art Auctions Inc., which, the previous year, had helped the restaurant hold two charity nights when reproduction items were sold for up to $1500 each.

The main characteristic of a drug-money laundering operation is that the front enterprise — be it a restaurant, an auction house or a carpet-cleaning company — doesn't have to make a genuine profit. Indeed, it can run at a heavy loss. However, it will show some profit because drug proceeds are being pumped into the sales figures. These figures are then declared to the tax authorities, and tax is duly paid. This way the drug money is laundered clean and can be safely used for other outwardly legitimate investment.

These days most police departments investigating organized crime have caught up with such tricks, so you can't run a cheap pizza parlour with no customers all year round and then declare a million-dollar profit. Someone is likely to notice. The operators of Splash therefore adopted the opposite tactics. The food was expensive, the decor plush, and the rich and spoilt of Hollywood flocked in. Unfortunately they weren't paying out enough greenbacks, and, it seems, Splash was plunging deep into debt.

Mine Host Ronnie Lorenzo was not a native Californian. He had arrived in 1982 from New York, where, federal authorities say, he was a made member of the Bonanno Mafia crime family and had risen to the rank of capo. Keeping up a Mafia tradition, Lorenzo had accumulated many personal friends in showbusiness, especially in Hollywood. Indeed, his best buddy was James Caan, who had played hot-tempered Sonny in *The Godfather*. The sentiment was reciprocated. In a statement Caan later released to the *Los Angeles Times*, the actor said 'Lorenzo is my best friend, and I love him. That's the way I was raised, and I know of no other way. I know of no crime this man has committed. And had he, he wouldn't be my best friend.' In court he would testify, 'If this man committed a crime, he would have to be Houdini. I'm with him all the time.' To the *Chicago Tribune* Caan ascended the ethical heights: 'I would never deny that my friend is my friend. Where's the morality in that?' And Caan put his money where his morals were. When his best buddy was in trouble with the law, Caan pledged his own Bel-Air home as collateral for Lorenzo's bail, set at $500,000.

Ron Farebrother may not have been quite as chummy with Lorenzo as was Caan, but when the English actor-turned-Ambassador showed up from London, these two Ronnies seem to have got on well.

'I used to go and visit Ronnie Lorenzo in Palm Springs, where he had a home. I attended a charity do with him there at the Ocotillo Lodge. Once a year the mayor, Sonny Bono (of Sonny and Cher fame), arranged for Palm Springs to be turned into a small car race track, and this function at the Ocotillo was on at the same time. So I was sitting with Lorenzo at one table and who should be sitting next to us but Frank Sinatra! Of course, he had a home in Palm Springs for years — in Sinatra Drive. We had a friendly conversation, and he even remembered me from London. Didn't say anything about the car door, though.'

By the time he became buddies with Lorenzo, Ron Farebrother knew exactly who — and what — he was dealing with.

'Whenever I went to America I'd be making contacts, meeting people, so they'd know who I was, socialising with the syndicate. I realised from very early on that I was meeting the mob, but it didn't bother me. I knew I was dealing with what some people call the Mafia, but we never called it that. I'd simply be told,

"He's in the family," or "Hes a family member." The person who usually told me this was Joe Pyle, who also laid down a firm code of conduct: "Don't embarrass him and don't embarrass us. You always have to be smart. And never swear in front of a woman." It was also on Joe's instruction that I made my first visits to see Lorenzo. My task was to set up meetings between his Family and our Office, to discuss what interests we had in common, and what might be done here in England that would be of mutual benefit.'

It wasn't long before the Office was asked to perform a very big service for another American friend targeted by a major law-enforcement investigation. This was an independent record-plugger named Joey Isgro, who, like Ronnie Lorenzo, was a Hollywood figure with alleged mob links. In his late 30s, Isgro had even more top showbusiness friends than Lorenzo. Actor/director Danny DeVito was a buddy — Isgro would later executive produce Hoffa, which DeVito directed — and when Isgro owned Bar One in Hollywood, Jack Nicholson, Sylvester Stallone, Charlie Sheen and Sean Penn used to patronise the joint and unknowingly drink alongside Mafiosi from New York and New Jersey.

In the mid-1980s Isgro was suspected of payola and supplying drugs: inducing radio-station programmers to play records he was plugging by giving them illicit and illegal payments and plying them with cocaine. Investigators believed the racket ran nationwide and involved all of $80 million supplied by major record companies desperate for air play, so they subpoenaed Isgro's closest associates to testify about his activities before a grand jury. One of these characters was British, David Michael Smith, who had been Isgros chauffeur and bodyguard.

Smith could never be portrayed as an untainted whistle-blower. Before the authorities even latched on to him, he had tried to sell dirt on his boss to the record companies themselves. He claimed that he had acted as a courier between Isgro and an accountant, Dennis di Ricco, who Smith said was laundering profits from the payola racket on Isgro's behalf. Smith was also claiming that in the mid-1980s he had met di Ricco several times to pick up briefcases stuffed with between $60,000 and $100,000 in cash.

The record companies turned Smith down, so he turned to the government instead. Federal investigators felt his life was in danger so he was quickly placed in the witness-protection program. Usually this would mean giving the witness a new name and identity, relocating him in a city where he knew nobody and so protecting him from the vengeance of the mob. In this case, however, things took a different turn. It seems Smith agreed to pretend he was a reluctant witness so he could flee back to his native England and beg protection from the underworld here, until the grand jury looking into payola had finished its sessions when his subpoena would become unenforceable.

Why indulge in all this subterfuge? Perhaps because there was an intelligence exchange deal between Scotland Yard and the federal agencies in California at this time. For it so happened that one record producer in Britain who had turned to Isgro for help in promoting his artistes on American radio stations was Joe Pyle. In researching this book, I spoke to Joe Pyle who confirmed this was true.

Joey Isgro had a very big company, which was in the way of selling air play for records. You're talking about $80 million going through his books every year, in legal turnover. What happens is this: when a big company has made a record of even a big star, they still need air play, because without air play, it's not a hit. So Joey would serve you a menu: 'You can have it played prime time four times a day, three times a week.' A different menu, a different fee. Now, let's say there are 2000 music stations in America, he would arrange for each station to play that record, so if he put a fee of, say, half a million dollars to the record company, that would be cheap for them, to get the record to number one. Whatever you think of it, that's the way the business is run all over the world — and that was Joey's business.

So that's how I came to know this guy, because I was a record producer here in London, and I would have wanted to get my records played on as many of those stations as I could afford.

And so it was that in November 1987 people in America seemingly close to Isgro asked the Office to house David Smith. He would fly to London on his own, but when he arrived he was to be watched over and protected until the grand jury threat was over. The scheme was simple — if Smith couldn't be found, he couldn't testify — but fulfilling the favour caused no end of trouble. Especially for Ron Farebrother.

I was at home when I got a phone call. It would have been from Joe Pyle who was in the US at the time. He told me to go up town to a boxing show to meet somebody. The show was at the Hotel London West in Fulham, and the big fight was between Rocky Kelly and a fellow named Kirkland Lane for the British welterweight title.

Joe said, 'Now this guy you're meeting, you're to keep an eye on him.' I said, 'Well, who is he?' and Joe said, 'His name's Dave Smith, and he'll be there at the show.' I said, 'Sure, I'll look after him. How long's he staying for?' 'Just for a few weeks.' 'All right, Joe, he can stay at my place.'

Did I ask why he needed looking after? You don't ask those questions: never on the phone, and not at all in these circumstances.

So then I said, 'How will I know who he is?' He said, 'You'll recognize him. He'll stick out of the crowd.' And he did stick out. He was a lump, a very big guy, tough-looking. I didn't have to go up to him, though, because he was introduced to me by Alex!

But right from the start he didn't seem quite right, because when I asked, 'Are you coming with me tonight?' he said, 'No, I'm going to see my sister.'

As I think about it now, he must have been an out-and-out plant. He was definitely put into us. I've stated that all along. Like I told Joe when he came back I told everybody — This guy, there's something wrong about him. If I were meant to be protecting him, how come he does this instant disappearing act?

I was meaning his 'going to see my sister' performance. So the next morning he turns up, good as gold, at my King's Cars office in the Studios with his bag. For the next two days he's following me around like a fucking lost dog, but I didn't ask him any questions.

Then, when I'm about to go off on some job, he volunteers, 'I can't come with you.' So I said, 'Yeah, I'm told you're not going anywhere.' 'Yeah, I'm on the run from a grand jury.' I said, 'I never asked you that.' He said, 'Well, I want to let you know that I am not a wrong 'un,' by which he meant he wasn't an informer or a grass. So I said, 'Don't you worry. I'll find out if you're a wrong 'un!'

Now this Dave Smith was an amazing guy. He was super fit. He was an Englishman who had been in some crack army regiment. He said he had served in Northern Ireland, and he even showed me his credentials, some proof he had been in the British army.

Looking back, I can see he was a wrong 'un even then, because he had already changed sides once: from being a defender of the state here in Britain to working in America for someone whom he had already told the cops was a crook, even before he came here. But we didn't know that for sure at the time. We understood that he was a genuine mob guy, on the run so he couldn't be jailed for refusing to testify against his boss. Therefore what we had to do was keep him out of the hands of any Scotland Yard cops, so he couldn't be sent back to the States and put on the witness stand.

Well, while he was staying at my house, he slept with a bulletproof vest on. So just as most people would get up in the morning, have a wash, clean their teeth, get dressed and polish their shoes, this guy would be standing there wearing his bulletproof vest. This was when I was living in the beautiful house in Frogmore, with my second wife, Pat, who knew nothing about Smith. We gave him a lovely guest room.

One morning he made me laugh. He'd got this little routine: he'd go out of the room, close the door behind him, I'd lock it, and then he'd get a little tiny leaf, wet it and put it by a certain part of the door. And I used to smile to myself and think, 'This is fucking going over the top, this geezer!' And he used to leave lots of little signs and easily disturbed indicators, to see if anybody had been around in my place while we were out.

Not that he was a little lost lamb with no friends whatever. He knew a few people. He made some calls from my home phone, to get money sent over from America. I just looked after him, as requested, until he got on my nerves.

That happened when he started pulling strokes. I had told him, 'Look. Dennis Andries has got another fight, against Hitman Hearns, so I'm going to Detroit, but don't worry. I'll find you another safe house.' Then I called the Office, and I said, 'There's a pub in Hendon that'll put him up, the Lower Midland.' So that was taken care of. He stayed at the pub. He loved the idea. He even worked there, because the publican, Bob Matthews, used to photograph boxing shows and often couldn't work nights.

But as soon as I got back from Detroit overnight I knew something was wrong. I went into King's Cars, and the atmosphere from my staff wasn't right, so I said to Pat, 'What's going on?' And the next thing I knew, I walked in my office, and there was all my gear all my gear, including all my ornaments from the house. So I said, 'What?!'

And Dave Smith was there, and he said, 'Oh, Pat doesn't want you to stay there any more.' I said, 'I'm her fucking husband, you silly cunt. And don't you try coming between me and my wife. Anyway, who moved my gear?' I was getting really angry. 'You moved my gear? Did you touch it?'

He said, 'Yeah, and one of your drivers,' so I gave that driver a fucking good slap, and I put a phone call in to Joe Pyle, and he went absolutely apeshit. He went really mad. And it was over all this that Dave Smith got very scared.

I told him, 'By five o'clock tonight you better fuck off,' because I was going apeshit too and I pulled a gun out on him, and as I knew he was wearing his body armour I said, 'The only place you haven't got protection is round your head!'

So he fucked off.

Now it turned out that Dave Smith had told Pat that I didn't go to America for the boxing show. He said I went because I had another wife out there. He had brainwashed her, and now she was completely blanking me.

I don't know who put him up to it, but the trouble was resolved within 24 hours. Pat found out I was telling the truth because, fortunately, a friend of mine had videoed the fight when it was shown over here, and when I showed it to her, she could see me clearly, getting into the ring as one of Dennis Andries's minders.

So Smith got fucked off out of King's, but he still carried on living and working down at the pub. What happened then was very fucking weird. When I phoned up Smith at the pub, I was told it had got raided for drugs, and Smith had been arrested. But there never were any fucking drugs in that pub. Smith wasn't dealing in drugs and nor was the publican. Anyway, the

Office got him a brief — a top solicitor — to see what the police were holding him on.

A couple of hours later Smith either got bail or he was freed without charge. So I went down to the pub, and, talking there, he made the biggest fuck-up of his life. He turned round, right in front of some of the other guys from the Office and said, 'They questioned me a lot. Thank goodness I'd got that brief representing me. I think perhaps Ronnie had me spun, he got me arrested.

So Dave Smith was trying to plant a seed, to ruin my credibility with the Office. So I said, 'Why would I want to do that? Bollocks! No way! I do not trust this cunt. I do not know where or who he's coming from, but it's something thats got to be looked into.'

So we called a meeting in the Office. Dave Smith and everyone was there. And I said, 'One of us has got to be found out. Who's the wrong 'un here? I think he's wrong, and he thinks I am.'

And then he made a very big mistake, which Joe and I picked up on straight away. He said he had been released from West Hendon Police Station with his property bag, and when he got back to the pub he had to check his property on the counter of the pub. So I said, 'What do you mean, property bag? Describe the property bag.' He said, 'Well, you know, the big bag. They put a label on it.' And I said, 'Who's doing all this? The custody officer?' And he said, 'Yeah, the guy by the desk there.' I said, 'What? He just gave you your bag?' He said, 'Yeah, I just picked up my bag, and I had to check if my watch and knife and all that were in there.'

I said, 'How did you open your bag then?' He

said, 'He pulled —' and then Joe kicked me under the table and said, 'Shush! Let the man talk.' And Joe asked, 'What, you just pulled the tag off, and the bag was sealed?' Smith said, 'The bag was sealed.' And Joe said, 'You're sure they didn't put anything in it?' And he said, 'No, the bag was dead sealed.'

That was when Smith fucked up, because that's not the way it's done. See, it doesn't matter what London station you're being kept in, you've got to go before a normal custody officer, who takes your property and writes it all down in a book: every item, even down to a comb, down to every penny, whatever you've got. Then it all goes in that bag, and it's sealed. There are two seals. And on those seals is a number, and that number goes in the book, so they know who it belongs to when it goes into the property room: 'Ah, property bag — blah blah blah.' And when you're free to leave the station, they rip the bag open in front of you — every villain knows this — they rip the bag open, and they say, 'Check the items.' And you sign for all the individual items that you received from your property bag.

Whereas Dave Smith is trying to tell us that the police just gave him the bag, which he opened when he got back to the pub!

And then I knew, then I knew — and so did Joe — that Smith must have been visited at that station by senior officers from Scotland Yard. What's more, a bent copper at West Hendon told us so. He said there were big heavy noises — a lot of people — in the offices at West Hendon, but to make it look good they had gone through the rigmarole of arresting him at the pub, then bringing him back to the station.

But then Smith had fucked all this elaborate protective smokescreen by telling us he had brought the bag back to the pub and only opened it up there! So, Joe called an end to the meeting but in an affable way — I'd managed to shut up for a while — leaving Smith thinking he was all right, in the clear.

Later, Smith and I made arrangements to go to a pub near Wimbledon.

Now I'm not saying who or what, but when we got there, and we were at the bar, a shot was fired, to the side of Dave Smith's head. He went down. Three guys picked him up — he was still walking — well, walkingish and took him out to a car.

And that was the last I ever saw of him.

It's curious. When this happened a load of people were in that place, but they just got up and walked out. It amazed me that nothing ever appeared in any newspaper except for one report about a mystery shooting in a mystery pub somewhere in south London. It said there were rumours of blood all over the place, but the victim was unknown. The police had checked all the hospitals, but they still didn't know whether the man had lived or died.

The only thing I ever heard was years later in California from someone very high up in the Mafia. I wanted to know if we really had done a fraternal service and stopped Smith testifying, so I said, 'I heard Dave Smith is still walking about.' The guy said, 'It's best not to mention that name. We don't know what he is or where he is, but we do apologise for the inconvenience he caused you.'

Inconvenience!!! He tried to ruin my marriage, and he nearly got me killed!

If Ron's American mob connections were not prepared to tell him what happened, I thought I should ask Joe Pyle. His version of events was wholly different from Ron's.

All I know is that Dave Smith was a chauffeur for Joey Isgro, and I never liked him at all. Then, some time later, I had a visit at my home because by then he was missing. The press even knocked on the door, and I told them to fuck off.

As for the story that he was shot and done away with — and I had something to do with it — that's rubbish. Definitely not. I don't think he even disappeared. He might have kept out of the way for a while, until he smelled a reward, and then he gave himself up for money. Later on, I understand, the guy turned up and gave his evidence after all.

Intrigued by this conflict, I tried to track down the mystery newspaper article that had hinted that Dave Smith had been shot to death in a south-west London drinking place. I failed to find it, but I have gone one better and discovered the fate of both Joey Isgro and his former chauffeur from the files of the *Los Angeles Times*. These show that despite the best endeavours of Farebrother and Co., Dave Smith did turn up and give evidence — not only to the grand jury. In August 1990 he appeared in open court to testify that he had been not just Isgro's bodyguard but also his bagman, collecting the laundered proceeds of payola. As Dennis di Ricco, the man who allegedly gave Smith the bulging briefcases, also provided sworn evidence to the grand jury that these transactions occurred, we might reasonably assume that Mr Isgro would now be serving a long jail sentence.

But no. For in 1988 di Ricco had faced trial himself — also over drugs and money-laundering — when he denied on oath that he had ever passed laundered money to either Isgro or Smith. This completely negated his grand-jury testimony because, either way, he was a perjurer. Even worse, the prosecution had failed to disclose it to Isgro's defence. When this came out in 1990 the judge had no real choice but to dismiss the case. It was revived but finally dropped again in March 1996 to the humiliation of the US Justice Department — and the fury of Joey Isgro at having been the subject of a ten-year-long investigation. 'I was wrongly accused, and, in the end, not one person ever testified that I provided them with drugs or payola or prostitutes or had any ties to organized crime. All those scandalous allegations that your reporters got so much mileage out of proved to have no substance whatever. The government spent 10 million bucks for this?'

But even if Dave Smith's act of betrayal came to nothing, this was through no lack of effort on his part. As he readily testified against Isgro to both the grand jury and in open court, it is reasonable to assume that his entire trip to Britain — which he claimed was to duck out of testifying — had been an elaborate deception in order to infiltrate the Office and entrap Joe Pyle, Ron Farebrother and others.

Later events would demonstrate that the intelligence wings of both US and British law enforcement were true believers in the old saw: if at first you don't succeed, try, try, try again!

As for that shooting incident in south-west London, Ron Farebrother still cannot figure out how Dave Smith survived. 'Well, if he did get back to America and testify, he must have had a nice hole in his head.'

RON THE GUN MEETS THE QUEEN

Ron did not always keep bad company. When not involved in underworld sit-downs and shoot-outs, he moved among the highest in the land — thanks to Alex Steene. One great advantage of being a top ticket agent is that you can get yourself easily to all the best events. Couple that with being well connected personally to many showbusiness stars and throw in the fact that you are a man of charity, then getting prime seats at the Royal Variety Show should be no problem.

And that was exactly how it was with Alex Steene well, almost, because, of course, the very best seats at the Royal Variety Show always go to just one very special group of people: the Royal Family.

There was one year when Alex Steene not only patronized the Royal Variety Show in the second-best seats but also acted in a most charitable way towards one of his favourite causes: ex-prisoners.

The ex-prisoner he especially favoured back in 1984 was none other than Ronald Patrick Farebrother otherwise known as the Ambassador (which would have been appropriate for a royal occasion) and as Ron the Gun (which would not). On 6 July 1984 Ron had been released from his prison sentence for possessing a firearm and burglary. On 10 July 1986 he would be arrested for attempted murder when a Mauser automatic pistol and ammunition clip was found in his office desk. In between he attended a very special occasion.

I had only been out of jail six months or so when Alex invited me and Pat to the Royal Variety Show. He told me that on such occasions — and he went to plenty of them — he was responsible for everyone he invites, for security reasons, so he had put my name up to the royal protection people so I could be vetted. Well, that seemed reasonable to me if I were just one of the thousands sitting in the main audience but, when we got there, I was staggered to find that Alex had booked the box right next to the Queen!

During the national anthem I couldn't believe it. I was standing no more than ten feet away from her. She was to our right in the tier below us in the next box, with Prince Philip. So I said to Alex, 'Are you sure you gave my name up?' He said he certainly had, so there was I, standing up in that box right by the Queen looking down on all the big showbiz people in the front row and in other boxes. I figured it was quite an honour to be there.

Not that the show itself was any good — in fact, it was bleeding boring — so, halfway through one of the acts I said to Alex, 'I'm just going out. I'm going to the toilet, to the bar.' We did have a waitress there serving us, but I just wanted a break.

As I came out the back door of the box, you can imagine the security I ran into in front of the door to the Royal Box. I had a pass to get through to the bar, but still one of these security guys right outside her box stopped me and asked, 'Mr Farebrother, where are you going?' Now he hadn't even looked at my pass, and yet he knew my surname. So I said, 'I'm going to the fucking bar, the service is bloody useless.'

He said, 'Well, I'm coming with you. I have to escort you wherever you go.' So I said, 'What? Just me? Are you having a go at me or at everyone in that box?' No, he said, putting on a sarcastic voice, as if he were talking to a kid, 'for the *Queen*. We're doing it for the *Queen*, for the *Country*,' taking the piss.

So we came into this private bar, and I'm standing there, when suddenly one guy got up and held up a tiny bell and rang it. At this moment my security man looked me straight in the eye and said, 'Members of the royal family will be coming in here. When they appear, just bow. Don't say nothing!' And I said, 'No! She can buy a drink just like anyone else can, mate!' I was trying to make a joke of it — but as I was saying this, in walked the Queen, and she kind of nodded to me. And I said 'Good evening, madam,' and gave a little smile, and all this time this security guy had his back to the Queen and was looking right into my face, and he said again, 'Don't you open your mouth.'

The guy was plain clothes, but he was sure tooled up — gun, the whole lot — and I guess he knew who I was because, if I had been given the pass, then I must have been vetted: my gun conviction and all. Otherwise the vetting system is a farce.

So after this break I went back into the show, and the guy said, 'Right. You're going back to your box? I'll escort you there.' So I said to him, 'Do you think I'm going to do anything with the Queen there, you silly bastard!' 'No,' he said, 'but, in case you do, when you go back in your box, just look across opposite.'

Now I'm curious. I'm thinking, what's he going on about? So I'm sat down in my chair, and the Queen looks as if she's dipping into her box of chocolates, but I can't keep gawping over to her side and making myself look a mug, so instead I'm looking across, like this guy told me.

And there's an empty box there, all in darkness, black curtains, the whole lot. And you can see, there's guys in there — obviously, security again, watching out for any potential assassination attempt. Anyhow, by the end of the evening, I had struck up quite a relationship with the security squad and was starting to have a laugh with them.

No ordinary anybody is allowed to take photographs at the Royal Variety Show, but the following day we got some photos that (I was told) the royal photographer had taken. These showed not just the Royal Box but the box next door as well, and there we all were! Alex and his wife, Anna — a lovely lady. Then there was Pat and me, but I'd been having a cigarette outside, so my chair was empty, and I could be seen in the shadows behind Alex.

And then there was an older lady, sitting beside me. It was Eva Brindle, the sister of Frankie Fraser — Mad Frankie — who was jailed for ten years as the torturer in the Charlie Richardson gang and whose lifetime total of years spent in jail would eventually reach 40. When he was sentenced, the judge said, 'You must be kept under lock and key. You terrorized those who cross your path in a way that was vicious, sadistic and a disgrace to society. It must be made clear to all those who set themselves up as gang leaders that they will be struck down by the law as you will be struck down.'

So now, right alongside the Queen, we have me fresh out of jail on a gun charge and the sister of the most dangerous man in England! Now don't get me wrong: Eva Brindle is a lovely lady, She was even trying to keep me under control. She was nudging me: 'Where've you been?' 'Sodding around.' 'Well, don't keep disappearing!'

I managed to stick the rest of the show out. It didn't get any better. But the experience was quite something: looking down on all those faces, all the connections — meantime, looking up at me, they must have thought, 'Who the fuck is he, standing up there?'

I don't know what was going through Alex Steene's mind when he invited me, but he does do a hell of a lot for charity. It was a generous gesture, and it was very soon after I had been over to his place to thank him for having supported me while I was inside. It was a very public display.

Ron may have appreciated the gesture, but this story — and the photograph — shows the system for protecting the royal family in a bad light. I hasten to add that the Ron Farebrother I know is not remotely likely to take a pot shot at Her Majesty or lunge at her with a knife, but I cannot see how any vetting officer could sensibly rely on the assurances of a man like Alex Steene who kept the company he did: the Kray Brothers, Charlie Richardson and Frankie Fraser, to name almost the entire criminal hierarchy of London in the 1960s, from whom he has never sought to disassociate himself. And even if one only considers Ron Farebrother's long-documented record held by Scotland Yard at that time — convicted of a gun crime, fresh out of jail and clearly prone to moments of irrational violence — he was hardly fit for royal company.

On the other hand, if a cat may look at a king, surely a con may look at a queen.

There were two queens in Ron Farebrother's life at this time. The other was his new wife, Pat Sherman. For a while she brought out the best in his tempestuous character. Yet even when Ron was trying to do good, he had a strange way of going about it. There was the bizarre incident of the kindness kidnap.

While I was at King's Cars, I would often get cranks ringing up, and one day I got a phone call from a guy who went to school with my son. He said he was in Bedford, which was 40 miles away, and he needed £200 to help him out. He was a crackhead or a heroin addict. I just put the phone down on him three times, which I thought was the best thing to do. Then he phoned up a fourth time. This time Pat was there, and I recorded the conversation. He said he'd sell the baby, then he asked, 'Do you know anyone who wants a baby?'

So I said to Pat, 'We can't stand by while this guy sells a baby! Who knows where it'll end up, or if it'll end up dead.' And with that Pat said, 'I don't see this as

right. We're walking into a trap. I don't believe this.'
Anyway, I felt we had no alternative so I told this guy
'Right, for £200 we'll buy the baby — just to find out
what the hell's going on.'

So I decided to drive straight to Bedford that
evening. We had two cars: Pat's Daimler, and I called a
couple of the lads over in a Mercedes as a back-up, and
we drove to Bedford. It took far longer than I'd
expected and we got there at nine or ten at night. But
when we pulled up to the address they gave us, it
turned out to be a cul-de-sac. Then I knew something
was wrong. It was my gut feeling — the hairs on my
neck, whatever — that made me feel, 'This is a set-up.'

So I said, 'Stay in the car, Pat.' And I was right
because — its scary thinking back on it — there was a
squat of these bastards. Then someone leaned out of a
window, and I recognized this kid as the schoolfriend
of my son.

He said, 'Did you bring the money?' And, with
that, the door was opened, and I walked in to find a
little yobbo in a leather jacket with a knife in his hands.
So one of the guys I brought with me — he wasn't the
kind to ask any questions — just pushed me out of
sight, and he let this yobbo have it in the legs. He
blasted him with a shotgun!

Then we went on up the stairs, and I'm thinking,
'This is fucking madness, this is all going wrong.' When
we got upstairs, there were about four people in the
room. And at this point I was absolutely sure it must be
a set-up, because there was no baby or nothing. And
they were all yelling because their guy's screaming
from the pain in his legs.

Then Pat got out of her car — in her wisdom —

and walked straight into this shit-hole, and the bloke said, 'Yeah, there is a baby.' And then I saw there was a dog, a little black mongrel, cowering away in a corner. It was terrified, doesn't know what's going on, and he said, 'It's over there, the baby.' Now I thought he meant that the dog was the baby. I thought he really thought the dog was a baby — that this guy was so high on drugs that his heads gone. So I said, 'It's a dog, you silly bastard!' He said, 'No, it is a baby.'

And blow me down! There was a baby, right next to the dog. And Pat just picked it up, put it in a blanket and said, 'Tell him we'll take it!' And we got straight in the car, and were driving away.

Then the guy I was with says, 'D'you realise, if we get stopped, there's two things wrong here? One, we don't know whose baby that is, and, two, we don't even know its name.' By this time Pat had sussed out it's a girl, and she said, 'Well, forget that! Just drive to a hospital.' I said, 'We can't go to a hospital.' She says, 'She looks ill. A doctor must see her straight away.' So we get in a private doctor, who said she was well under-weight.

Now, of course, any moment I'm expecting a visit from the police. After all, a guy's just been shot in the leg, his friend knows exactly who I am, and I've got the form for this kind of thing. And also we've gone off with someone else's baby. But we never got a visit, funnily enough. It turned out the guy had only got a few pellets in his leg.

I didn't know that at the time — I was still expecting a bang on the door and a spell in the cells — so Pat had to get a move on and make this entire thing legal. She did. She arranged for us both to go to court the following day.

That was the funniest thing ever: me, standing in front of a High Court judge in chambers, asking for a 28-day order to sort things out, when all we had was the baby's first name, Carly, and we'd only just got that. Amazingly, we got the order. We took her home, and, after six weeks she was in great shape, up to the right weight and looking lovely.

Then all of a sudden the squatter's consciences had been pricked. They'd been overcome by parental feelings at last, and now they wanted the baby back. So I said to Pat, 'No way the baby's going back there. She's sticking with us!'

So now were back at the High Court, and this time the social-services people made representations and reversed the order, which had been in our favour. Now the judge was ordering us to hand over the baby to the welfare people. So, right there in court, in front of the judge, I asked them if the baby was going to be put into care. They said, no, it wasn't that simple. First they had to give back the baby to the rightful mother, then they must go and get another court order to state that the baby is on the warning list. I went mad. I said, 'What do you mean? The baby is on the warning list. It was on the warning list before it was even born.'

At this point I turned round and said to the judge, 'Now you've heard that, Your Honour, do you want to think again? The baby's not being handed over to anybody, not till we get this mess sorted out.' So he gave me just four hours to hand over the baby. So I said, 'Right! You might as well send me back to prison, cos the baby isn't going back there. It's like a sentence of death.'

Somehow we managed to keep the baby for another two weeks. Social workers kept following me, but here I give the police their due. After the four-hour limit that the judge had imposed, there was supposed to be a warrant out for my arrest. Then I got a phone call from Borehamwood nick — I don't know who the copper was — and he said, 'If we don't see you, we can't arrest you.' I said, 'Well, I'm not fucking running from anybody.'

By this time I had decided that publicity and public opinion were our greatest allies. I was appearing on local radio stations, and people were asking what had I done with the baby, and I was saying, 'She's in a safe place, until we get something sorted out with the social services.'

Then I set up quite a cunning trap. I arranged that we would be interviewed for the local Anglia Television news programme, so I knew the film crew would be at our house at a particular time. Then I deliberately tipped off the baby's parents and grandparents about where the baby would be at that time, but I didn't tell them a TV team was going to be there too! My idea was that they would witness these people grabbing the baby, record it on video and put it out that night on the local news.

The idea worked almost like clockwork. The TV crew and reporter arrived on time and started interviewing Pat and me, with the baby in the shot. Then there was a bang on the front door, and it was the parent posse. I let them in, but I hadn't allowed for another silly bastard coming over the back door.

At that moment you don't know how close the real Ron came to breaking out, but then I remembered the fucking camera was rolling, and I stopped myself. That little shit! I actually had a taped conversation of his wife or girlfriend, where she said he had burned the baby for a laugh — I state that on the TV interview. I said, 'What about the taped conversation about you hurting the baby?' I tell you, any normal man would have beat the shit out of him on television, but I couldn't show any thuggery.

Anyway, with the film crew there and me having to be seen behaving properly, we let them get away, but we had foreseen this development, too, and we instantly tipped off the social services. Within 45 minutes, they were on to the parents and had rescued the baby. Of course, in normal circumstances they would have had every right to keep their own baby but not after the way they had been looking after her. Until they had possession of the baby, the Social couldn't do sod all, but once we'd tipped off the Social that the parents had possession of that baby, the Social were on to them straight away. They had all the correct court papers to take the kid back off them.

The whole thing was ludicrous — it was fucking madness but I went along with all that shit, and at the end of the day I felt happy about it. Except for my solicitor presenting me with a fucking great bill for his services! I'm sure it was within the normal hourly rate — it was totally legitimate — only, on this occasion, I told him, 'Kiss the money goodbye, for Christ's sake! This one's for charity.'

With the help of local TV and radio stations, Ron was now recreating himself in the likeness of St George: slaying dragons, saving babies and making the streets safe. He had a loving, public-spirited, upmarket wife. He was even hobnobbing with the Queen. So could Ron at last be on the verge of total long-term rehabilitation?

Not in the eyes of the local police who had recently failed to nail him for either attempted murder or possessing a gun. Detective Inspector Morse and Co. still believed he was a cold killer, so when Pat went away on holiday without telling a woman friend, they thought their worst suspicions had been realised.

Off she went on holiday, and a few days later this friend rang up and asked, 'Is Pat there?' and I said, 'No.' Well, Pat was away for a full month, so by the time the friend had rung up four or five times, she thought I had killed her. Then, unknown to me, she called the police, so one day they knocked on the door and asked 'Is Mrs Sherman there?', and I said, 'No.' I wouldn't even talk to them, and I closed the door on them. Then they came back again and said, 'We have reason to believe she's missing,' but I still wouldn't tell them nothing — after all, these are bastards who had just been trying to get me locked up for ten years. So then they came in, waving a warrant to search the place. And it so happened that I'd just moved something in the conservatory — I'd shifted the carpets and everything so they dug it up: floor tiles, foundations and all.

And at that, in walked Pat! On the very day they were digging it up! And so I said, 'Carry on digging!'

Well, of course, there were red faces on the boys in blue. They had to compensate her, and we got the top firm in to make it all good again. I hadn't really done it deliberately, but it was one little victory in a long, long war.

Mind you, my life with Pat was always tempestuous, and sometimes I played rotten tricks on her. There was one time when I was taking some 'Reader's Wives'-type photos of her in her Janet Reger undies in the house, when I suddenly said, 'Let's have one out in the garden,' So out she went, in her undies, when I flicked on all the lights and then turned on the alarm. 'Come on!' she was going. 'Let me in!' while the people living in the other wings of the mansion must have been looking out of the windows and wondering what the hell we were up to.

The stunt had its effect because, not long after, a neighbour came in to say goodbye to us. He was moving out, and he said, 'It has been an eye-opener living next door to you!' So Pat said, 'Yes, I'm sorry about him.' He said, 'No, it must be exciting living with him. You never know what he's going to do next!'

The neighbour was too right. Ron would soon shock Pat by ditching her for a woman of outrageous bad character. Far from curbing Ron's criminal tendencies, as Pat had tried to do, his new girlfriend would only encourage them.

THE MILLION-POUND NOTE

At Elstree Studios Ron had moved way beyond just booking cars for the stars. He had established himself as the person to come to for extra services. In this capacity he met a woman who would turn his entire life upside down.

I first met Sylvia when she walked in my office at King's Cars. One of my sidelines was supplying strippers and strippogram girls to entertain the stars, directors and crews at the end of film shoots. So one day this woman showed up to do a strippogram, and I went over to watch her. She was pretty spectacular and became a frequent visitor because people often asked for her in particular.

When Jim Henson was filming *Labyrinth* at the studios, with David Bowie, I was asked to get a stripper for his birthday to surprise him right on the set. The crew approached me and said, 'It has to be Sylvia.' I knew what they meant. She had rather large tits and was very convincing with them. To accost Henson she dressed up in her favourite role: a policewoman.

He must have half-sussed the crew would be up to something as it was the last shoot of the film. The signal was when he said, 'Everyone, break for lunch.' Then in walked Sylvia with a notepad and pen. I could see he didn't really fall for it — he knew she was a strippogram — but he went along with it anyway.

Henson was a straight guy, as far as I know. He was a family entertainer, what with *Sesame Street* and *The Muppets*, so strippers weren't really his scene. This didn't make any difference to Sylvia. Never mind his blushes, she went at him as if he were game for anything. She took off his earphones, flung her tits into his face, then made sure he couldn't hear by putting each tit over each of his ears. He just laughed and smiled because they were filming it, and I guess he didn't want to look a prude.

Then along comes my own birthday — 19 January — and my mates turned the tables on me. I was playing pool in the bar there at the Studios when she turned up. I thought she'd just popped down to see me because she was in normal clothes, not dressed as a copper or anything else.

I still didn't catch on when she started playing pool with me. Then she said, 'I can get it in that pocket! — with my tit!' and I thought, 'Here we go.' It was a crowded bar, and I told her, 'You ain't stripping me in no fuckin' bar.' So that's how it was. I gave her £50 to keep her clothes on!

It wasn't long before we were going to bed

together, because she was overpowering. She did have an amazing figure, but that wasn't her main attraction. She was just so exciting — in a mad way — compared to my new wife Pat. Whenever we met I never knew what Sylv was up to, what scam she had dreamed up or was about to pull off. She was totally unpredictable and outrageous. With her, life was one long surprise. Always on the edge.

The first time I visited her house I was sitting in a chair, having a look at the little knick-knacks around the place, when I registered that this same chair was definitely a bloke's — where he always sat. So I asked Sylvia, and she coughed to me that she was still married. Till then I'd thought she must have been married some time previously, but I assumed she was now on her own. So that was surprise number one. Number two came straight after.

Suddenly I see these lights coming in the drive and seconds later this man walks in. Now I know he's the husband — when only 30 seconds ago I didn't even know she had one!

So I went, 'All right?' and I was thinking, any minute it's going to go off — and he just went, 'Yeah, all right, mate.' And he's got a snooker cue in his hand. Now I just happened to be watching the snooker on TV, and he went, 'You don't know the score, do you?' And I thought, 'What do you mean, the fucking score, mate?' So I said, 'I'm in your house, and you want to know the fucking score? In the snooker? Are you sure?'

Anyway he just sat there while Sylvia was floating around, in and out of the kitchen, then she just said, 'I'm going to bed in a minute, I'm tired.' And I said,

'Yeah, you better get me a cab.' And she said, 'No, no, no. You can stay.' I said, 'No, no, no. I'll get a cab, fuck it.' Then she said 'No. Peter! You can sleep on the couch!'

And I thought, 'Yeah! I am going upstairs with this fucking dodgy couple. There's something definitely wrong about this pair of cunts.'

So I said, 'Sylv, can I speak to you in private?' I said, 'I'm not being rude, mate. I know it's your house.' I was being very polite with him. And I went into the kitchen with her, and I said, 'This is fucking wrong. This is his house. I'm going!' She said, 'No. If you do go, he'll kill me!'

So I walked back into the lounge and asked him, 'Are you going to touch her when I go?' 'No, mate, no. I'll sit in my chair, watch a bit of videos. Don't mind me.'

Then he seemed to lean down by the side of the couch, and I thought he must have been going for a tool, so without warning I laid into him, I gave him a beating.

And Sylvia said, 'I told you! Now you will stay!'

I didn't feel any easier when, after Id given him this beating, he said, 'Yeah, go on, mate. Use my bed. I don't mind.' Fucking weird cunt, he was. I kept my eyes open all night long.

Then in the morning she threw him out!

It was two years after Ron and Sylvia began their bizarre relationship that I first met them. It was in that August 1988 at Hampstead's Bull and Bush pub. There they were: racketeering Ron and statuesque Sylvia. As I've already mentioned she was striking, no doubt about it. Big, busty, bubbly and blonde — at least on that occasion. They made an extraordinary pair: Ron, the bleary-eyed ex-actor-cum-street-fighter, glass of vodka in hand and Sylv, whose personality was even greater than her breasts. Meeting this pair in the Bull and Bush seemed highly appropriate. 'Come, come, come and make eyes at me . . .'

In conversation it emerged that Ron was still living with his wife, Pat, who was standing by him and continuing to support him, despite his philandering and the deep trouble that now threatened to get him locked up in jail for the heaviest sentence of his life.

It was this matter that had encouraged Ron to speak to me. Maybe he thought that catching the prior interest of an investigative reporter would be some kind of insurance policy if he were convicted. For all I knew, he was as guilty as sin. Equally, he might have been innocent and facing a genuine miscarriage of justice. At that stage I did not know.

Certainly the charges on the sheet Ron now passed me looked formidable. These alleged that:

1. On a day unknown before the 18th day of November 1987 he stole a cheque number 014668 drawn on the Corporate Trust Office FIS Collection Account Number 1 belonging to the National Westminster Bank plc.

2. On a day unknown etc he dishonestly received certain stolen goods, namely the cheque number 014668 etc knowing or believing the same to be stolen.

3. On the 17th day of November 1987 he used an instrument, namely the cheque number 014668 etc in the sum of £2,190,000 which was and which he knew or believed to be false with the intention of inducing

somebody to accept it as genuine and by reason of so accepting it to do or not to do some act to his own or any other people's prejudice.

These charges alone indicated that if Ron Farebrother were not innocent, he must be a criminal of style and ingenuity — a suave white-collar fraudster who, like some wayward product of our finest public schools, chooses to rob banks from within rather than off the pavement. I was thinking that Ron should have chosen a career in the City. This was the Eighties, after all, when everyone there seemed to be at it. But the charges gave no hint of the extraordinary events that had led to his arrest. Ron proceeded to enlighten me.

I'm not going to tell you how these bits of paper came into my possession. There were obviously people on the inside, but I can't say who they are because the police would go straight round and nick them. Just let the starting-point be that somehow I've acquired this very special cheque, which is called a town clearance cheque.

There were two signatures on the cheque and under each signature were code numbers stating the amount, to whom it was to be paid and under what conditions. And the amount really was £2.2 million! Of course, I knew no branch of a bank ever holds £2.2 million in cash — certainly not the Borehamwood branch of the Natwest — but I wasn't aiming to pull off a smash-and-grab. This was a cool and measured operation.

Before I attempted to get my hands on any money, I made an appointment to see the manager at that branch. His name was Mr Baby. First I told him I wished to check on something. This way I was planting the seed, laying the groundwork, ready for the big cheque. I said I had been approached at a boxing show by a financial broker who wanted to use me as an agent. So I asked Mr Baby, 'Would you look into this? Look into this thoroughly because I want your advice on it. Obviously I'm going to get paid for helping him, so I want to know if its really OK for me to act as his agent to clear this cheque.'

Baby then explained that this kind of thing was not unheard of. Stockbrokers do use other companies that have been going for a while to clear such cheques, but he advised me that I could only do it once.

He then asked, 'Who will the cheque be made out to?'

I said, 'It'll be made out to me. I want to put it in my account and these are the conditions of the transfer. Oh, and it'll be for £2.2 million.'

Well! The bank manager nearly fell through the back of the chair when I said that. But I went on. 'Once you've got it cleared — there won't be any trouble about clearing it, it's all legit — I want you to check it out for me, check every legal angle.'

So now, I figure, I've got him on my side.

Then I continued, 'I want £1 million delivered the first day — and £1 million the second day — and the balance left in my account. That's just the conditions.'

'Fine,' he said.

'And I want it all in 20s. It's got to be in cash, the first million.'

He then asked me, who was the guy. I said, 'I dunno. I only know him as Jo Jo — Japanese Joe.

I also told him how I'd met this Japanese Joe. You

meet all sorts of people in boxing, lots of them — very rich, which is well known.

He said, 'Well, until we get the cheque, there's nothing for me to check on.'

A week later he rang me up and asked, 'Is there any more news about that cheque?' I said, 'Na, na. We're not rushing it. I've taken the guy round the Studios as my guest,' which I allegedly had done. I really had made a big thing of taking an oriental gentleman around the Studios.

Then the day came when I gave the bank manager the cheque. I went in his office, I handed it to him, and he said, 'I could check it right now, in front of you.'

Now what made this cheque special was that it had two Ts in the left corner and the right corner, and these numbers underneath the signatures. It was a five-digit number — and he punched these numbers into his computer, and the printout came back straight away: where it was issued, who issued it, where it was going to, the time — all these little code numbers came up, verified.

So he had gone through all the safeguards, and then he said: 'I've verified the signatures, and I've verified the cheque. It's the highest we can get, it's what we call a town clearance cheque. It's better than a bankers draft, because you can steal a bankers draft.'

So I said, 'Right, leave it for a while. The guy's away for three or four days. I'll give you a call on Monday.'

In the meantime what I'd done was set up a party for the Friday night before that Monday — a special midnight announcement party, invitation only, at my house. And on this occasion I gave out bullshit that I had sold my life story for £1 million. That's how I was explaining to my friends why I was going to get all this money. And I went ahead and gave this elaborate party on Friday, 13 November 1987.

So, after all this carefully paced rigmarole, it was all cleared: the cheque, everything, all pukka — thanks to someone somewhere in the banking chain. The cheque really was genuine. It had been properly issued. Those people really did sign it with their own monickers. They weren't forgeries.

Naturally the subject of security had come up in my discussions with Mr Baby. I told him that, when it came to my collecting the money, I did not want anyone else on the bank staff to know. I explained this was for my own physical safety. And that's what he, too, was most worried about: my security. But I said, firmly and clearly, that I had my own personal security staff, and I didn't want anyone else involved.

I told him I would be in there on the Monday, 17 November, at one o'clock. So when I turned up — with my driver as security — I received an apology from Baby. He said he had an appointment for lunch, but another employee, an assistant manager, would be handling the transaction. Baby himself said he would pop down to the Studios after his lunch, to make sure everything was all right.

I'll never forget what happened next. It was unbelievable. There was the £1 million! It was all in a big brown holdall with two locks. The assistant manager said he and Mr Baby had already checked and counted it. 'Right,' I told him, 'now I'm going straight to meet this guy and give him his money.'

In reality I was going to do nothing of the sort. In

fact I had already cancelled the following days million because there was never going to be a following day. I knew that once I'd got hold of this first million, I had only 72 hours. Once the money was out, it would be just that amount of time before someone shouted, 'There's something fucking wrong here!' I knew there'd be no scream-up about the cheque before then, because it was covered all the way. That's why I'd always told the manager to take his time, and why I'd said, 'No, leave it for a week, the guy's away,' because this would disarm any suspicions, and because there was no chance of anyone spotting anything wrong until three days after the money had been paid out. Once I had it, I knew for sure there'd be a scream. But by then I'd be well gone.

My scheme was to go straight to the airport with the money. There were one or two other people involved in the conspiracy, but I was still going to get half of the million. I'd even thought up a way for me to reappear. I was going to leave indicators that I had been kidnapped. As I had thrown that Friday-night party, where I'd announced to dozens of people how much money I was getting for my life story, this would have explained the kidnapping. Then some time later I would have been found somewhere, all tied up, without any of the money, and I could have blamed it on a leak from the party.

So now I picked up the money, in this big protective brown holdall, and it was an amazing feeling. Fucking amazing! But what happened then was even more amazing. Coming out of the bank, standing on the steps, in Borehamwood's main street, I see four or five police cars, all with their lights flashing.

So I stood there thinking, I wonder what's going on here then!

Now my driver was right in the middle of it. So I said, making a joke of it, 'I hope someone's not trying to rob the bank.'

'No,' said the assistant manager gently, 'Don't worry, Mr Farebrother, Mr Baby's taken care of it. The bank's paying for this.'

I said, 'Paying for what?' And I remember having a conversation with this silly cunt on the steps of the Natwest Bank and him mentioning a figure of £12 a head for each policeman, or £12 a minute for them all, to be an escort. He thought I was concerned only about the cost of the cops!

I said, 'Oh, bollocks! No, I'm going back in! I didn't want all this! I don't need an escort. I told you, I've got my own security.'

But, as I was trying to get back in the bank, this big, uniformed sergeant came forward. He was in charge, but the bank hadn't even told him whom he was meant to escort. So now he asked what's going on. The assistant manager said, 'It's all right. You're to escort Mr Farebrother here, he's got rather a large amount of money.'

'Yeah?' said the sergeant. 'Mr Farebrother, is it? Well, the only place we're escorting Mr Farebrother to is the station, so we can find out whose money it is!'

'No, no, it's perfectly all right,' said the assistant manager. 'Well, how much is it?' asked the sergeant. The bank man said, '£1 million.' And the copper said, 'Oh, no, no, no!'

And that was it. Bang! So I said, 'Well, it's a fucking fit-up then!'

Oh, for fuck's sake, I was almost there! It was just a case of walking from the steps of the bank to that street into that car with a million pounds. And it was all fucked up because this bloody bank manager was genuinely trying to help me! Of course, I hadn't told him not to tell the police — that might have made him suspicious — but equally I hadn't mentioned hiring the police, or needing an escort, because I said I had my own security! What is that old saying, 'the road to hell is paved with good intentions?' Well, that day the road to Borehamwood Police Station was bleeding with good intentions!

So I'm trooped into the station back door as usual by these uniform guys, then this sergeant went up to the CID office and had a word with them. Meantime I'm put in a cell, and the money goes straight back into the bank.

So, of course, who should come and greet me in my cell but my old sparring partner, Detective Inspector Dennis Morse. Well, Morsey was over the moon, wasn't he? Old Morse! 'Come on, Mr Farebrother,' he asked, in his usual gloomy drone, 'Whose money is it?'

I said, 'It belongs to Jo Jo. I'm acting as a fucking agent. Don't take my word for it. Go back and ask the bank manager! I asked him to check the fucking thing out. I hope it's not fucking stolen! If it was, you know, I wouldn't have had anything to do with it, and I wouldn't be here.'

He said, 'Well, we'll find out, Mr Farebrother, through our own inquiries, and until we do, we'll keep you here.'

'Oh, fuck it!' I thought, 'this isn't looking too

good.' So I said, 'Don't be stupid, Morsey, I've been set up like a fucking kipper here. If there's anything wrong with this cheque, then this has been a right fucking fit-up, and it's all down to Japanese JoJo.'

'Are you offering a statement?'

'No, listen. Take this down quickly, Morsey. Or get your sidekick. This is the only thing I am going to say! I've been fitted up by a Japanese guy who's with the boxing. He's been using me as an agent to clear his money. If I've been hoodwinked — caught with the baby — you'd better have his number.'

So I gave him that phone number, but it was obvious he didn't believe me. For all the harassment he'd been giving me, he himself had never managed to get me convicted, so this time he was bursting to lock me away. He saw this £2.2 million as his chance to do me good and proper.

For sure, Detective Inspector Morse was not impressed with Ron's story. He gave him the benefit of no doubt whatever, for in his mind there was none. Instead and straight away he came up with the charge of attempted criminal deception: Farebrother had presented a stolen National Westminster Bank cheque and attempted to obtain £1 million cash — an offence that, he told Ron with the faintest trace of glee, could bring him six or even twelve years in jail.

The charge sheet written out that day recorded this verbal snapshot of the defendant. The 40 year old's ethnic appearance was described as white, his height as 5 ft 10 in, weight 12 stone, build medium, eyes blue, eyebrows normal, hair brown/greying and collar length, his voice strong and his accent London. His dress was given as dark two-piece suit, blue shirt and tie and black shoes. His occupation was shown as managing director, King's Car Town and Country Hire, and his address as South Wing, Frogmore House, Park Street, St Albans. The charge sheet also noted two warning signals shown on the police national computer: Farebrother was disqualified from driving, and he was violent.

The following day he appeared at Barnet Magistrates Court, to find yet more indignities heaped on him.

'They demanded £100,000 bail — the highest bail ever demanded at Barnet — and all in cash. Unheard of! I was in jail for four weeks until we talked it down to £50,000 in cash from Pat and a £50,000 surety from my brother.

'So when I got bail, came out of jail and walked into the bar at the Studios, you could have heard a pin drop. The rumours were already flying. At the time Steven Spielberg was producing *Who Framed Roger Rabbit?* there, so he came over and whispered, "They all think you stole my cheque!" I said, "Let them fucking think that. I stole nothing! It's a misunderstanding." "But my office is getting wind of all these rumours," said Spielberg. "They're all saying it's my cheque, my million!" It seemed everybody was phoning him up, but he wouldn't comment, so I told him, "You should be making *Who Framed Ronnie Farebrother?!*"

'Then I benefited from a lovely gesture by Andrew Mitchell, the managing director of Elstree Studios, which were then owned by the Cannon group. While I was on bail, a lot of people were shit-stirring, saying what was I doing in the studios while there was this heavy charge hanging over me. So Andrew had a lovely sign put up in the restaurant: PEOPLE WHO LIVE IN GLASS HOUSES SHOULDN'T THROW STONES — REF RON FAREBROTHER, signed ANDREW MITCHELL. I thought it was very nice of him to do that.'

Such gestures were getting rarer, as Ron's support dwindled. The ups-and-downs of his life were more precipitous than ever. One minute he had £1 million in cash in his hands, the next he was lucky to get bail and was now facing a very long stretch in prison. Could there be any escape? he wondered. The odds weren't encouraging, but, with the love of two good women well, one good and one entertainingly wicked — surely something was possible.

To Ron's horror, the two women had come to know each other, though one was playing naughty tricks on the other. 'They had first bumped into each other in the King's Cars office. Pat was usually there, because it was still her business, but Sylvia had a perfectly good excuse to drop in from time to time because she was running round doing errands for Joe Pyle and Alex Steene. At least, that was what I told Pat, and she was satisfied with that explanation — only Sylvia had to go one better.

'One day I walked in my house — the one owned by Pat — and I saw Sylvia sitting there with Pat. I shat myself — it was just like those scenes in *Play Misty for Me* and *Fatal Attraction*, where the man is suddenly confronted with the sight of his wife or regular girlfriend chattering happily with the nutty screw-on-the-side.

'I thought I was in big trouble until Pat announced that Sylvia would now be working in King's Cars, to help me out. She said that, because I still had a disqualification for drink-driving, Sylvia would now be working as my chauffeur. Pat added that she wasn't in the slightest bit worried about any hanky-panky between us because Sylvia had confessed she was a lesbian so she wouldn't be interested in me. Pat said that right in front of Sylvia! I could hardly keep my jaw from dropping off.'

Ron's trial for the attempted bank fraud did not take place until almost ten months after the attempt itself. Throughout that time he had to live at his marital home, to fulfil his bail conditions, but the marriage was now a sham. In every other respect he was hitched up with Sylvia — although Pat still didn't know the truth.

What she did know was that King's Cars — the business she owned — was not in good shape. It wasn't so much Ron's criminal activities that had hit the firm's turnover. It was much more the sad shape of the Studios. After so many changes of ownership — ABPC, EMI, Cannon — Elstree was finally going down. Fortunately, Ron had received a tip-off from Andrew Mitchell that Cannon was going to quit the Studios in six months at the most, and Brent Walker was going to take it over.

'Andrew told me that Brent Walker would simply pull the whole lot down and turn the site into a supermarket. He said, "There won't be any studios here, so if you can, try and sell it." So I sold it as a going concern to another firm, which lasted there three months. Sure enough, Brent Walker did buy the

Studios and sell most of the land on to Tesco and the like. Andrew and another guy called Paul Walsh fought hammer and tongs to keep part of the site as studios, and eventually the council bought what was left back off Brent Walker. In the eight years between it was completely run down. So I got out at the time.'

Despite selling off the business, losing his job and surely soon to lose his liberty, Ron did enjoy lighter moments, especially as the trial approached.

'The very night before the £2.2 million trial was going to start, Sylvia arranged for one of her friends called Maria to pull a sex stunt on me. She came in the Bull and Tiger pub in Borehamwood where I was playing pool. The first I saw of her, she was dressed as a judge — long wig and all — when suddenly she and Sylvia had stripped me down to my socks and handcuffed me to the pool table. Then the pair of them produced a big iced cake with cherries all over, and Maria wiped it all over me.

'At that moment my son walked in, with his girlfriend. That was pretty embarrassing for me, but my son just shrugged it off. He just told this girl — who had never seen me before — "Oh, that's my Dad down there."

'Now Maria had really got into this judge role so she sentenced me to a hundred lashes and produced a whip to inflict them on me. And the silly bastard was really whipping me, and there were marks all over my back. So at this point a good mate of mine called Kimi Hall took the whip off her, which was a good thing, because this was the night before my court case. If any prison officers had seen me with the marks of a hundred lashes all over my back, they would have thought I was a right nutter.'

And so Ronald Patrick Farebrother survived ordeal by whiplash at the Bull and Tiger to face up to his real trial at Wood Green Crown Court in North London. It began on Wednesday, 31 August 1988, and I turned up to see what proved to be a complete farce. Indeed, in many respects Ron's experience at the Bull and Tiger bore a closer resemblance to justice than anything that occurred at Wood Green.

First there was the sight of Ron's wife and girlfriend sitting within a few rows of each other. Pat, I was told, still had no idea Sylvia was Ron's lover and continued to regard her as a dedicated lesbian. The two women had agreed not to acknowledge each other in court, lest Sylvia disturb the jury's image of Pat as a prim and proper wife.

Once the jury was sworn in, we heard the story of this extraordinary crime, as told by the prosecution. In a judicially dry and compressed version, it seemed even more like a fairy tale than it was in reality: how Ron was captured with £1 million in cash, which a bank had just willingly handed over, and what the status of this massive Natwest cheque really was. In plain language it seemed like a £1 million note, which some dishonest person had diverted out of the bank's headquarters, that had fallen into the hands of Ron Farebrother, who did what any red-blooded thief would do: he tried to cash it.

The prosecutor argued with impeccable logic that Ron must have known the cheque was stolen and that he had no right to the money. Sure, there had to be at least one co-conspirator, but the mystery of why he stood alone in the dock did not diminish his own criminal involvement and intent.

There seemed no way Ron could walk out of this open-and-shut case. All his barrister could do was peg away methodically at the Crown's presentation, hoping as Mr Micawber used to say — for something to turn up. Something did.

On the first day I didn't really know what was going on because I'd been told that, if I was found guilty, I'd get a minimum of six or twelve years. This made me feel pretty shaky, but I know the system about courts, so throughout the first day I'm coughing like a good 'un.

Each time I cough I'm asking the usher for some water for my bad throat. Then every time there's an important question I'm coughing again so he kept on bringing me cups of water. All this is to set up a scene where I ask, 'Can I have a plastic cup, then I won't disturb you any more?' So he gave me the cup, but on day two I've brought in a big plastic bottle of lemonade, which is only 25 per cent lemonade and 75 per cent vodka. Very soon I was three-quarters pissed.

Now although my situation looked grim there were a few surprises for the prosecution buried within their own case. Some I knew about, others I didn't. For instance, when DI Morse got in the witness box, he was looking pretty pleased with himself, in control. He was even wearing a silly police club tie adorned with the scales of justice. Then my barrister asked him, 'Did you follow up the assistance Mr Farebrother gave you, by supplying the phone number of this man he knew as Japanese Jo?'

So Morse said, yes, he did. And it turned out that the phone number belonged to a caravan that had been parked on a semi-permanent basis in a car park in Camden Town. And it was registered to some Japanese man, whose first name was Jo! Now I knew that all along, but the way it came out, it must have looked to the jury that Morse was giving evidence for me! He was reluctantly backing up my story that this JoJo existed, and I'd been duped. It was very clever, the whole way it was put together.

Then the judge — who must have thought Morsey was out of his depth — had a go at him: Why was this case handled by the CID in Borehamwood? Why wasn't it given to the Serious Fraud Squad? So Morsey replied with something like, 'We thought we had the whole case sewn up, Your Honour.'

By now my barrister — my brief, as I call him — was on to something. Before Morsey stepped in the box, three uniform officers who had helped arrest me had given evidence. Each one asked, 'Can I refer to my notebook?', and the judge said yes. Now these books contained the officers' handwritten accounts of what they had seen and done relating to my arrest on that same day, and judges almost always let coppers refer to their notebooks as they give evidence. Nothing odd about that.

But then my brief was asking to see each notebook in turn, and he kept them by him while he was cross-examining the next ones. Then when Morsey gave evidence, he took charge of Morsey's notebook as well.

It was only after the fifth officer — Morsey's sidekick, another detective — had finished giving his evidence and handed over his notebook, too, that my brief moved in for the kill. He called this guy back in the witness box and said, 'You are still under oath. Would you like to refer to your notebook again?' Then my brief handed him his notebook and asked this detective sergeant, 'Did you write this?' 'Yes, I did.'

Suddenly my brief stopped questioning the detective and asked the judge to send the jury out of the court for a while because he wanted to raise a point of law. The judge sent them out; then my brief said he believed that he had discovered something that should lead either to the case being dismissed or, at least, to a retrial.

Now all this time I did not know what the fuck was going on. But once the jury was out, my brief went at it hammer and tongs. First he produced all the notebooks, except Morsey's, one by one, then he asked the detective, 'Who wrote the notes in these other notebooks?'

'I did.'

At this point the mystery of my brief's discovery all became clear — even to me in the dock. While the junior uniform officers had been giving evidence, he had been scrutinising all their notebooks. Now he revealed that not only did these books contain identical evidence but they were all also written in the same handwriting! Morsey's sidekick's.

The judge himself then asked for the notebooks, looked at all the handwriting and agreed it was all the same. He then intervened to ask the detective, 'Was this on your own initiative?'

Then this guy dropped Morsey in the shit, saying it was Morsey's idea: 'He said that, as it was open and shut, I had to make sure there were no mistakes in this case with Farebrother.'

Now, while this had no bearing on whether I had tried to bilk a bank of £1 million, it pole-axed the prosecution case. So in a matter of minutes, the judge called the jury back in and started addressing them through the foreman. He said, 'I am instructing you to find the defendant not guilty, even though it would have been a pleasure to hear Mr Farebrother testify in the witness box.'

At one point he turned to me and said, 'You are either an innocent person involved in a major scam or you are a Machiavellian character.' I acted as if I thought Machiavellian was another witness, and my brief just looked at me and smiled. I said, 'Who's Machiavellian then?' And I had a laugh in court — all to myself I suppose — because I was still three-quarters pissed from drinking all this vodka.

And Morsey just looked devastated.

My solicitor was adamant I would have got off anyway. The jury could well have believed that this Japanese JoJo had set me up. And the signatures of the top bank officials on the cheque were genuine — at one point I'd been charged with forgery, but this was later dropped down to obtaining. Also there must have been someone involved on the inside — someone far more important than me. This might have gained me some sympathy because it entirely ruled out theft. An expert from Natwest's own security unit gave evidence that it was impossible to break into the office where that particular cheque book was held, because it was so securely protected. And there was only one cheque book from which this cheque had definitely come.

Then there was the local bank manager, Mr Baby. He was a great help in court because the first thing my barrister asked him was, 'Did Mr Farebrother have suspicions and did he ask you to check this out?' And, of course, he had to agree. But the thing that would save me all along was that I had asked to have it put in my own account, not a false or dodgy one. So if I'm supposed to be such a brilliant criminal, how come I would have been so dumb as to put everything in my own named account?

The judge then recommended that the Crown Prosecution Service should look into why Borehamwood CID had handled this major crime itself, instead of calling in the Serious Fraud Office. But it all came down to the fact that Morse had his private vendetta against me; he saw this as his big chance to put me in jail and effectively throw away the key.

I later found out what had happened from a friend inside the Borehamwood police. The problem was that Morsey did not want any angle going wrong through the incompetence of junior uniform officers. It seemed he didn't think much of their abilities. That's why he wanted all their evidence notes written up by the same person. He fucked it up badly. By doing what he did, far from nailing me and jailing me, he let me walk free, the very opposite of what he wanted! And his sidekick — the hapless detective — was back in uniform a few weeks later!

It seems that a serious breach of regulations had led to catastrophic humiliation in court and a high-ranking villain walking free after being caught red-handed stealing £1 million in cash! The fact that four officers' notebooks contained identical evidence was no great problem. Surprising as it may seem, such co-ordination rarely upsets judges. They scarcely blink an eye at tightly-orchestrated police scripts, even when they are bitterly contested by defendants crying, 'Fit-up!' However, on this occasion the fact that all four accounts had been written by the same hand was both bizarre and unacceptable. The entire point about an officers' notebook is that it must contain that individual's own version of events, however concocted it may be. Not even this pretence can be maintained when the writing is someone else's.

'Of course,' Ron says, 'however carefully I'd plotted my defence, it was all irrelevant. Not even I had foreseen the police's joint kamikaze act, thanks to Morsey. That was a gift. And what a gift!'

So Ron walked out of Wood Green Crown Court a free man, despite almost pulling off a bank job bolder than any ever performed by Billy the Kid. This had been nothing so crude as a robbery, of course — the only weapon Ron had used was his brain — but he had displayed extraordinary nerve to walk into a bank and walk out again with a crisp million that wasn't his. There could be no reasonable doubt of his guilt, yet here he was back on the streets with no further stain on his character. To their chagrin the police themselves had to stamp NOT TO BE CITED AS A CONVICTION on Ron's record.

Now Ron received the thankful embrace of his wife, Pat. Three rows behind, Sylvia was chuckling to herself. Both women had sat in court throughout the trial, but now Ron had been acquitted, he no longer needed the respectability of a marital address to get bail. Within hours he told Pat he was leaving her for good. The marriage was over. He was now free to move in with Sylvia.

BONNIE AND RONNIE

Some things go together. Peaches and cream. Fish and chips. Sodom and Gomorrah. It was the same with Ronald Patrick Farebrother and Sylvia Lucie Helga Barnes. They brought out the worst in each other.

Just as they were capable of having outrageous sex, so they matched each other for criminal inventiveness. Now that Ron had failed as a white-collar fraudsman, he and Sylvia turned themselves into south Hertfordshire's answer to Bonnie and Clyde. They became Bonnie and Ronnie!

'After the £2.2 million trial I left Pat and her lovely home. I had no job and no money at all, but Sylvia and I still liked a little luxury, so we would book into a hotel on a stolen credit card and stay there for two or three days. Then in would walk Sylvia wearing her stripper's police uniform and arrest me. She'd pick a time when no staff on duty might recognise her, then she'd tell the receptionist or night porter she was carting me off to the station for credit-card fraud.

'Before anyone realised what was going on, we'd be gone, off the planet, nowhere to be found.'

In October 1988 a mere month after his acquittal for attempted bank fraud Ron took Sylvia to the Red Lion Hotel in Watling Street, Radlett, and checked in for the night. So far, so good, except that Ron had claimed he was an employee of the BBC and completed the registration form with false particulars. The Red Lion's staff were not beguiled, and they called the police. The couple were carted off to Bushey Police Station where Ron was charged with forging a hotel registration form and obtaining property and services (a room, a meal and drinks) by deception. Unflinching and showing a typical touch of wit, Ron gave his occupation as self-employed security adviser.

The Bushey police were not amused. They recorded that Ron was strongly suspected of similar offences. He contested the charges so the trial was put off to a later date.

'That one at the Red Lion in Radlett was legitimate. I paid cash, but I did claim a BBC discount: I got a double room at £45, not £65. I'd simply made use of a BBC account number that I'd come across while working with the *EastEnders* production team. As for forging a hotel registration form, all we did was use false names. Is it really an offence to check into a hotel using false names? People do it all the time. On that basis they'd have to convict half the MPs in Britain and their secretaries.'

Two weeks later, on 14 November 1988, security adviser Farebrother and Sylvia Barnes turned up at a

DER shop in North London pretending to be officers of the law. Ron claimed to be a Detective Sergeant Jefferies while WPC Sylv strutted round in her strippogram kit. This lent overwhelming authority to the deception. The staff were totally taken in, and when Ron asked to borrow a video-camera for social purposes — filming a police ball — he was instantly supplied with one worth £1399. Off went the bogus cops and the camera was never seen again — at least not by DER.

So dazzled was Ron by the ease with which the pair had carried out this scam that the very next day, 15 November, he telephoned another DER shop, a few miles away in Golders Green, purporting to be a detective sergeant from the local station. This time he arranged to hire a video recorder and later turned up at the shop to fill out a rental form. When asked for some identification, he replied that CID officers in his squad did not carry identification as they worked undercover. This made the staff suspicious so they rang the local CID office. Alerted by the delay, Ron suddenly made off, but five weeks later he was arrested by detectives from the very same squad to which he had claimed to belong.

The arresting officers were none too flattering, recording that Ron is a compulsive liar and will attempt to obtain immunity from prosecution by offering information. They added, 'He should always be dealt with by senior officers.' Again there was no immediate trial so Ron was restored to liberty, free to perpetrate a series of ever more ingenious scams, which — says Ron — were usually inspired by Sylvia.

'She was a crazy woman. We did quite a few shops, and quite a few we got away with. That was because Sylv was so convincing as a policewoman in uniform. I just trailed in behind as CID. She would walk into a jeweller's shop and convince him that a load of secondhand 'tom' he'd just bought from someone else was bent. This made him a receiver of stolen goods — which he probably was anyway — and that's a very serious offence. Then she'd handcuff the guy and suddenly announce to me we're robbing him, when a few moments earlier all she had said was she was just popping in to do a strippogram. Then we'd clear the window of trays full of rings and watches.

'It was Sylv herself who had sent in the first guy with the bent gear, so she could be sure the shopkeeper already had a guilty conscience. Of course, when he sees this strapping woman copper bearing down on him, he's caught on tenterhooks. She says, "You're under arrest," and in no time she handcuffs him to a radiator. Then she says, "Right, well take all this stuff," and that was it. Out! Gone!

'I won't say which jewellers that was, because he didn't report it — well, a guy in his position isn't going to run to the police, is he? — but it was quite a big shop. Later we were questioned about it because some copper had heard tell on the grapevine, but there was no evidence so we just denied it. We did this kind of thing all over London in loads of places, so I guess that whenever Scotland Yard received a report of a couple of confidence tricksters claiming to be cops and whipping out handcuffs, they must have put it down to us.'

By now Ron was so besotted with his partner-in-crime that he vowed to make her his partner-in-life. On 13 December 1988 at Watford Register Office he married Sylvia.

'That night we were in our hotel room when Sylvia starts giving me a serious talking-to. She looks me in the eye and says, "If ever I catch you with another woman, I'll kill you. So if you want another woman, I'll get you one. Now to show you how good I am, I've got you one for our wedding night!" And she brought in Maria, with a blue ribbon tied round her. Maria! The woman who, on the eve of my trial, had dressed up as a judge, stripped and handcuffed me, then wiped a big iced cake all over me. What a woman.

'So it was three in the bed on our wedding night. I had both of them! Mind you, they were both bisexuals.

'Sylvia had other hobbies. She bred greyhounds, and, in these early romantic days, she kept a pair of greyhound puppies at home. One was called Ron the Gun, the other, I Love You So. These were their officially registered names, but people in the local park must have been bemused to hear Sylvia calling out: "Ron the Gun . . . I Love You So" to a pair of dogs or, even worse, "I Love You So, Ron the Gun."

This marriage would have been just fine, except that Ron was still married to Pat. If his record was not diverse enough already, he had now committed the crime of bigamy. So had Sylvia, for she had failed to dispose legally of her husband. 'What the hell,' thought Ron. By the time anyone spotted their shared offence, the newly-weds would be beyond the reach of England's courts. Ron had already decided that, rather than face two trials for the video-recorder and hotel charges, they would flee abroad. As this country was no longer receptive to their activities, Ron and Sylv vowed to go west to Heathrow Airport.

On 26 January 1989 they took a taxi to Terminal Four where Ron bought two return British Airways tickets to Los Angeles, worth £2000. Nothing became this couple like the way they left England, for Ron had bought the tickets using a company account number. The company again was the BBC. It was yet another fraud, with Ron obtaining services by deception, but it was so easy.

Like millions of others without profit or honour in their own country, Ron and Sylvia headed for the land of opportunity. But where some folk in their position might have tried to make a new beginning by going straight, this pair of grifters aimed right from the start to carry on where they had left off. Farewell, Borehamwood. Hallo, Hollywood!

Ron chose Los Angeles because of his long-standing connections with Mafia members active in that city. He also had a semi-legitimate business excuse to be on that side of America. One month later, on 25 February in Las Vegas, British boxer Frank Bruno would be fighting Mike Tyson for the world heavyweight title. The occasion not only gave Ron a plausible reason for visiting America (should anyone in US law enforcement choose to ask) but also meant that all the faces would be in town: all the characters from the overlapping worlds of prize-fighting, gambling, showbusiness and organized crime. Ron would be in his element and Sylvia would be the perfect companion.

When I went to Vegas for the Tyson-Bruno fight, I just showed up. I wasn't sent by Joe Pyle. I hustled my way in through connections I had already made. I was comped — given a free room and meals — at one of the plushest casino hotels. I even had a ringside seat.

Being known in those circles was working to my advantage, but it all backfired. One day we picked up a paper from back home. It was the *Daily Mirror*, and it had a full-page picture of me and Sylvia, saying we were married. It also said we were wanted for bigamy, and there couldn't be much doubt because it was a wedding photo! A photographer/reporter I knew named Ron Fairley had turned up on the day. Before I left England I had made the mistake of telling my friends, including Fairley, that I was going to the States with Sylvia. Then her husband found out we were married, and all hell was let loose. Someone went and told the police we were bigamists, then this damned photo appeared, with some comment revealing where we were.

As it happened, we weren't bundled home on the next plane. Once the big fight was over, we didn't stay in Vegas, so if anyone acting for Scotland Yard was looking for us, we would have been hard to find. Besides, even the Yard can see bigamy isn't worth an extradition warrant.

Not that we were off the hook. Back home there were now five arrest warrants out for me: five reasons for us to stay in America and carry on conning. We ran all over the country, and Sylv was a fantastic asset. She was excellent at drawing getaway maps. If we did a little con job, she would always know the quickest way out of town. She even made sure we had sets of different number plates, to switch, if we thought the cops were on to us.

You wouldn't believe what she would get away with. Neither did I, even when I saw her do it right before my eyes. Sometimes we'd be driving a car we'd rented in Los Angeles, and we'd enter another state where California plates were like red rags to the local cops. They assumed we must be drug-crazed hippies or

Charlie Manson types. So sometimes we'd be driving along when they would creep up behind us, flash their lights and start wailing their sirens. And shit! The last thing I wanted was my car searched, because I usually had something on me, whatever it may have been. So I'd say, 'Right, Sylvia, quick! Get out and do the English tourist bit! Have your tits hanging out!'

So, of course, she'd get out and be flaunting herself in front of this sheriff or Highway Patrol guy and give him the old tourist act — 'Oh, hi! We're from England!' — and all you could see was his eyes on her tits. He'd be mesmerised. Oh, well, haeve a nayece daey and all that Yeeah. And all the time I'd got a fucking gun on me or something stupid. I always had a gun over there. That's the norm, not just for people like me — for straight folk, too — but it still might take some explaining to a redneck cop.

Sometimes just for the fun of it Sylv would take the battle right to the police. She had brought her WPCs uniform with her to America, so we'd stop in some small town, and she'd go into the tiny police HQ or county sheriff's office and say, 'Hi! I'm a British bobbie on holiday over here, and I'd love to make fraternal contact with you.' And all of a sudden the police chief or sheriff would do anything for her! She'd put on her uniform, strut around the town, jump in a patrol car and have her photo taken leaning on the bonnet. Then she'd say goodbye, and we'd leave town chuckling at the con she'd pulled on these hicks.

Not content with taking the mickey out of small-town cops in America, Ron did not forget his old adversary back in Borehamwood. Detective Inspector Dennis

Morse was still smarting over the £2.2 million bank fraud trial fiasco, so Ron vowed to show he was making the most of the freedom that only Morse's excess of zeal had permitted.

'While I was in the States on the run from all those warrants, I knew Morsey would be doing everything he could to find me and bring me back (even if the intelligence boys at the Yard wanted me to stay there). As he was always driving me mad when I was in Britain, I decided I'd wind him up by sending cards from all over America, saying, "Wish you was here, Morsey!" I even had photos taken of me leaning on the gates of Fulsom Prison outside Sacramento, so he could be in no doubt I really had been there.

'Meantime I found out from a friendly source inside Borehamwood station that Morse was keeping all my cards and trying to plot my movements from the postmarks. So when my daughter came over to the States to visit me, I gave her another photo showing me somewhere in America. I made this into a postcard and addressed it to Morsey, and I told my daughter, "Take this card with you and, when you get back, mail it from Borehamwood." As ever, I'd written on it, "Wish you was here!"

'Bloody hell! After my daughter got home and posted it, she rang me up and said, "He's gone into every pub in Borehamwood looking for you. He's convinced you've never been away!"'

Still in America, Ron had more things on his mind than upsetting Morsey. Most of the time the couple had to stay in southern California because Ron was trying to set up new scams with Ronnie Lorenzo, his Hollywood contact, but sometimes Sylvia's tempestuous temperament got in the way. In America the Mafia tradition is for wives to be kept barefoot and pregnant while the wiseguys make whoopee with their girlfriends. Sylvia was a wife, of course, but hardly a conventional Mafia mamma — more like a gangster's moll. Either way, her presence was not required when the two Rons were discussing business — a fact she grew to resent with ill-suppressed fury.

We were living in Palm Springs, but most days I had things to discuss in Los Angeles. Now from Palm Springs to LA takes three hours, and it's a bastard drive, but for weeks I had to make that journey every morning. I'd usually take Sylvia with me, but, understandably, she was getting fed up with it.

On this particular day I was heading for a restaurant where, as usual, Sylvia wasn't allowed to sit at the table while I was discussing business with Ronnie Lorenzo and other heavies. It was getting late so Sylvia walked over and asked how much longer I was going to be. I told her we'd be talking for a couple more hours. A little while later she walked over again and said, 'Right, we're going now. We've been here too long!' So I said, 'Well, you're getting on a plane back to England!'

I was acting like a cunt, I admit, but suddenly she opened her bag and pulled out a small white gun. She did not hesitate. She just went Toohh! She fired the bloody thing! And I was sitting right next to Lorenzo at the time, and the slug went into my leg and came out the other side. I've still got the mark there.

And there were other people in the restaurant! Ordinary working stiffs! I couldn't believe it! But, of course, I couldn't go to hospital with a bullet wound —

they're bound to ask who, where, when and why — so I put my leg in a plastic bucket. Strangely, it was hardly bleeding. So she said, 'Sorry,' and put the gun back in her bag, and Lorenzo said, 'Some woman! From now on she can sit at the table any time she likes!'

She went to the kitchen and got a rag, but cleaning up hurt more than the bullet did because it happened to be full of bleach, which went straight in the tiny little hole. Fucked up a good pair of trousers, that did!

Then things started going a bit wrong. I had a row with Lorenzo's right-hand man, Tommy, who was from Boston. He and I did not get on. So Sylvia poked her nose in again and threatened him, too.

Now Sylvia had become too hot to handle. She was a liability after that. I wasn't cast out. I was still accepted in that circle, but I was told, 'You've got to keep your woman in check.' So I just drifted away; I couldn't go back to England, and that's when things began to go boss-eyed.

For a while we got work managing a Palm Springs motel. The trouble was that Big Sylv couldn't resist sunbathing topless by the motel pool. Apparently this breached a local decency law, then someone complained, so we both got fired.

We moved to another motel, where we had a fight. Sylvia threw a golfclub at the car windscreen and cracked it. The motel staff called a cop who caught me driving off and booked me for a defective back light. Then he told me I was under arrest, and he took me down to the precinct.

Now this was a hired car that we had got on a BBC account, like the air tickets. Then he started checking our documents, and he saw immediately that we had overstayed our six-month visas. He must have done further checks and discovered I was wanted by the law back home. So that was me done for!

Now Ron came face to face with a law man who already knew a vast amount about Ron's criminal liaisons in Hollywood, and who would figure in many of his upsets during the next two years. Felix Rocha was a Special Agent in America's Immigration and Naturalization Service (INS). He had particular responsibility for liaising with UK police forces, above all Scotland Yard, about the activities of British felons in California. As he questioned Ron, he dropped gnomic hints that he knew exactly what Ron's game was, before taking him to Los Angeles Airport for deportation back home. In a strange turn of events, Sylvia was allowed to stay.

'As he put me on the plane, Rocha said, "See you in five years!" and I said, "Bollocks! I'll be back in three or four weeks!" Cocky bastard, I was. He just laughed. In no time I was stuck on a plane back to Heathrow and found myself facing the music. And how!

As a matter of course Rocha had told Scotland Yard what flight Ron was on. As soon as he landed, he was put through the legal wringer.

'I was taken straight to Borehamwood Police Station. As usual I was brought in the back way, but hanging there to greet me — right above the custody area — was a big blanket, and on it someone had stuck the American flag in one corner and the English flag in another. And they had hung up a big sign saying, WELCOME HOME, RON!

'And when I was taken to the cell, I found DI Dennis Morse there waiting for me — silly old Morsey.

He had laid out some freshly laundered towels along with three of the day's newspapers, and he said, "There you are, sir. Your suite is waiting. I always look after you, don't I?" He was taking the piss, his way.'

Due perhaps to the relentless zeal of DI Morse, English justice would now prosecute Ron with conveyor-belt efficiency. On 7 September 1989 at Staines Magistrates Court he was charged with obtaining those British Airways tickets by fraudulently using a BBC account number. The following day he was in Hendon Magistrates Court, being fined £500 for his 1988 attempt to obtain the video recorder from DER in Golders Green. Five weeks later, on 13 October, he was up before the beaks at Watford over the offences at the Red Lion Hotel, also in 1988. He was told to pay £150 costs but given a conditional discharge.

Enough of courtrooms and fines, Ron was thinking. He aimed to skip all his further trials and get straight back to California especially with the English winter coming on. But after his recent deportation, and the fact that his criminal record was now well known to Special Agent Rocha in LA, there was surely no way back in. But, yes, there was, thought Ron: by using a forged or stolen passport in someone else's name! Within days he had acquired one in the name of Ronald Walker, and by early November he was back in Palm Springs and living at 271 Monterey Road with Sylvia. He then used his real name to acquire a State of California ID and driving licence. Rocha and the Yard had been completely outwitted, or so Ron thought.

For a few weeks the couple were doing fine and back to their old tricks, but it soon went wrong all over again.

'We were quickly picked up in Palm Springs for some blistering argument I had with Sylvia. She had got a job in a Wendy's hamburger restaurant, but her boss kept making her work extra hours at night. One evening I got so fed up I went down and yanked her out, saying, "You're coming NOW!" The boss called the sheriff, and I was arrested. It was like before. This lot of cops decided to look over my car and check if I was wanted for any driving offences anywhere in the USA. Then they took my fingerprints and sent them electronically back to England. And within five to eight minutes I saw my face come up on a fax that said, "Wanted back in England." There was a warrant out for me for jumping bail. I had missed my trial for the airline ticket fraud!

'So who should come up to Palm Springs but Felix Rocha of the Immigration Service, laughing and smiling and saying, "I didn't think I'd see you so soon!"

Even sooner, Rocha put Ron on another plane back to England. This time Sylvia was shipped back with him. At Heathrow, Scotland Yard was ready for them both, but not for what Sylvia had brought with her.

'When we arrived we were immediately arrested by the police but we still had to go through Customs. So the police asked Customs to search our cases there and then, rather than doing it themselves in their own area. I don't know why. Perhaps they feared I would shout, "Fit-up!", if they found anything in our bags.

'So when they opened up Sylvia's case, out fell all these vibrators. They rolled all over the floor, and the cops and Customs guys seemed to think Sylvia should pick them up. But she made a big thing of it. She picked on this poor, bleeding low-ranking copper and said, 'I'm not picking them up, YOU pick them up!' Now Sylvia was really embarrassing him. He was going bright red. But it ended up with him having to retrieve four of these huge things and stick them back in her case.

'The copper wasn't the only one who was embarrassed. So was I because I didn't know she had any vibrators. You don't take vibrators across the fucking world, do you? At least, not when you've got a real man beside you? So I said, "Why the fuck are you taking vibrators round the world with you?" I don't remember her answer. What a girl she was. Definitely lively when I was with her.'

On 6 February 1990 Ron Farebrother was brought back before the Staines magistrates for the ticket fraud and for failing to appear at the previous hearing. He was fined £550 and ordered to pay £2000 compensation. But he had the satisfaction of knowing that he had cost the BBC far more in other ways. Whenever he and Sylvia had wanted accommodation anywhere in America they used to call a woman friend back in England who would send out faxes claiming to come from the BBC. This deluded not only hotels but house-rental agencies too.

'We would say, "We're from the BBC, and we're researching film locations in this area, and we'll take this accommodation." Then we'd ring up our woman in England who had run up the BBC letterhead on a computer. We would give her the fax number of the house agency, and she would fax back a letter confirming our BBC status, and the agency would say, fine. In America the BBC helped us out a great deal. I love the BBC! I'll always be indebted to it.'

But now America — and Palm Springs most of all — seemed a long way away. Ron was flat broke, though at least he had Sylvia. They spent Christmas and the New Year living in Tomkins Close, Borehamwood, but it was there on 12 January 1990 that the police struck again. They were both arrested and charged with bigamy. In one of life's ironies that art cannot afford, the arresting officers name was Husband.

They would both be tried by St Albans magistrates but not at the same time. Sylvia was up first, in April 1990. She was fined £100. In May it was Ron's turn. He portrayed the offence as a minor folly perpetrated by a hopeless romantic. His solicitor, Errol Shulman, explained that the loving couple felt committed to each other and wished to make a public declaration of that fact. However, Shulman went on, 'There was a problem about him getting a divorce, and he was impatient.'

To sway the magistrates Ron felt he should elaborate, so he told the touching tale of how he had fallen for this busty strippogram girl when she popped up at the party to perform on him. 'She was about to peel off her clothes for me, but I paid her £50 to keep them on.' The beaks were unimpressed. They imposed the same fine on Ron as on Sylvia: just £100 — a tiny, derisory sum, but such is the value English law places on monogamy.

It places a far higher value on property, of course. In the same proceedings the magistrates fined Ron £500 with £300 costs for the occasion when this loving couple, posing as cops, deluded shop staff into giving them a £1399 video-camera.

For such an obscure case, the press interest was enormous. One national newspaper described Ron as Dirty Den's former chauffeur, another as the cousin of Costa del Crime fugitive Ronnie Knight. This coverage seemed to have been stimulated by Ron Farebrother himself. He was not Knight's cousin, but occasionally he claimed he was, for the publicity. In June 1987 he had turned up in Spain when Knight married his second wife, Sue (after his divorce from actress Barbara Windsor). Ronnie F. even had his photo taken with the couple at their reception. In 1993 I asked Sue about this incident. She told me that Ronnie F. was never a cousin of Ronnie K. — he was a bloody liar who had gatecrashed the do.

Now both the worry and excitement of their bigamy trials were over, the banality of marriage in deepest, dullest Borehamwood was eating into Sylvia. The contrast with life in Palm Springs could not have been greater. She got hold of a notebook and poured out her feelings.

'I came home one day and found this notebook open where she'd been writing me a letter. In it she said she loved me but could not forgive me for insisting on dragging her out to the pub when she didn't feel well or sociable. She moaned on about how much she hated "this fucking Borehamwood" and the "fucking people in it". This "shit-hole town" had come between us before we'd gone to America and was doing it again. As soon as I had any money in my pocket I'd spend it "mixing with arseholes", while we were stuck living in a pigsty.

'She said she'd never have peace of mind till we left England. She was at the end of her tether, she had 'had it', and my family was "the last straw, typical of the idiots round here". Now I had to choose between them, this town and her.

'She was sure we still loved each other, but why did I have to get pissed in Palm Springs, have a row at her workplace and get us shipped back here? In America we'd been so close, so happy and so lucky but, back on English soil, all we were doing was arguing and fighting when she just wanted loving and being happy together. She ended the letter saying she felt like death. When I read this, I was worried she might have topped herself. I ran into the bathroom expecting to see her lying dead in the water, with her wrists slashed. But then in she breezed as bright as ever! I should have known she was as tough as old boots. I guess she was just making sure I knew I couldn't take her for granted.'

Under this sort of emotional pressure, even hard-hearted, hard-drinking Ron buckled. All through the summer of 1990 he was figuring how to get back to America. He had been thrown out twice, but he was game for another go. He submitted a formal application to the Passport Office in the name of Reginald John Atkinson. Astonishingly, he was given a spanking new passport in that identity! On 28 September 1990 he flew into Los Angeles with that document and was waved through immigration. Sylvia Barnes was on his arm. She had even more false passports — in five different names — and used one on this trip. Landing (they thought) without attracting suspicion, the pair set about reconstituting their lives as confidence tricksters in the land of the gullible. The first thing Ron did was take a trip to Honolulu courtesy of the BBC, checking into a resort hotel as Atkinson at the Beeb's corporate discount rate.

He slipped back to California and was soon setting up major crimes with his Hollywood mob connections, but within three months he was again stopped by police. This time it was an arranged arrest. The couple had been under surveillance since soon after their arrival. Their

Atkinson passport ruse had been allowed to continue until the Feds felt it was time to pull Ron in.

The arresting officers were told, 'Hold him!' until who should appear but Ron's nemesis, Special Agent Felix Rocha. After twice giving the Englishman the easy ride home in 1989, Rocha felt Ron should now taste how most illegal aliens get treated. Entering America on a false passport is a serious crime, especially when you have just been deported. To do it twice is suicidal. You don't get flown home again. This time you get stuck in jail.

I was charged with entering the country illegally and taken down to a detention centre in Los Angeles, where illegal aliens are held pending a decision on their fate. I was held there for four or five days while Felix Rocha kept coming back saying, We're trying to process you now. It won't take long. I don't think it was Rocha's fault, but, while I was going through this procedure, the authorities kept on fucking around. I just wanted to get out of this place and go home but no such luck.

Instead I was kept stuck in this cage with 30 or 40 other guys. It was so crowded they couldn't keep us all there for long, so one day I found myself on a roll-call of people being sent to El Centro, an immigration jail down on the Mexican border. As I heard all the names, it struck me that the only guys going to El Centro were guys the LA staff didn't like, the troublemakers. There was me, there was an Israeli and an Iranian called Jehan Jehan. Now all of us were being punished with an 18-hour drive on a fucking bus. We even passed through Palm Springs on our way. Almost all the other prisoners on the bus were Mexicans who were being taken there so they could be quickly dumped over the border when their appeals failed. That doesn't explain why all of us were kept in shackles, chainlinked together.

Now on this bus I'm sitting beside Jehan Jehan. Then a guy in the seat in front of us leaned up and over and said, 'Have you got a smoke?' As it happened, I had already given this guy a Marlboro, but JJ gave me a bit of advice. He said, 'Don't do that again cos they'll rob you. Seriously, don't even talk to these Mexicans!' So this Mexican said, 'My friend wants a cigarette.' So I said, 'Well, tell your friend to fuck off.'

Now I'm getting really pissed off, but I kind of forget that I'm chained to this poor bastard JJ. So when the Mexican leaned over again in front of me, I thought he was going to do something (like hit me!), and so I lifted my hand and whacked him. But I'm still handcuffed to JJ on my left. And, as I hit this guy in front, I pulled JJs hand up as well and accidentally bust it. I broke his left thumb! This caused a riot on the bus, which was a good start, but eventually we got to El Centro.

El Centro was bad enough, but the trouble was that they kept on bringing us back to Los Angeles, the bastards, every Monday morning to be processed all over again. Up to 18 hours each fucking way. JJ was in the same boat as me: just fighting against being deported. Meantime we had to go back and forth to this hellhole on the Mexican border.

In El Centro I got pally with this Israeli guy who was in for murder, so he and JJ were telling me all about the US jail system. They told me to take care when we were allowed out of the cage to walk round the exercise yard. I had to be especially wary of the fucking Mexicans, dodgy cunts. So it was my first day in there, I was really pissed off, and this Mexican comes up and says, 'How you going, Homey!' And straight away I thought, Fuck, I've had enough of all this bollocks. I'm not having this! So I just lost my cool completely and started belting the shit out of this Mexican guy.

So the other guys broke it up, then another Mexican guy came up. He was covered in tattoos — they do like tattoos, these Mexicans — and he was built like a gorilla. And he said, 'Why did you do that? He was only trying to be friendly'. And I said, 'Just tell your mate, being friendly? I am not a fucking homo!' He said, 'He never called you a homo. He called you Homey.' I said, 'That means fucking homo.' He said, 'No, Homey means "Home Boy" friend.'

I was gob smacked. I said, 'Oh, I made a bit of a fuck-up there, didn't I!' So everybody was laughing. Because of my accent they accepted that I had got it wrong, and I apologized. They called me Mad English Dog after that.

It was fucking horrible in El Centro. When eventually I came back home and spent my next spell in jail it was the first time I was ever pleased to get into an English cell. Because 80 per cent of the prisoners are Mexicans, all you get is Mexican food. So as for JJ, he was a Muslim; well, you don't get any food prepared according to Muslim law. It's all just shit. I wasn't allowed to make any phone calls. There were only three phones in this block that I was in, and those three were all monitored. In fact I did get JJ (who was speaking to his sister) to pass a message over to England that I was in the prison there. That was vital because, until that point, my family did not even know I was in jail because I, wasn't allowed to make any phone calls. Eventually I did get a call out to England just to let the Office know that I was banged up.

On 13 December 1990 Ron had been ordered to be detained at government expense until he could be brought before an immigration judge. Next day a judge was produced. He ordered Ron's deportation, which was what Ron was asking for. Yet instead of being flown home straight away, he was told he would be kept in custody in California for further investigation.

'They are clever fuckers. They're very good at fucking you around. When they asked me, was I prepared to go back voluntarily? I always went, 'Yeah. Course I am.' Or they'd ask, 'Are you fighting extradition?' and I'd say, 'No, I want to go straight back.' So this nice old judge would stamp the order to send me back within 28 days.

'Then dear old Felix Rocha would come up and say, "We haven't processed you," so then I had to go to the British Consul to get all the paperwork and the photographs done for a travel permit because, of course, I did not have a passport. They'd even managed to lose the Atkinson one! "We'll try and get it done," I was told, but, of course, I was down in El Centro, and I could only get to LA twice a week with an 18-hour trip each way bridged by an overnight stay in that infested LA immigration holding cage.

'Of course, the minute I got into LA I said, "Let's get on with this fucking thing!" So the guy who did the photo said, "Well, once we get that stamped, you'll be on the next available flight out." But I think they deliberately fucked up the system. I got the passport photo done once, then they said, "No, it's not clear enough. They won't pass that. You'll have to go back again. Ah! The office is closed at four o'clock. You'll have to do it next week. Monday. So it's back to El Centro tonight!" Now, out of pride, I couldn't let these guys know I was getting pissed off, but they knew.

'Eventually, in April 1991, I was taken to LA airport where Felix saw me off again. I was flown back to Heathrow, handcuffed to another US immigration officer, dressed all in green. When I got off the plane this guy told UK immigration, "I'm handing over your prisoner." Everything had been arranged between all these cops, so as soon as I arrived I was arrested over the Atkinson passport.'

Ron sensed something wasn't right. Someone was missing from the proceedings. Why wasn't Morsey around to enjoy Ron's latest humiliation?

'I was surprised that it was another officer who arrested me at the airport, so I asked, "Where's Morsey?" And the guy said, "Well, he was looking forward to arresting you, but, sadly, he was out jogging a few weeks ago and died of a heart attack."

'And I had a little grin and said to myself, "Fucking Morseys done this on purpose. Getting fit just because I was coming home, getting ready to wind me up, going jogging, dropping dead. Silly really." Even I felt upset.'

In a curious twist, although Ron had been arrested over the passport on arriving at Heathrow, he was not instantly charged. There was surely no problem in defining a criminal offence. For obtaining a passport by applying in another name, he could have been prosecuted under Section 15 of the 1968 Theft Act or Section 36 of the 1925 Criminal Justice Act. There was no doubt he had committed a crime, and he was in no position to deny it.

Strangely, no immediate action was taken. The reason may be found on a sheet added to Ron's criminal record held at Scotland Yard on 18 January 1991 while he was still locked up in El Centro. Under Section 29, reserved for other useful information, were typed the words that according to US law enforcement, Ronald Farebrother was a 'member of Joey Pyle organised crime group, London.'

Joey Pyle? Organised crime? Why were the Americans telling Scotland Yard all this? Surely there was no intelligence coming out of the USA about a London syndicate that the Yard did not possess already? Not necessarily. Not if the Feds in California had developed their own sources — their own informers — within the Joey Pyle OC group. Or in the circle of mobsters in LA with whom visiting members of this Pyle group were doing regular business.

For at least a year before his third deportation from LA, Ron Farebrother had suspected he was being informed on. It wasn't just the speed with which a brief encounter with small-town cops or a county sheriff could end with him dumped back in England. There were other indicators. Indeed, while Ron was looking for a way out of El Centro, the Special Agent from Immigration gave him all the proof he needed.

'Now Felix Rocha had got me over a barrel. Coming in on the false Atkinson passport, I was in deep shit. Then he pulled out all these intelligence reports revealing my connection with Ronnie Lorenzo. They had photographs of me coming out of restaurants with him. They showed me all this evidence. It was like a diary of my entire life. Someone had to be grassing me up.'

But who would know everything Ron was doing? Who could be that close to him? There was one obvious person: the person Ron had not seen since he was thrown in El Centro, who had disappeared from his life the moment he had been picked up on the Atkinson passport, and who was not by his side when he was flown back to Heathrow in handcuffs: Sylvia Barnes.

US law enforcement had been showing Sylvia a lot of favour ever since she and Ron were first arrested back in 1989 for over-staying their six-month visas.

'You might think Sylvia would have got chucked out with me, and been put on the same plane back home. In fact she was allowed to stay another three months. At the time this was a mystery to me. I couldn't figure it out. I thought she was being kept there under duress to put pressure on me, to blackmail me into co-operating with the Feds. Later I realised this wasn't a punishment for her. It was a reward.'

An earlier mystery had first aroused Ron's suspicions. After their visas had expired (but before they were caught), he overheard Sylvia making a call to her teenage son Peter back in England.

'After a little while I heard her saying, "No, no, no, no!" So I thought maybe someone had been picking on him, and I asked, "What's the problem?" Then I took the phone, and Peter said, "A fine mess bloody Mum's left me in. She's turned my best mate over, some credit-card con!"

At the time I couldn't work it out because, all the while this credit-card thing he was talking about had allegedly happened back in England, Sylvia had been with me in America. But later I realized there had been a spell of two weeks when we'd been apart while I did some business I couldn't let her be anywhere near. She was quite relaxed about this, saying she'd take the opportunity to do some travelling around America by herself. But during these weeks she was completely out of reach. I couldn't trace her. What she must have done was go back to England, and that was when she pulled a wicked con trick on the family of her son's best mate.

The trick was neat but nasty. Peter had a friend called Robbie. His parents liked Peter, who was always welcome in their house. Indeed he was considered part of the family. One day in waltzed Sylvia on the pretext of seeing Peter who was there at the time. She started chatting to Robbie's mother, who had never met her before. She stayed for a coffee and left. She visited the house just once more before disappearing as mysteriously as she had appeared. That was all the family ever saw of her, but her shadow lingered for months, as Robbie's mother explains.

We went on holiday for two or three weeks but, soon after we came back, we noticed that our monthly poll-tax payments weren't being deducted from our bank account. We got in touch with the council who told us we had been completely wiped off the computer. We investigated further and found out that, according to council records, we weren't living here any longer. Sylvia Barnes was!

What she had done was tell the council — in writing or in person — that we had moved out of our house, and she had moved in. That's why we were taken off the poll-tax list. The council had taken our names off the computer, which in turn cancelled our direct-debit order. They had simply believed what she said. They relied on her word alone.

Of course, she never did live here, but now she had our address she could easily con a bank into giving her an Access card. All it required was proof she had a permanent residence, so she waved a poll-tax bill in her name. She was then given the Access card with a credit limit of £1200, which she promptly spent on all sorts of goods and services.

I only found this out when I opened a letter that arrived here in her name. It was an Access bill for £1200! I called them up straight away to say she didn't live here, but they didn't believe me. I had terrible trouble convincing them, until we found out what she'd done and how she'd done it.

We also had calls from different firms saying she'd ordered lots of stuff from this address. I had to tell them to get lost, no such person lived here, so she must have run up a lot more debts. Thank goodness she used our address and not our names, otherwise we would have been blacklisted by credit-rating firms.

For a few weeks it was a nightmare, but my husband used to laugh about it. What wasn't so funny was that the police did nothing about it. My husband went to the police station and reported what she had done, but we never heard a word back. They never said they'd investigated it or anything.

And we scarcely knew her! She just breezed in here one day, had a coffee and breezed out again. And that was it!

It seems that not only was Sylvia pulling all sorts of

confidence tricks on both sides of the Atlantic but she must have been getting protection as well. How else could she fly out from America and back again, when she had already exceeded her visa? The protection continued even after Ron Farebrother had been deported back to England.

US Immigration and Naturalization Service documents confirm that, while Ron was taking the rap in England for some of their joint crimes, Sylvia Lucie Helga Barnes was allowed to remain at the Cypress Hotel, Highway 111, Palm Springs, despite the fact that she had been caught violating her visa. Just as surprising, she was given INS authorisation to stay working in America for three further months from 14 September 1989. But there really should be no surprise, for it is clear that she had been acting as an informer, against not only her bigamous husband but also the high-ranking mobsters with whom they had both been associating in Hollywood and Palm Springs. On 23 June 1989 she had accepted a subpoena to appear before a federal grand jury investigating the Ronnie Lorenzo group on 29 June. Any testimony she gave on that occasion is sealed secret, unavailable for public scrutiny but much later when Ron eventually saw Sylvia's grand jury subpoena it made a lot of things clear.

'Look at the date: 23 June 1989. This is the first time I've seen this. She never told me. I can't fucking believe it. Our arses were getting pulled left, right and centre. And she must have known all along. The strokes she's pulled!

'Now it all fits into place. A couple of years later I remember ringing up a copper in St Albans, because he always kept bugging me about her. I came straight out with it. I said, "How long has she been your informant?" He said, "You must be blind. She was put into you very early." '

But if Sylvia were a police informant who had she been informing on? On Ron, of course, but who else? On the alleged Malibu Mafioso, Ronnie Lorenzo? On the Joey Pyle organised crime group? And what did she know about any of them?

THE GRASS MENAGERIE

Sylvia Barnes knew a fair amount about Joe Pyle, but little involving crime. Certainly Ron had used her on Office business, and she would attend meetings at the Russell Hotel, where Charlie Richardson would sometimes join Joe and Alex Steene discussing business. One meeting is etched in Ron's memory. 'I'm a bit deaf in one ear, and so is Charlie Richardson, so most of the time either I was saying, "Would you mind repeating that?" or "Sorry, I didn't catch that," or Charlie was. Maybe we were talking in whispers that day because we thought the room was bugged. To Sylvia the scene was hilarious, and in the middle of it all she said, "I'm going to get Charlie and Ron a present: one Walkman between the two of them." '

Despite Ron's detailed accounts of working with Joe Pyle, Joe himself says he kept his dealings with Ron to a minimum:

I met him years ago through the boxing, but I've never done no business deals with Mr Ronnie. I've never had anything to do with him, and anything else is rubbish. Knowing people is one thing, doing business with them is another. And he was no nominee of mine. OK? He kept coming to me and trying to get me involved, but I used to just ignore him. As for Sylvia, yeah, I met her. He said she was his wife. I regarded them both as fucking nutters, the way they used to go on, a pair of loons. He could have brought her to a meeting when we were talking about property or something, but nothing illegal, I can assure you.

To Scotland Yard's exasperation, that had always been the way with Joey. Every time it developed a line of information on him, he turned out to be no more crooked than any other entrepreneur. Whatever his gangster activities, through a long career he had always appeared to be a legitimate businessman, a straight goer involved in betting shops and the car trade. Indeed, he fulfilled the classic redemptive image of someone who has survived a very tough start in life to become a straight and successful citizen.

You know why they wanted to set me up, from the days of Sgt Harold Hannigan [whose pursuit of Pyle ended in fiasco, and who was convicted of corruption in 1975]. They just didn't like me, so what can you say to that? I can't get inside their minds. All I've ever said, and I've said it to police and judges, 'Listen, all my life, I've had no twin brothers, I've got no brothers except one who's an invalid, and I've never let any villains bully me. If that makes me a bad guy, then I'm a bad guy.

All baloney, according to the Yard, which had been gunning for Joseph Henry Pyle for over 30 years. Within its intelligence files lay a mass of reports indicating he was the biggest London crime boss to have outlasted the gang-busting fever that overcame the Metropolitan force in the 1960s and 1970s. Indeed, he had barely been scratched since a notorious gangland murder in 1960, involving the death at the Pen Club in Spitalfields of Selwyn Cooney, a middle-ranking clubland figure, first brought him to the Yard's attention. As an accessory to grievous bodily harm, Pyle was jailed for 18 months.

In the eyes of the police Pyle had got off light, but in London gangland so heavy a sentence was a mark of honour. For the next 30 years these diametrically opposed views would bring Pyle no end of trouble. His status in the underworld was unequalled. He was the only peer of the Nash

Brothers (who had been linked to the Pen Club affair) and their more notorious gangland rivals, the Krays and Richardsons, and was on good terms with all of them. While the Krays and Richardsons fought vicious turf battles and were all jailed by the end of the 1960s, so Pyle emerged as the underworld's leading survivor and its supreme diplomat. Yet at the same time his very survival, his apparent untouchability, irked the gang-busters of Scotland Yard; the longer he stayed at liberty, the guiltier and more powerful a criminal he must be.

By the late 1970s Joe Pyle was back under the Yard's microscope, though this time the investigating squad was a special intelligence section, hermetically sealed from the rest of 'C11', the Yards Criminal Intelligence Department. This incorruptible unit (consisting then of only four handpicked officers) tried to track down all Pyle's assets. If he were as big a villain as the Yard's gangbusters had claimed, he must have something to show for it, however well hidden.

Yet, no matter how hard they searched, this crack squad could find nothing. It appeared that Pyle was essentially skint, with no assets except a small legitimate business. His lifestyle was so modest as to be unexceptionable. He made no secret of associating with the major-league crooks he had known since Pen Club days — he would visit Ronnie and Reggie Kray in jail — but where he had stashed any assets, nobody had an inkling.

By the late 1980s Joe Pyle had established

himself in the recording and management business (collaborating with Alex Steene) and had become a film producer, running a successful production company called Touchdown, based at Pinewood Studios. But the Scotland Yard intelligence officers who now had the brief of monitoring organized crime had got it in their heads that Pyle still was a Mr Big. That view was reinforced when law-enforcement colleagues in California claimed he was on visiting terms with suspected Mafiosi in Hollywood. Of course, it can now be argued that his dealings with record promoter Joey Isgro were legitimate as he has always maintained and as the 1996 verdict in Isgro's trial would appear to confirm. But back in November 1987, when Isgro's bodyguard Dave Smith was due to testify against him, US investigators were adamant Isgro was a Mafia guy, extorting and corrupting the record industry at its most vulnerable point.

For that reason the Yard's intelligence boys would have been overjoyed to sponsor Smith's spell in London when (pretending to duck his subpoena) he infiltrated Pyle's circle. But if the Smith scenario weren't enough, another inside track emerged the same year. The mob connection this time was Hollywood restaurateur Ronnie Lorenzo. He, too, had a spy in his camp, 32-year-old Robert Franchi, later described by Paul Lieberman in the *Los Angeles Times* as 'a bull-necked Bostonian, who had worked at the fringes of the mob in New England. He had come west to flee loan sharks and then, when he heard they might be headed this way, volunteered his services to the FBI. Soon the feds were paying Franchi $5000 a month to eavesdrop on local mob figures.'

Franchi's favoured technique was to hang around the bars of smart restaurants, wired up and letting anyone know he had piles of cash to buy kilos of cocaine. This proved so successful that his tapes would win convictions against six restaurant owners. One was Lorenzo. In 1989 he had bought a kilo through Franchi for $19,000. The FBI did not reveal they knew about this for three years, after Franchi had snared Lorenzo six times over.

Lorenzo took Franchi wholly into his trust. So did a crew of robbers tied in with Lorenzo, who were looting and beating their way through scores of grand California homes. They, too, gabbled away carelessly while Franchi's recorder was turning. In all he gathered 10,000 pages of taped evidence for the FBI. On some tapes you could hear an Englishman. It was Ron Farebrother. He had no idea Franchi was an informer until I showed him the proof in 1996. So what dirt had Robert Franchi gathered on Ron?

I knew Roberto Franchi through Ronnie Lorenzo. I met him in Splash, just as I met the rest of the crew hanging round Ronnie. This was in 1989 from January till I got chucked out in September. Of course Sylvia was there, too, most of the time. And when we went back to the States as Mr and Mrs Atkinson, it was Franchi whom Lorenzo's man, Boston Tommy, had told to arrange our hotel in Beverly Hills. From that moment on, our false passports were no use at all. We must have been watched morning, noon and night.

This must also have kicked back on Joe Pyle because, remember, although I was in LA on my own initiative, I was claiming to represent the Office: doing anything for them in the States, like I had years before as the Ambassador. This gave me the status I needed, but where I really scored was doing the work, getting my hands dirty. Lots of mobsters can sit around offices and restaurants talking big, but when it comes to action, you'd be surprised how useless they can be.

So don't think I just sat in Splash drinking vodkas or Bacardis. I was going everywhere, with Sylvia and without. I had to put my face around, get myself known. If you want to do business with the people who have business to do, it's no use being a voice on the end of a phone. That's why we went to Boston, New York, Texas and back to LA, seeing businessmen. On a Friday, we'd ring up and say, 'When can we see you?' They'd say, 'Monday,' so over the weekend we'd fly 1000, maybe 3000 miles, and turn up at their door on Monday.

When I say businessmen, I mean guys with connections: family members, or friends of the family, or individuals with problems or propositions. I couldnt have done this by myself. My connection was Tommy, from Boston, where we had our strongest and longest connections. It was Tommy who had originally introduced me to Ronnie Lorenzo. If he hadn't vouched for me, I would never have got near Ronnie.

So Tommy would be sitting beside me saying, 'This guy's gotta see you, *this* guy's gotta see you, this guy's *gotta* see you!' Different trips, different strokes.

Why me, rather than one of their own? It's all about face, about front. I've got more arsehole than a lot of those mob guys. In the States I can bullshit my way into more places and get more information, just from my accent. And if we pulled a job and got away with a lot of money or whatever, the cops would be looking for an Englishman or Australian not a typical Italian-American Mafioso. An example: if they wanted someone warned off — even someone in another crime family — they didn't want to send one of their own to do it. They would send me in instead.

Think about it, it's brilliant. Send an English guy in there Can I see so-and-so? I'm from England — and they don't know the fuck what's going on. And so I see the problem person, and I give him the message: 'Stay out of this shit because you're upsetting people — and you're fucking with London too.' Now, of course, these people may not care about London, but most of them do hope to do business there in the future. Some have to. If they want to be players, they've all got to do business in London some time or other.

So what job did Tommy really have in mind for Ron,

the smoothtalking front man from London Town?

'There was one job we were planning for months — me, Tommy, Ronnie Lorenzo and six other guys, including Roberto Franchi (who, you now tell me, was a grass). This was massive, involving not just LA and Boston but other American families — and London too. We were going to break open a safe deposit in northern California containing 530 boxes, some known to have huge amounts of cash and jewels in them. My role was crucial — until we hit a big problem.'

The problem was that the Americans, Tommy in particular, resented London's agreed share of the action: 50 per cent. They felt London was not putting in enough money to justify what it was going to get out.

'Tommy was trying to fuck up. He said, "Fuck London." So I'd say, "You can't just fuck London." He'd say, "Yeah, fuck London! Why is your corner getting 50 per cent?" I'd say, "Because my corner has 25 per cent for me and 25 per cent for Joe Pyle." He'd say, "Well, now you're on your own over here." The guy was driving me mad. We'd started years before on good terms — after all he had sponsored me with Lorenzo — but now I was calling him 'Evil Tommy'. In the end I just told him and his *compares* what a bunch of cunts they were.

This is where Sylvia Barnes felt she should intervene. She wrote a letter to Joey Pyle laying out the entire argument. Pyle does not recall receiving the letter. If he did, he says, he would have thrown it away, as it would have meant nothing to him. But Sylvia's draft survives.

As you know, Ron has told Boston and Tommy to their faces that they are the biggest load of amateurs again, and he's going to punch Tommy all around California. Ron's loyalty to you and Charlie — Ron has got to do this thing and fuck them, but they've now said that if he does, he's dead. They are saying that they have financed this for $4000, Tommy has spent far more than us, and Ron owes them, and that he should fuck England and JP and work for them.

What is he supposed to do? We now owe them money and have had no real help or anything in return. They just cannot believe how loyal and respectful he is to you, and if it wasn't for you he would probably be dead. Then they say, London hasn't helped Ron out financially and laugh at him and tell him to work for them, and they're saying that you and England don't care and haven't given him any support at all. They're saying that we've wasted time and money when it's them that have kept dilly-dallying around. Ron is really uptight and convinced he's being set up.

The dispute festered on. The safe-deposit job was delayed and delayed, until the incident when Sylvia shot Ron in the foot, in front of Lorenzo. Next she had a flaming row with Tommy and threatened him. After that, the job had to be abandoned — or, at least, Ron was no longer involved. He was, as they say in Hollywood, off the picture.

That turned out to be his good fortune. If he had stayed on the picture, he would have been arrested in 1992 with the rest of the crew. Thanks to their partner-in-crime, undercover snoop Robert Franchi, in 1996 most were given long jail terms. One is doing life.

Back in 1989, when it first became clear (through Franchi, probably) that the Englishman Farebrother was associating with one of the leading Mafiosi in Hollywood, Special Agent Felix Rocha promptly alerted Scotland Yard. So, when Ron was deported back to Britain for the third time in 1991, there to greet him was no ordinary Yard detective but Peter Cox of S011, the Criminal Intelligence Branch formerly known as C11.

'When I first met Coxy at Heathrow, he said, "We'll get your mess sorted out, and then you can go back to America and be there with Sylvia . . . blah blah blah." At the time I thought, This is a bit odd. Why is the Yard giving me instructions on my private life, and saying how I can live with my girlfriend in America? It made me wonder, even then, whether she was working with them.

'I told him, "Fuck off, Coxy. I'll sort out my

own mess and fuck off whenever and wherever I want." Coxy said, "You'll go back to America when we tell you to go back there." I said, "No, I won't!" '

But Ron was not as free as he liked to talk. When he had arrived at Heathrow on 2 April 1991 he was arrested for the passport offence but not charged. He was released on police bail. This meant the authorities still had room for discretion: either to charge him or to let the matter drop. His passport deception really could get him jailed for years — but what if he now co-operated? That might make a difference — or so he felt led to believe. He was now wedged between the proverbial rock and hard place. What was his way out? What was on offer?

There was a task for him back in Los Angeles. If he did it, any little difficulties in England could be ironed out. He might even be allowed to stay in America after all — with Sylvia (if she showed up again) or without.

The job was to act as a courier between Ronnie Lorenzo and Joey Pyle: to carry a consignment of cocaine supplied by Lorenzo in LA back to London and deliver it safely into Pyle's hands. Joe's film-production company would provide the perfect cover: Ron would bring the cocaine through Heathrow concealed in film-stock cans. His police minders would give advance warning to Customs who would allow the consignment through the airport. This would avoid the embarrassment and recrimination of some previous controlled runs when Customs had seized drugs from police informers coming through Heathrow, owing to a lack of prior candour on the part of the police.

Once the cans had been delivered into Pyle's indisputable care and control, the cops would arrest him, charge him with a huge cocaine conspiracy, then watch him go down for at least 20 years in jail. The plan appeared immaculate; Ron was claiming he had the trust of both Pyle and Lorenzo, and was indicating he was pliable, prepared to help out in return for a clean start in America.

Or so law enforcement in both Britain and America were led to believe. To the Yard's LA counterparts, the scheme was irresistible. Through Rons co-operation, they would bag Lorenzo and his soldiers in the same sting and at the same moment as Pyle was bagged in London. Both men would rot in jail for the rest of their lives, and it would be brownie points all round in the joint US-UK war against international organized crime.

The Yard was so keen for success that SO1, its central detective office and Serious Crime Branch, took a direct interest. From its elite ranks Detective Chief Inspector David Morgan was chosen to supervise the operation: a controlled delivery, in law-enforcement terms. Morgan had his concerns. He knew little of the background, though to him the job never looked like a goer. He doubted if Ron had the credibility to carry off such a remarkable double-headed sting.

The operation went ahead anyway, but before it could get going, one big obstacle had to be overcome. How was triple-deportee Ron going to get into America when his own passport had been confiscated, and his false Atkinson passport had disappeared? Once again, he says, the enthusiasts in the Yard had the answer.

They said, 'Don't worry, we've got you a passport. We'll give it to you when we get to the airport. You're going back to LA.' So they told me to go to Gatwick because we were flying out on Virgin Airlines. So I arrive at Gatwick. No ticket, no passport! Then one of the Yard officers walked over to the first-class check-in counter and came back saying, 'All right! You're going through that way.' Then I go straight through Customs!

And then from his pocket Peter Cox pulled out a plastic sleeve containing an old passport of mine with the corners cut off, and with big, red letters stamped on every page — CANCELLED — even across my photograph. I looked at it, and I realized this was the passport I had surrendered at fucking court as a condition of bail on the BA ticket charge! What's more, it had run out! So surely this passport was no use to anyone.

So I looked at this guy, and even he laughed. I said, 'You cannot get on a fucking train with that fucking Mickey Mouse passport, and you expect me to get on a fucking plane with it? That ain't gonna get me nowhere!'

And he said, 'Well, you're not gonna be able to fuck off with that, are you!' So already, at that stage, they had sussed that I might have the idea I was gonna fuck off, but they'd fixed it — or so they thought — so I couldn't. And, of course, I did have that idea because I never had any intention of entrapping either Joe Pyle or Ronnie Lorenzo. All I wanted to do was get to America and fuck off.

Anyway, I was astonished: I got through on to the plane! So I was sitting there in economy class. We took off, and I couldn't see anyone from Scotland Yard. Then suddenly up popped Peter Cox from some other section of the plane with a smile on his face. But I was still trying to figure out what was going to happen when we got to the States.

You just imagine queueing up at LA immigration, when all you've got is a fucking passport completely disfigured! When I handed this to an immigration officer, I though it would be all over, and I'd be sent straight back to England. But suddenly my old sparring partner Special Agent Felix Rocha showed up! He pressed in some numbers, and I was let through. And then they had the nerve to take even that crummy passport off me again.

So Rocha picked me up, took me right out of the airport and told me I was booked into a hotel close by. Now it was going through my mind: I'm going to get out of this hotel, I've got connections in this town, and I can lose myself in the system here.

I walked into the hotel with Rocha, and I was still thinking, so far, so good. Great, give it a couple of hours and fuck off! I'll have had one over on Scotland Yard! Then I realized: everyone in the hotel from the porter to the pastry cook (for all I know) was from one US cop agency or another. Talk about overkill: these cunts virtually took over the hotel!

So I went up into my bedroom, and it looked pretty normal, like any other hotel room. Then I noticed a door into the next room. It was unlocked so I went through, and that room was like a TV studio. There were cameras, recording machines and earphones all over the place, and a couple of TV monitor screens. Then I realized my bedroom was being shown on these monitors.

The monitoring room was full of people. I met about ten guys in there, and I was told, 'You've already come through immigration so you don't need to be searched again. But you're not allowed to move out of this hotel.' Fat chance, I thought, because I can see my entire room on these fucking monitors! There was no angle that wasn't covered.

So I went back in my room, curious to see where the camera was. I couldn't find it·so I started moving things around, then going back next door and checking the monitors, thinking: this camera's hidden somewhere. Stuck in some ornament maybe. Then these guys barked at me, 'Leave the equipment alone!' Don't look for things you shouldn't be looking for!'

So I slept there overnight, wondering whether I

dare take a crap without them having a camera up my arse. The next morning they said, 'You're under our jurisdiction now, not Scotland Yard's.'

Then I saw my minder Coxy — Peter Cox — just sitting on the bed. So they said, 'What do you do now?' I said, 'Nothing, mate. I just stay here. I stay here in this hotel.' Then they said, 'Well, don't you want to go down to the restaurant? Ain't you gotta make a few phone calls?' I said, 'No. I've gotta do fuck all, mate. I'm just sitting here. I'm not leaving.'

But there was no way I was going to help them, partly because I had fallen out with Peter Cox. To put it bluntly, I always called him a horrible four-letter word beginning with c.

Then they turned round and said, 'Well, you've got to put a call in,' so I said, 'Right. I'll put a call in from this room.' Then I emphasized it: 'From this room. That phone.' They said, 'Yeah, fine.' 'Right. I'll do it in the morning.' Now I'm agreeing to do something for them, they're fucking over the moon.

So the following morning — don't forget, I've flown all the way from England, I'm jet-lagged, and I get just three hours sleep with all them silly cunts in the other room — now I was thinking, I'll go down and have breakfast in the hotel restaurant or coffee shop. But they said, 'We prefer you to have breakfast in your room.' So I said, 'No, I'm going downstairs.' They thought about it, then they said, 'All right. They went straight on the radio, and suddenly everyone was there to meet me: in the lift, discreetly all over the place, while I was having breakfast, all these cops and agents!' And as I approached the hotel entrance one guy said, 'Don't even attempt to go through those doors!' So I took him at his word. I thought, OK then. So when I got back upstairs, this same guy said, 'Right. You'll put a call through now.' I said, 'OK. From this room.' He said, 'All right.'

Then I said, 'This is what I've got to say. I'll tell Joe — I'm in the hotel room, Joe, and I'm here.' He said, 'That'll be it? It'll be taken care of then, will it?' I said, 'Yeah, it'll be taken care of.'

So I put the call in. I said, I better get him on his mobile. They said, OK. But that's another thing you'd never do: talk on a mobile. I phoned up from the hotel room, and the first thing Joe said was, 'Where are you?' I said, 'I'm at the airport, in a HOTEL!' He said, 'You're phoning from a hotel phone?' I said, 'Yeah, in my room!' He said, 'All right, mate. What's the weather like?' I said, 'It's pissing with rain, believe it or not!' And he said, 'Oh, right, I'll hear from you later, mate?' I said, 'No. I think I might stay in the hotel, mate. I'm not leaving the hotel. Get it over with. I'll stay in the hotel! All right, see you later.'

Now they're all sitting there congratulating themselves, thinking: contact's made, Joe's gonna make a phone call, blah, blah blah (to whichever villains or crooks or associates he has in America), and it will be delivered.

Some time later I made a second call to Joe, and he asked me, 'Are you going to the restaurant?' and I said, 'No, I'm staying in the hotel room.' Well, from that answer alone he knew I was in right shit, because we had a system. We would never discuss anything, unless it was Office One to Office Two. In other words, the first thing I'd do is go to a payphone. That's because payphones can't be bugged as easily as subscriber phones. Cops can't usually get wiretap orders from American judges or British Home Secretaries on them because they can't bug unknown private citizens, just because they happen to pick up a payphone to make a personal call.

So usually I'd use a public payphone to call Joe at his office, then he'd go round to another payphone near him, which we would call Office Two. I already had that phone's number, which I would now ring. This way, we hoped to avoid any police taps, but, even so, we wouldn't say anything directly. And even if we met each other face to face, we'd never discuss anything in so many words. We'd do it in a roundabout way. I mean, anyone who thinks you say words like COCAINE on the phone or in person, is up the creek. It's just a no-no. You don't mention the word, any word like drugs!

Perhaps that's what they thought I'd say when I had my conversations with Joe. Maybe I would have talked about films or cans of film instead. I'm not saying this is very subtle, or that, over a long period of listening in to our phone calls, the cops or the customs might not have cracked our codes and precautions. On the other hand, in this case, the way I was talking to Joe and what I was telling him was so out of line from our normal way of doing business that he must have known for sure I was acting under duress and even deliberately letting him know that.

This went on for two days, and each time they're going, 'Shouldn't you be doing something?', and I'm saying, 'No, just sit here, mate.'

Well, of course, I should have been either on a payphone to Ronnie Lorenzo, or, better still, I should have gone straight down to his restaurants, Splash One or Splash Two, or headed over to see him in Palm Springs if he was there at that time. I mean, this was stupid. It's not as if this kind of guy sells drugs by mail order or on a TV shopping-channel line. Anyhow, I'm not saying that I know anything about Lorenzo dealing in drugs, but, for sure, no one was going to have any dealings with me so long as I stayed in an airport hotel. For a start, no LA connection of mine even knew I was there, and, for sure, Joe wasn't going to tell them. I don't think I ever told him which hotel I was in, so how was anyone else to find me?

So this waiting went on for days. Now you can imagine, all that lot, they got so bored, some of them were coming in my room chatting to me, saying, 'Here's my card' all dishing out cards as if they were fucking salesmen!

I was staggered. There weren't only cards from guys in the Los Angeles Police Department (LAPD), the Drug Enforcement Administration (DEA), and someone from Felix Rochas INS. There were also agents from the FBI and even the CIA! But why the CIA? What conceivable relevance did my activities, or Joey Pyle's or Ronnie Lorenzo's have to do with the US governments strategic international interests? Did they think any of us were spies? And, if so, who for?

One CIA guy told me he was there just to monitor, standing back, not getting directly involved. A lot of the agents were very young, and, frankly, they were naive. So now I'm showing a little cooperation, they were cock-a-hoop, talking to Coxy there on the bed.

And because I appeared to be co-operating, they allowed me once, on the second night, to go down into the bar, but they said, 'You cannot move, because we'll have people in there, at the entrances, so don't try to fuck off.'

Well, I got talking to the girl behind the bar, trying to embarrass her so she would call security. I thought if she did, it might give me a way out of the hotel So I said I was a salesman for male dolls. They're really lifelike: squeeze their balls, and they come! But this girl, far from getting upset and calling security, she was laughing her head off. Fucking hell! But I still thought that if somehow I could get out of the place, I could get into the system and disappear, with the help of my contacts with Lorenzo or whoever.

Most of the time Peter Cox didn't seem to be around. I scarcely saw him. I think he told me he was off playing golf, but that might have been an intelligence ploy to put me off guard. I do recall that when we had an argument, and he kept pointing his finger, I said, 'Don't keep pointing your finger at me. Anyway, I'm fucking off Friday,' and he replied, 'You can't fuck off anywhere! We've got your passport.' But even if I tried to go, Coxy didn't have to be there because I always had some armed Yank looking after me. Dave Morgan was also around most of the time. Somehow his presence was reassuring. For once I was pleased to see a face from Scotland Yard keeping an eye on things.

But there was this one LAPD guy. He half-sussed I was fucking about, and he said, 'I think you're taking us all for fools. Nobody in organised crime would come to a hotel anywhere.' I said, 'Why?' I was pretending to pick his brain but taking the piss out of him really. He said, 'Every time you've been over here you've always been met. The worst place you'd go to is a hotel, and an airport hotel is the worst of all.' I just laughed at him, and he told the other guys he thought I was taking the piss.

And then on the third day, they said, 'Right, we'll give you a car, and you can go to the restaurant.' I said, 'No, I'm not leaving the hotel. I'm staying here. I don't know what you think is going to happen.' They said, 'We know you're getting drugs.' I said, 'Bollocks!' They said, 'We know you're getting them and taking them back inside film cans.' I said, 'I'm not prepared to go ahead with any of this. I'm going back to England. In fact, I'm going back tomorrow. Bollocks to all of you! I'm not leaving this hotel. The only way I'm leaving this hotel is on a plane. On my Mickey Mouse bloody passport.'

At this point up piped the guy from the DEA. Now, if you had seen this guy! He had a tracksuit on, and he had bleepers — one in each foot, in his socks, and on each bleeper he had a little tag with the name of the villain who's supposed to be calling him up on it. He had five bleepers altogether! And two guns! He looked ridiculous. So anyway, I said, 'I'm going.' He said, 'No. We've had word it's being delivered to you.' 'It's being delivered?' I said. He said, 'We know its coming here tonight.' And then I turned round and said, 'Whatever you've heard, it's all bollocks.'

Then, out of the blue, the phone rings, and everyone's jumping around saying, 'That's it!' And they're going, 'Hold on, hold on, make sure it's monitored!' and all that shit. Then the DEA guy says, 'Now answer it.' So I pick up the receiver, and there's a voice that was half-English and trying to be a bit American, and he said, 'Your pizzas, sir?' And I turn the phone away, and I look at Dave Morgan, and I say, 'Did anyone of those clowns out there order pizzas?' And they keep going, silently mouthing the words and gesturing like, 'Keep talking!' I say, 'No, bollocks, who's ordered pizzas? It's a pizza delivery! Look, there's five pizzas coming up to the room.' I say, 'I haven't ordered any, it might be some of the clowns in the other room there!' And I put the phone down.

Then the DEA guys jumping for joy saying,

'That's it! That's the fucking delivery!' But I say to Dave Morgan, 'It's a fit-up. I'm not answering that fucking door. I say, I ain't ordered no pizzas. Especially five pizzas. I know what you're talking about. You're talking about five kilos of cocaine, and you're expecting me to take it back through British Customs to give it to Joe Pyle! It's a set-up!'

And Morgan's looked at the guy, and he turned round and asked, 'Are you sure this is the delivery?' And the DEA guy said, 'Yes, our intelligence tells us, it's coming through this way.'

It wasn't from Ronnie Lorenzo, I know it wasn't. These agents must have been delivering some of their own stuff. I know that because they actually said it afterwards — this DEA guy, the one with all the bleepers on him.

So the door rang, and I refused to answer: 'Bollocks! I ain't answering.' It was like in boxes. I knew what was in it, because they took it in next door, and I said again, 'Morgan, it's a fit-up!'

And I must give Morgan his due: he said, 'It might be the American way, but it's certainly not Scotland Yard's way.'

And I said,' Thank you, Scotland fucking Yard!'

I said, 'Right, now let's fuck off! You've had a fucking good laugh, I'm going back to England, I'm not helping you lot.'

So they turned round and said, 'Right, we'll have to talk this through with Peter Cox and everybody else,' and they fucked off into the other room. Then in came these other two cunts and the one who had previously sussed me and knew I was taking the piss, said, 'I was right about you,' and I had a go at him. I said, 'I've found your camera, you wanker! It's in that lamp, and I threw it on the floor'.

And that's when he said, 'Right! Fuck you!,' and he pulled out his gun. And I was baiting him to use it. I called him a cowardly cunt, and I said, 'Fucking use it!', so he said, 'You fuckin' bastard, we'll get you put back in El Centro.'

And Morgan turned round and said, 'Excuse me, this man is under our protection.' So the LAPD guy said, 'No, he's not. Scotland Yard has got no say over here. He's under our jurisdiction now. He's under arrest.'

So I had a scuffle with the silly bod, and he hit me over the head with the gun. It looked worse than it was, but there was a cut on my head and blood all over the place. 'Right, you'd better put him in custody,' someone said, and I was arrested.

By now I didn't give a fuck about them because I thought, That's all right, I'll be fucked off back to England. Only now I was like a live wire — fucking furious — so they had to put me in custody. Then one of the guys, from another agency, said that when he wrote up his report of this incident he was going to say how badly I was treated. Brutality, he called it. He told them all, 'You will get my report.' Meantime Dave Morgan demanded a copy of the tape they had made of the pizza telephone call, and he was given one.

Anyway, when I was arrested, and they took me down to some police station, the desk sergeant guy had to do everything by the book. He obviously put down that I had been arrested at the hotel. Then he asked, 'How did you get into this country?'

Well, I looked at the other guys with me, including Felix Rocha and Peter Cox, and I was about to say that I had been brought in on a mutilated passport under the control of Scotland Yard. So you can imagine what was going through the minds of Rocha and Cox! Fortunately, Dave Morgan was there too. He saved my bacon, by getting me out of LAPD custody and making sure I was immediately put on a plane back to London. If it hadn't been for him, I could still be in El Centro, with all those crazy Mexicans.

On the flight home, Ron was looking forward to a comparatively quiet life. True, he wouldn't get a chance to set himself up again in America. He'd blown that option for all time. And he wouldn't be seeing Sylvia any more unless she returned to Britain, which seemed unlikely. Rather, it seemed that she had got the deal that he had been looking for. By becoming an informer to US law enforcement, she now seemed to have secured permanent residence, despite a British criminal record that should have got her thrown out. And were the Yanks aware, he pondered, of her five false passports? Anyhow he hadn't seen her since before he was carted off to El Centro some five months earlier. She had never even bothered to visit him. And so, good riddance.

But far from a quiet life, Ron was rearrested soon after he landed at Heathrow. Police records show that on 8 May 1991 he was taken to Barnet Police Station and charged with obtaining the Atkinson passport by deception. On 20 May he appeared at the local magistrates court and indicated he would plead not guilty. Furious at what he regarded as an act of vengeance for his failure to co-operate in the Pyle-Lorenzo sting, he mounted a convincing argument for the case to be dropped.

When I got back I told the police, 'Right, you cunts, I've gone through all that bollocks in America where you got me into LA on a cancelled passport with all the corners cut off! — and now you've got the fucking cheek to arrest me for the previous one! And you've sent this poor DS from Barnet who is just told in a phone call, "Arrest Farebrother at Heathrow!" Right. You can tell your governor that I am dragging fucking Scotland Yard through all the courts. I'm going to plead not guilty to this, and I'm going to fight it all the way.'

Then I told Dave Morgan. I rang him up to say I'd been nicked over the passport at Barnet. He couldn't believe it. He said it was out of order, and he'd have a word with someone. Whether he said anything I don't know. Anyhow, it did no good because the charge wasn't dropped. Then the legal guys told me, just plead guilty, and you'll get a £50 fine. I was going to plead guilty? 'Bollocks,' I said, 'I ain't pleading guilty.'

This went on for about a year. The police were in no hurry to face this kind of music, and whenever my solicitor contacted the Crown Prosecution Service (CPS), it seemed they kept delaying and delaying it.

Some of the delay was down to me because I was always on bail for some fucking thing. But when you're on bail and you break bail, they bang you up again. With me failing to show up at all these court hearings, we could argue that I've obviously got a memory problem, and this was partly how the passport charge was eventually swept under the carpet.

Even the CPS seemed convinced I must have had some lapse of memory. They questioned me at length, then they told my solicitor that I didn't even remember going over to the States with a passport, so if I could get medical proof of a memory-lapse condition, they would drop the prosecution.

I said to my solicitor, 'Well, do you want me to get that? I'll get a letter for you.' So I went to see a doctor, and I gave him £25, and he came up with this letter confirming I had been attending a neurologist at the Royal Free Hospital [in Hampstead, north-west London] in connection with an episode of loss of consciousness last December, cereballar ataxia, and significant loss of memory. The letter went on to say that as I was due to have a more formal assessment . . . in the near future . . . it might be better to postpone things for the time being, if possible.

This worked like a treat. By the time I eventually was due to face trial over the passport offence on 27 July 1992, the CPS had lost all enthusiasm to pursue it.

The CPS then sent a letter to Ron dropping the prosecution but saying nothing about his memory loss. This entire ploy — as false as the passport itself — had been introduced just to confuse the issue. One agency that must have seen through the sham was the Passport Office, furious that Ron had pulled some devious stroke to get off the charge.

'The Passport Office still wanted to go ahead. Yet they were the ones who had given the Yard that cancelled Mickey Mouse passport with the corners cut off, so I could go through Virgin Airlines at Gatwick. They can't deny that.'

'There was a Passport Office official who liaised with Scotland Yard over serious offences like mine. I was going to get this official in court and ask her straight, "Why did your organization reissue that passport?" See, I would have made it a real stink of a court case. I was going the whole hog. Even though it was only going to be a measly magistrates court hearing, I would have made sure it got publicity. Then the whole shit about the sting on Lorenzo and Pyle would have come out — blowing the undercover jobs that were still going on against both these guys in both countries. No wonder everyone wanted me to plead guilty and shut up!'

Whatever the reasons why the CPS dropped the case, it certainly spared the Yard's blushes. And if Ron had gone public back in May 1991, it would undoubtedly have scuppered another Yard sting on Pyle, which, it hoped, would bring its public enemy number one down at last.

And Ronnie Lorenzo? Despite the fiasco of the Farebrother sting, the FBI were able to gather enough dirt on Lorenzo through its own informant, Robert Franchi, whom they were paying $5000 a month to eavesdrop on the Hollywood mob. Lorenzo was arrested in June 1992 for helping Franchi to buy nearly six kilos of cocaine. Lorenzo's trial attorney branded Franchi a high-priced mercenary . . . a walking definition of entrapment, but the jury found Lorenzo guilty anyway. Not even actor James Caan's supportive character evidence could save the restaurateur from a sentence of 11 years in jail.

THE TRIALS OF JOEY PYLE

By May 1991 Ron Farebrother was in limbo. From the moment he had resolved to screw up the LA sting, he was also screwing any hope of a new life in America, with all the protection he would otherwise have earned for helping to nail Ronnie Lorenzo. Instead of starting afresh anywhere in the USA with a new identity and even a new officially faked past (courtesy of the federal witness security program), he would probably never, ever be allowed back in the country.

Back in England things were scarcely any better. No sooner had he been deported home than he blew any chance of protection from Scotland Yard by refusing to plead guilty over the Atkinson passport and threatening to reveal how the Yard had sponsored his LA adventure courtesy of another invalid passport knowingly supplied by the same Passport Office that was now prosecuting him. This tactic would ensure the

201

case's evaporation but it was no way to win friends and influence people in the Big House, without whom no turncoat London crook could reasonably expect to survive.

Nor could he turn to his old sponsor Joe Pyle for relief. Within two months of Ron's repatriation, Joe was arrested and locked up over a drug deal. He was in no position to help Ron. If anyone needed help, it was Joe himself. Ron might have supplied that help by telling Joe what had happened in LA, but what could he really say? Even if he could wangle his way into Belmarsh jail to see Joe (and ex-convicts cannot visit top-security, Category-A prisoners unless they are related), could he ever look him in the face?

Just when Ron had been in Los Angeles, wrestling with British police and American agents trying to bag Joe Pyle and Ronnie Lorenzo together, another individual in London was proving far more co-operative.

Richard John Ledingham, a failed businessman, had recently been caught trying a series of massive scams. In October 1990 he was arrested for conspiring to steal £5,340,377 from Barclays Bank. He had also presented three stolen Natwest cheques worth £610,122 to the City of London branch of the Banca della Svizzera Italiana, intending to get them credited to an account that he controlled. On 12 March 1991 he was committed for trial to Knightsbridge Crown Court later that year, on 21 June.

He was now in deep trouble. The evidence was overwhelming, and he had no choice but to plead guilty. He was facing years in jail and was looking for a way out. Fortunately for him, a friend who had helped him greatly in the past was one of Scotland Yard's longest-standing targets. The friend was Joey Pyle, and, as Jesus Christ almost said, 'Greater love hath no man for himself than this, that he lay down his friends for his life.'

Ledingham mentioned Pyle to his captors from the City of London Police, and they handed the lead to the Yard's Criminal Intelligence Branch, 5011, who tipped off a squad of operational detectives.

The police version begins early in June 1991 when they say Ledingham (whom they would later call Greene to protect his identity) was asked by Pyle if he could find purchasers for heroin at £28,000 per kilo. By 12 June — just nine days before he was to be sentenced for the £6 million fraud — he had put himself under the Yard's control.

In much the same way as Ron Farebrother had been encouraged to make that call from the airport hotel room, to whichever contacts he might have had in the States, Ledingham's police handler now instructed him to tell Pyle in his Pinewood film office that he had a purchaser. Pyle replied that his supplier had between five and twenty kilos and gave him a sample of what he said was inferior brown Turkish heroin with a lower market price. Ledingham handed the sample to his handler and was told to say his buyer was interested. Pyle asked £25,000 for an initial kilo and suggested a rendezvous.

After various changes of plan, the deal was fixed for Wednesday, 19 June. Only on this day did Ledingham meet his buyer, Dave, from Manchester. He was (surprise, surprise) an undercover cop, as was the man who would drive an old gold Ford Escort to the rendezvous, where Pyle's alleged runner was to dump the drugs. But due to a breakdown in communication, the deal had collapsed. No-one on the police side had ensured that the Escort's boot was unlocked, so the runner, Warwick Willers, could not deposit the heroin. Willers was arrested anyway, still in possession.

Pyle's version of events is rather different. For him the story began back in 1985 when a friend had asked him if he would lend some money to Ledingham. Pyle did not know him but was led to believe that he was a safe risk. Ledingham said he needed £20,000 immediately but would pay it back at £500 a week just half his takings from his club's gaming machines.

Pyle handed over the £20,000 in late October 1985. After one week Ledingham repaid the first £500, then closed the club and disappeared, failing to make any more repayments or offering any explanation to his creditor. He went missing for almost three years, but Pyle failed to exert the kind of pressure on Ledingham's relatives to be expected from an organised crime boss of the status he was accorded by the Yard. Sure he tried to find out where Ledingham was, but no one near-and-dear to the defaulter was wounded or slain.

In August 1988 the opposite happened. Out of the blue Pyle received a phone call hinting that Ledingham wanted to come out of hiding and settle his debts. Looking back, Joe Pyle says he treated his prodigal debtor with a forgiveness verging on folly.

I was asked to ring some fellow who was a born-again Christian. And he's telling me that he knows this Richard Ledingham and says he's become a born-again Christian too. And he says, 'The fellow wants to give you that money back. He feels very bad about it. But he wants to know that there'll be no problems, Joe.' I said, 'There'll be no problems. Just give me my money back. I don't want any interest.'

I don't know. I thought, Well, the guy must have a good heart to go out of his way to get someone else to get in touch with me to say he wants to pay me back. The guy can't be all that bad. To come back and say, 'Look, I had a breakdown. I tried to commit suicide. I've been in a bad way, and here's your money, I thought he wasn't a bad guy. May sound silly on my part, but when it happens to you, it's pretty easy to accept.

After that, he became a personal friend to me and my family. He wasn't somebody who came on the scene where I had to sit down and say, 'Ah, can I trust this man or can't I trust him?' We were just pals, and I trusted him as a friend. And then he did what he did.

Sometime later, in October 1990, Ledingham was arrested for his failed £6 million fraud. He was given bail, but in May 1991 he was again begging a loan off Pyle, this time for his son-in-law in desperate need of £10,000. Pyle (who, if his claim to have trusted this rogue again is true, was a big softie) could not come up with the full amount but did come up with £4000. Pyle says it was not his money, so he had given a personal guarantee to the lenders who wanted it all back in four weeks, plus £600 interest.

When the four weeks were up, Ledingham

sheepishly admitted the money could not be repaid. Instead he produced some uncut precious stones and asked Pyle to sell them to repay the loan. Pyle spurned the offer, but he says that by 18 June Ledingham told him he was now selling drugs to repay the debt and indicated he could pay Pyle back all the money in cash the following day, 19 June.

Early that afternoon, says Pyle, he went to the Driftbridge Hotel, Epsom, where he spotted Ledingham having lunch with another man. Ledingham took Pyle aside and told him this was Dave, his buyer friend from Manchester, but the drugs had not arrived so Dave had not paid him. Not to worry, the deal would soon be sorted, and Ledingham would pay his debts. Pyle says he was annoyed at this waste of time and drove off.

The accounts of Pyle and the police are diametrically opposed. Clearly, if Pyle is lying, he has lied to excuse any references to drugs in subsequent chats with Dave, taped by the police. However, as Ledingham was a master conman and fraudster, desperate to please any police who might speak up for him at his sentencing, could he have set up the entire event, as Pyle alleges?

According to Pyle, Ledingham phoned up next day, 20 June, to lament that something had gone wrong with the deal, and so Manchester Dave thought he was taking him for a ride. Now Ledingham wanted Pyle to reassure Dave that everything was OK, and there would be no further hitches. He also said he had told Dave that Pyle was supplying the drugs, so when Pyle was talking to Dave, he should stick to that story.

Pyle claims he was perturbed by the huge danger in this lie and 'was very reluctant' to maintain it, but after a lot of heated conversation he agreed to tell Dave that story, 'on the basis that if it was resolved I would get my money.'

Pyle then met Dave at the Forte Crest Hotel at Heathrow. 'We both sat down, he wanted confirmation that he wasn't being ripped off. I told him precisely what Ledingham had told me to say. I then left, telling him that Ledingham would contact him. The conversation couldn't have lasted more than five minutes.'

The next day, 21 June, Ledingham had to appear at Knightsbridge over the fraud. He pleaded guilty and was given two years for each of seven charges. These were made concurrent, so he received a mere two years in all. As 18 months was suspended, he ended up with a modest six months and so (with remission) would serve just four.

That same day — Pyle says — he called Ledingham's home, not only to commiserate with his wife but also to mention his latest £4000 loan to Ledingham. The wife knew nothing of it. Nor did the son-in-law on whose behalf Ledingham had claimed he was borrowing the money. Later, Pyle says, Mrs Ledingham rang to ask him to collect a note from her husband. This contained instructions to tell Dave that his supplier [Willers] had been arrested, but when the supplier was bailed, everything would be sorted: 'You can pay off my debts, I am sorry about this, Richard.'

Whichever way we look at what happened next, Pyle behaved naively. If, as he says, Ledingham had told him his supplier had been arrested, Pyle should have realised the deal had become far too risky, and promptly pulled out. On the other hand, if Willers was working for Pyle, he must have known of the arrest. Even if the police had suppressed that news, surely Pyle would have found out from his own sources that both Willers and the kilo had disappeared. Pyle claims he did not even know Willers.

Whatever the truth, Pyle says he duly phoned Dave and explained things according to Ledingham's script. But even if this deal fell through, Pyle was still desperate to recoup the money he had lent the conman. His opportunity arose almost instantly when up popped a man called Peter Gillett, with prescription painkillers for sale. Pyle knew Gillett as the young, blond, bodybuilder-cum-male-model-cum-singer whom Pyle's friend Reggie Kray had formally adopted. The brand was Omnipom which, Gillett said, was often used by athletes, footballers and other sportsmen. He had 7000 tablets (or ampoules as they are resolutely described in police papers), all British army Iraqi War surplus. Pyle says he told Gillett he might be able to get rid of them. He then arranged to meet Dave at another Heathrow hotel, the Skyline, on 27 June.

Pyle says Dave had already told him to get in touch if ever he got hold of other drugs. On reflection, he says, 'I did not like Dave, there was something about him. . . . I thought he was a bit thick.' When showing Dave a sample, 'I made up a lot of lies about street prices and going to help him to sell it. This was all sales talk to get him to buy.' Pyle also recalls, 'to my surprise, during this meeting Dave kept asking about heroin.'

As far as Pyle was concerned, Omnipom was not a controlled drug — Class A or B — even though it contains an opiate. It was merely a painkiller and had no estimable street value as no-one had ever been arrested for possessing it on the street! It had little use outside the medical profession with whom it is popular as a pre-operation analgesic. It has been around since 1908 and is often prescribed to pregnant women suffering from back pains.

Besides, this consignment was out of date. All in all, hardly a best buy for the aspiring drug-dealer. Worth 11 pence a tab at the most, not the £2 dumb Dave was prepared to pay for it. Caveat emptor. Let the buyer beware, not the seller!

Pyle's attitude was simple: if Dave were mug enough to buy them thinking they were controlled, fair enough. 'I was relieved that the deal was going through as my profit was £3500, which [with other funds] would pay off Ledingham's debt. Pyle had another reason for relief: 'The people I took the money from . . . were not the type of people we mix with, and, quite frankly, I was in fear for my own safety and for the safety and lives of my own family. . . . Ledingham's family were equally at risk.'

On 3 July Pyle met Dave at the Heathrow Sheraton Skyline to hand over all 7000 pills for £14,000. Dave kept demanding heroin. He did not want to be fobbed off with Omnipom, which he claimed Pyle was dangling like a carrot. 'He made it perfectly clear that he wouldn't buy the Omnipom if he couldn't get the heroin. Of course, I was not concerned with any heroin. I did not trust this man who was only interested in the heroin of which I had no interest, knowledge or connection.'

During this meeting Dave called his friend Alan to arrange the money. Alan duly arrived with £14,000 in a carrier bag. Dave then asked Pyle to wait till Alan had driven away and had checked the goods. A little later Dave telephoned Alan who confirmed the goods were OK. With the £14,000 safely in the carrier bag, Pyle felt he had finally sorted out the fine financial mess Ledingham had landed him in.

Or had he?

'I went to leave the hotel and, as I walked through the door, I was attacked from behind, hit over the head, pinned to the floor, with blood streaming down my face, with someone's knee in the back of my neck, informing me that they were police officers.'

Pyle had been well and truly stung. Dave was an undercover cop, and so was Alan. Where SO11 and the Americans had failed to nail Pyle through Ron only months before, these boys also under SO11's guidance had succeeded through the far more malleable Ledingham.

Pyle, Gillett and two others were charged with conspiracy to supply 7000 ampoules of opium and morphine (the Omnipom pills). Pyle alone was charged with giving Dave the sample ampoule and, far worse, of conspiring to supply five kilos of heroin. He was denied bail, guaranteeing him a year inside before the trial, whatever the verdict.

When the trial finally began, Ledingham admitted that, as soon as he had been arrested for fraud in October 1990, he began informing on Joe Pyle. The police asked 'if I knew Pyle: in what connection, how long? Drugs were either mentioned first to the police or by the police to me. I've never dealt in drugs, and that's what I told them. I had no access to drugs. By the time I appeared in court [on the fraud] I had helped in relation to a drug matter. The fact I had given information was not made available to the judge. I believe a letter was given to the court concerning other matters on which I had assisted.'

Pyle's counsel now enquired why Ledingham would have taken so active a role against Pyle, if the police had not offered to help him? 'I felt it was the right thing to do: I've got seven kids, twelve grand-kids — drugs are disgusting. I suppose morality played a part being dragged into drugs. That's why I talked to police.'

But Ledingham could scarcely talk about morality. His spasm of alleged conscience over drugs illsuited someone who had not only attempted to pull off a £6-million bank fraud but also bilked a lot of private individuals whom he had beguiled into investing hundreds of thousands in a Sierra Leone diamond scheme.

The police denied trying to influence the judge to minimise his fraud sentence. They sent no letters of mitigation and made no pleas in chambers. Even when the moment came for Pyle to stand trial, the Crown continued to maintain that 'no credit was given for information supplied by [Ledingham] in relation to this case when he was sentenced at Knightsbridge Crown Court on 21 June 1991.'

His reward came later, in a form he must have appreciated far more than a good word. In August 1991 police seized 40 kilograms of heroin in a Wimbledon warehouse. This was the biggest heroin haul ever found in Britain, but although Wimbledon, south-west London, was regarded as Joe Pyle territory in the gangland map of the capital, there was no evidence to link him to this consignment. Instead, during his trial, the Crown did admit:

> The operational team, which dealt with the seizure of 40 kilos of heroin from Abbey Storage in Wimbledon in 1991, have submitted a report to the Deputy Assistant Commissioner recommending that he [Ledingham] be paid a sum of money for information which led to that seizure. On 30 April 1992 he was paid £5000.

If Ledingham got the reward, might a jury have believed the 40 kilos belonged to Pyle? If they did, they were wrong, says Pyle.

> I've always maintained that Ledingham's supplier, Willers, made a statement confessing about the heroin and telling the police where to find it. They tried to tie the 40 kilos in with me, but it didn't wash. Right up until the committal they were saying it was mine, but there was no evidence, and it was impossible for there to be any. It was a shock to me when I read about the find, and I thought, They're gonna fucking put this on me. And sure enough they tried. But he got the reward because Willers was arrested on his information. Willers died before the trial, so the truth never came out.

In December 1992 Pyle was found guilty of the Omnipom conspiracy. He was also convicted for the heroin. The judge said he was a 'mainstream, class-A drug dealer. Those who are involved in the supply of drugs peddle degradation and despair, and cause others to commit crimes to feed their addiction.' He jailed Pyle for 14 years.

The police were exultant — and relieved — at securing Joe Pyle's first conviction for 32 years. Now came a torrent of unattributed quotes placing him at the top of British gangsterdom. Reporters were told he had spent years 'running a huge crime empire that has links with villains all over the world,' but to say he had now been 'caught red-handed masterminding a multimillion pound drug-dealing operation' was laughable. In addition, claimed detectives, 'He has built up a south London crime empire which he controls through fear.' One senior officer said, 'Like many top gangsters, he has managed to escape justice for a long time by distancing himself from his criminal activities. He always got others to do the dirty work for him. This is a real breakthrough in the fight against organised crime.'

These remarks directly contradicted the evidence in this case. Far from Pyle distancing himself, it showed him doing the dirty work himself, risking his own skin to meet a buyer when common sense would have told him the person might be an undercover cop and should be met only by underlings. That way he would have been insulated from meeting not just undercover cops but even the perfidious Ledingham, the source of all his woes.

In contrast, newspapers portrayed Ledingham as a smalltime crook, so deserving of public gratitude that they called him Richard Greene, his alias, to protect him, as he was now in hiding with a £100,000 contract on his head. He was a helpless victim, unable to afford Pyle's extortionate interest demands. There was no mention of him bilking Pyle of all interest on a £20,000

loan during three years when even bank interest rates
verged on the extortionate. Nor was it reported that he
himself had been convicted of trying to defraud banks
of £6 million. In short he came over as a half-decent
victim of a monstrous mobster on a par with Al
Capone or Lucky Luciano.

As the hue and cry over Pyle's conviction
subsided, and Joe himself submitted to the grind of a
convict's life for the first time in 30 years, many of
Ledingham's respectable victims felt he should have
been locked up for as long as Pyle, not for the measly
six-month term that, with remission, he had finished a
year before Pyle was even convicted. What is clear is
that this Walter Mitty character was a chronic thief
with no principles whatever. He was therefore a perfect
police informer!

The sum total he ripped off in all his scams and
frauds is greater than anything ever plundered by the
man he helped trap. One principle that ought to guide
any detectives genuinely committed to combating
crime is that informers should always be lesser
criminals than the people against whom they are
informing. With Ledingham that is questionable. For
sure, his name is not inscribed in thick, gold letters in
the annals of London gangland, nor was he a friend of
the Krays or the Richardsons, yet he had defrauded
many honest people of large amounts and should have
been done no favours by the police.

Certainly the police did no favours for Joe Pyle.
Not only did they pincer him with two near
simultaneous stings, in London and Los Angeles, but
also, over the same period, they bugged his offices at
Pinewood Studios. By late May 1991 a listening device

had been planted in the suite rented by his production company, Touchdown. A few feet away sat Lucy, a secretary, who unknown to Pyle was really a cop. Under her control was a cassette recorder, into which she placed and removed at least 140 tapes over a period of at least six weeks. If the eavesdroppers in SO11were hoping these would yield information confirming Pyle as an organized crime godfather, they were disappointed. With the exception of a six-minute exchange between Pyle and Ledingham, which may relate to drugs (but which Ledingham could just as well have gathered, if he had worn a body mike), the tapes consist of banal office chat with only occasional asides about crime.

Someone asks Joe the going rate for 'dodgy' (forged) £10 notes. He says it is £3, and he can get as many as he wants. He then explains how they can be faked on a colour photocopier. 'They've even got the watermark in them,' but adds that he has never printed such money himself. Driving licences can be faked the same way, he points out.

There is talk of the documents needed to put together a false identity; of someone else doing a share swindle; of getting a million out of Zambia; and of various mortgage schemes. There is mention of porn films, but (as the eavesdroppers felt obliged to note) there is no suggestion that Pyle intended to get involved in the trade. There is something about someone owing Joe £250,000 and reference to a time when Reggie Kray was in Lewes jail, and Joe got Reggie to put pressure on someone. Occasionally Pyle tells war stories about the Twins, like when he had dinner in the 1960s with Ronnie, Reggie and the faded

Hollywood star George Raft, who specialised in gangster roles.

There are calls to and from Joe's chum Alex Steene about boxing, both in the old times and in 1991, when Alex's son Greg was managing a string of fighters. On one tape the conversation turns to the drink and drug problems of various entertainers. According to the summary notes of an SO11 officer: 'Pyle is dismissive of the fears about film stars drug habits and refers to his own visits to Diana Dors's house in the past where drugs were always available at the bar.' There is then further discussion on the cocaine habits of American film stars, but nothing on the tapes indicates Pyle or his associates are involved in supplying drugs to show-business personalities.

What the tapes do reveal is a legitimate film business getting so little work that it may be forced into all-too-genuine bankruptcy. One suggestion is to get investment funds from pension funds (little luck there) or from some rich Saudi Arabians who are doing £13 billion worth of deals. Cash is so short that Joe asks an actor friend, Derren Nesbitt, to work at Pinewood for almost nothing for the next six months. Once Nesbitt is employed, according to police notes, he explains that Joe is aware of how serious the position is and the urgent need to start getting work in. Then general conversation: whether Joe really knew how dire the situation is. The firm cannot complete the sale of a feature film project, and there is a worrying overspend on the one production currently on location: a documentary in the Seychelles.

What did this long and costly bugging operation achieve? As an exercise it was successful, for it showed that Scotland Yard can match the FBI in covert surveillance techniques. As an evidence-gathering device, it was a near total failure. Even the snatch relating to the Ledingham drug deal did not strengthen the case against Pyle. Indeed it is arguable that the absence of incriminating conversation on the other 100 hours material showed him to be a reasonably law-abiding citizen.

The material did not support the claims of the detectives rejoicing in his conviction. Far from showing he ran a huge crime empire which has links with villains all over the world, it proved he ran a small firm likely to go bust. The case against him was no real breakthrough in the fight against organised crime. If he really is one of Britain's top gangsters, then, on the evidence of the Pinewood bug, organised crime in Britain scarcely exists.

Concerns about the quality of the evidence won him a retrial in 1995. At Woolwich Crown Court he was again found guilty, but his sentence was reduced to nine years. It seems the jury rejected the defence claims that the police had used the fraudster Ledingham as an agent provocateur, to entrap Pyle into a drug deal he would not otherwise have committed.

Ron Farebrother's experience in Los Angeles would tend to back up the agent provocateur-entrapment interpretation, but his tale was never told at any of Joe Pyle's three trials, for he had never told Pyle what had happened. Ron had troubles enough of his own. He could not risk getting caught in the no man's land between his long-time sponsor and the people with whom he was now enmeshed: the police.

A TURN FOR THE BETTER

Ron Farebrother was wrestling with his conscience, especially when he realized that SO11 had run the LA and Ledingham stings in tandem. Privately he took comfort in his saboteur role, but he had left it too late to tell all to Joe. Telling him now he was banged up would only infuriate him, for if Ron had come straight from the airport and marked his card, Joe would surely have spotted the parallel and shied away from Ledingham. So while Joe fretted in Belmarsh, Ron tried to get his own life straight by resorting to the vodka bottle.

'This was a very bad period for me. The whole thing was bad, from the El Centro shit to the pizza set-up in Los Angeles and the passport arrest when I came home. No sooner have I got a solicitor sorting that out, than I find they've put Joe inside on the drugs charge. No bail. So do I tell him? In the end I felt it wouldn't have helped him, knowing about that shit. Maybe I was wrong.'

Even at this late stage, Ron could have helped his *padrone* by disclosing a pattern of entrapment that might well have assisted Pyle's defence. But what would Pyle make of it? How would he react? For sure, Ron could tell no-one except Joe — no lawyer, henchman or relative — so he sat on the knowledge. He was now on his own, but he had to survive. He had to find a way to make a living without help from either the cops or the crime lords.

If organised crime was out, it had to be back to disorganised crime, so Ron returned to his old habits. On 11 August 1991 he went into the Kilburn branch of Threshers, the wine merchants, and racked up a stack of purchases on a stolen Mastercard in the name of R. Connolly and a stolen Visa card in the name of D. D. Carter.

Emboldened with success, six days later he returned to the same branch and tried to purchase £1617 worth of wines and spirits on a stolen Nationwide Anglia cheque. The counter staff were suspicious, as even the heaviest drinkers in County Kilburn rarely order the entire stock in one go. Ron's order was not accepted, and at 6.50 that evening he was arrested and taken to the local station where officers thought they had bagged a biggie. On the charge sheet they said he was believed to be actively involved in high value fraud, though this escapade scarcely deserved such a rating. They also noted he was still claiming to be a security adviser, though his chances of advising Threshers on security were now greatly diminished. He was told to appear at Harrow Crown

Court four months later, on 2 January 1992, where he could expect to be jailed because the offences breached the conditions of his discharge over the deception at the Red Lion Hotel back in 1988.

Desperate diseases desperate remedies need. And no remedy could have been more desperate — or more unlikely — than the one that now just happened to turn up: a contract to kill a housewife.

The full story of Malcolm Stanfield's grotesque plot to have his wife murdered so he could claim £560,000 worth of life insurance has been told in chapter 1. But when the offer was first made to Ron the Gun in September 1991 — a mere month after his Threshers arrest — he treated it with deep suspicion verging on total disbelief.

Suddenly getting a contract killing offered, after all I've been through. My brains are going 100 miles an hour, and I'm thinking, Well, who's fitting who up here? Cos at this fucking time I am not trusting fucking nobody, cos this offer comes up too quick. So who would want to get me involved as a hired hitman? This isn't tiddlywinks. If it goes wrong, we're looking at least ten years in the slammer. Could it be an act of vengeance — a reverse sting — by some of the cops I've just fucked off in LA? Putting a fake contract into me to see how I'd react? If I show any intention to take it, then bang! I'm arrested and stuck in a cell right next to Joe Pyle!

Or could it be a genuine contract but one that some other cops know about? What if some Surrey cops have heard that this Stanfield wants to kill his wife, and they're tailing all his contacts? What if the two men who have come to me with the offer are under surveillance even now as I'm meeting them, discussing it all?

And then when I first meet this Stanfield, boy! Is he fucking indiscreet! He's a loudmouth, spelling it all out in every detail at our very first encounter! What if the cops have got a bug under the table? Christ! I could be nicked as soon as I step out of this pub. Why should the cops believe I'm just stringing this bastard along just to test the strength of it?

And what if Stanfield is another Ledingham? Ready to set me up like he set up Pyle to get off some other rap? A guy like Stanfield could easily be under the hammer for a bogus fire claim or fraudulent bankruptcy or a tax dodge, and be trying to get a light sentence by delivering up a professional killer.

And what if these guys who've brought me the contract are setting me up? I've already got enough enemies in gangland who'd like me locked up till the end of the century. It'd be the easiest thing for them to set an elaborate trap, then tell some gullible detectives about it at the last moment, leaving me to take the blame. Maybe these guys even know about the LA sting! Perhaps there's been a deliberate leak from America. I upset so many Yankee cops on that job, those guys wouldn't care if I live or die. To a cop there's nothing more disposable than a canary that won't sing.

The trouble is, when you're in the underworld — when you're part of it — you get to think about treachery every waking hour, every day, every week. You suspect everybody and everything. You're perpetually saying to yourself, Is this a set-up? Why is this guy saying this? Where is he coming from? Who is he working for? Is he with the police? Would he shop you as soon as look at you? And is this scheme so fucking lunatic that it's bound to go wrong anyway?

And there's another thing. There may be no honour among thieves, but it's even truer that, when it comes to crime, you can never trust a straight man. Take this guy Stanfield: while he was an absolute shit in business and marriage, he still thought like an honest man. How else could he be so dumb as to write out a £30,000 cheque in his own name and draw a plan of the pub in his own hand? He was so open, he could not be trusted. And what if, years later, the guy gets an attack of conscience, goes to the police and tells all? Where does that leave the hitman, whether its Ron the Gun or Joe Blow? No, I couldn't risk working with a man who was that naive.

Don't get me wrong. I still would never have done the hit because I really do believe you shouldn't kill a woman — even for thirty grand! Christ, I wouldn't kill Sylvia for that much, wouldn't kill her for any amount, despite everything she did to me, so there was absolutely no question I'd kill poor Lorraine Stanfield. I was far more likely to shoot her bastard husband.

My girlfriend at the time — she's still married so I can't mention her name — she went mad. She said, 'To kill a woman you've got to be the scummiest, lowest thing going.' And my golden rule has always been never to see a woman or a child hurt. But, if it had been the other way round — a woman wanting her husband killed — God knows what might have happened!

So let's restate the obvious. I couldn't go to Old Bill with this contract killing, because Old Bill didn't want to know me. Anyway, after the LA fiasco, I was no longer talking to Old Bill. They were the last people I could trust. They were doing anything they could to get me involved in lots of old bollocks. It could even be them setting me up on this murder.

As for the guys who brought me the proposition, just let me say they were persons unknown who I knew! Now why they thought of me as a hitman, I don't know. It must be my aura. But these fellows know me very well. Maybe they had heard the same rumours that resulted in me being called Ron the Gun. I've no idea where they got their fucking ideas from. I'm not a killer. I've never killed no one.

From the outside looking in, this contract killing was proposed by good sources, and the money was good too, but, again, were my sources being taken in by this Stanfield? Was Stanfield being put into me? There was nobody I could trust. So that was my first reaction: this was another set-up.

But I couldn't let it go at that. As soon as I was told a woman's life was at stake, I had to get involved to make sure she stayed alive. Remember, at this point, I still did not know the name of the man who wanted the hit. I still didn't know he was called Stanfield, so, if I was going to stop this job happening, I had to find out who this murderous shit was!

And when I'd found that out, I thought, Right, there's only one place I can go with this information: the media newspapers, television, the highest bidder. That way I can save the woman's life, and I can get protection, recognition and some cash. For once my judgment turned out to be right.

The *News of the World* was prepared to pay me. And it was the *News of the World* that got in touch with the South East Regional Crime Squad, the section headed by Chief Inspector Chris Simpson at Surbiton.

With the newspaper as a buffer, I knew I was secure.

Until I was guaranteed that buffer, I would have nothing to do with the police. No fucking way would I talk to the fucking Old Bill. I hated the sight of them after the LA blow-out over that ludicrous passport charge. But as time went on, I got on better with the RCS [Regional Crime Squad], because I found a lot of them distrusted the usual Metropolitan detective just like I did. They did not seem to trust any officer outside the RCS. Which is why I found it so easy to work with them. They didn't trust no fucker.

These were the cops the *News of the World* used to work with, time and again. The paper could call on them almost 24 hours a day, so when Gary Jones [their crime reporter] called them at 11 that same Friday night I first told him about the murder plot, they leapt straight into action. Gary, quite rightly, used the best people he knew.

As you know, the Stanfield story worked like clockwork: for the cops, the newspaper and for me. And, of course, it worked out perfect for Lorraine Stanield, though she must have had a terrible shock when she realised her husband of 28 years just wanted her dead.

Detective Inspector Des Cooke, who headed the team that nabbed Stanfield, was quoted as saying, 'The co-operation of the *News of the World* is greatly appreciated . . . I'd like to thank the paper for it's assistance in bringing Stanfield to justice.'

The co-operation was mutually beneficial. With Stanfield arrested on a Saturday afternoon the story could be splashed next day without the newspaper running a serious risk of being accused of contempt of court by prejudicing his right to a fair trial.

Ron was thoroughly chuffed. He had prevented Lorraine Stanfield's murder and earned himself a huge stack of brownie points with a fresh set of police officers. On the downside, he was not happy at being named. He felt they had gone back on an understanding not to connect him with the story, but at least he had not been branded an informer, with all the life-threatening consequences that might bring.

In his overnight report Gary Jones wrote that the newspaper was 'tipped off that a cousin of Costa del Crime fugitive Ronnie Knight' had been offered money to commit the murder. Then this 'bit-part actor Ron Farebrother agreed to co-operate with us.' The same diversionary account was given in the post-trial spread six months later, but with the addition of Ron's genuine protest that he did not 'agree with killing women. It's out of order. You may hate your wife as much as you like — but you don't murder the mother of your kids.'

The cover was bogus, for who had tipped off the *News of the World* about Ron Farebrother but Ron himself? The device allowed him to continue meeting Joe Pyle's friends without stigma. He could also knock back any slurs that he was a grass by pointing out that Stanfield was 'not one of us': not a professional criminal or gangster or paid-up member of the underworld but a working stiff who was out of order, a danger to the genuine thief. In short, Ron had done everyone a favour by getting this guy locked up.

There are circumstances when, even in the underworld, being an informer is an honourable calling. Ron could think back to the mid-1980s, when, if he had not informed, the ageing, unlicensed fighter Lenny McLean might have been murdered.

'I was at a meeting, and Lenny's name came up. It was over a guy Lenny had hurt in a club he was looking after. The guy was a nothing, who had been behaving disgustingly, but I was contacted by someone else who was acting as a go-between: Gypsy John.

'Now this Gypsy John knew me as "Ron the Gun", so obviously he thought I was a hitman, a contract killer. I've no idea what gave him that idea. Sure, I'd got a conviction and been to jail for possessing a gun, but killing people really wasn't my game.

'My reputation was something else, as I could tell whenever I rang up Gypsy John. His missus would go, "It's Ron the fucking Gun on the phone for you." And so when Gypsy John came on the phone, I'd say, "Ron the Gun here." He'd go, "Hallo, Ron the Gun, how you going?" and I'd say, "Cheers, thanks very much."

'On this occasion Gypsy John told me that £5000 was on offer. "What for?" I asked. And he said, "Put one in his head." I said, "Who?" "Lenny McLean." I said, "I know Lenny! Fucking hell! He's never caused me no problems."

'So I went up to Lenny's warehouse and told him, "Ill just mark your card. Someone has asked me to kill you.

'So we sat down. He was quite shocked really. He called his mate, Billy, a body builder, who came down and sat there with Lenny. And Lenny said, "You come in to sit down and tell me this? That you've been approached to kill me?" He seemed a bit upset with me, even though it was me who had done him the favour of tipping him off. So I said, "Well, I'm not doing it, so at least you fucking know about it!" And we stayed around afterwards in this pub, and eventually he appreciated it.

'Of course, I knew Lenny was a phenomenal fighter. But I'm sure even Lenny would have agreed with me that huge powerful men like him are just as easy to get rid of as pathetic little creeps. I haven't met a man yet, no matter how tough he is, who can stop a bullet in the head.

'Of course, Lenny's dead now but when this book first came out he was still alive. Some reporter asked him whether it was true — that I had tipped him off about being offered £5,000 to kill him. He didn't deny it. He just refused to answer. Later his own book came out but he didn't say anything in it about me saving his life. Not so much as a thank you. The least he could have said was, "Thanks Ron for not putting one in my head".

For Ron, marking Lenny's card was a matter of honour. Informing on this planned hit was private and personal, for the victim's ears only — not for media consumption and certainly not for a fee. By 1991 his position had changed, but even then he vowed that any money had to come from information generated especially for his newspaper outlet. No old friends would be sacrificed or sold or embarrassed just for a few tabloid quid, or so Ron liked to kid himself.

The truth was that by now the *News of the World* was becoming Ron's lifeline, financially, even literally. Here was a way he could earn a living without reverting to the life of crime at which he had never been particularly successful. This way he could exploit his old criminal contacts and apply his aberrant instincts to justify his place on the payroll of a paper that thrived on crime, corruption and scandal. All right. It would not be a contract killing every week, but there was enough human degradation around for Ron to dig up a slice of it almost to order, every few weeks.

In April 1992, just as Stanfield was pleading guilty, Ron was helping out on the tale of a pervert vicar — for decades the archetypal *News of the World* story. He then turned his skills to exposing paedophiles, following up numbers that he prised out through various gay chat-lines, and recording every call. Few homosexuals may have pederastic tendencies, but Ron's persistent calls to one gay chat-line after another yielded more perverts than he could cope with.

I got names, addresses, phone numbers, the lot but it took a whole year, on and off. What takes the time is eliminating the dirty talkers, the guys who just wank on the phone. So what I would do is drop in a phrase like 'young puppies', and a pervert would pick up on that. He'd know what 'young puppies' meant.

There was a magistrate called Robert who had the technique of hanging round swimming pools. Nothing unusual about that, but he had also become a charity worker working with kids. What's more, he was a football referee in charge of under-12s, and under-14s. He even told me the name of the school where he used to ref games and coach. That bastard even claimed he'd had his paper-delivery boy. He was definitely genuine. He was hard to break, but once I'd got his confidence, he poured out all this filth. He had been recommended to me by another guy called Dave from Leeds. All these guys would recommend others in their dirty rings until I was able to build up a thick file and create a map connecting them all. Out of every 100 perverts I spoke to, I would say that 20 were hard-core paedophiles. These weren't just talkers, they were doers.

They'd go on about all the dreadful things they'd done to young boys, and what the young boys had done to them. This stuff is so sickening, it can't go in the book, but the detail that this 20 per cent would give me was so specific that it had to be truth, not fantasy. And they weren't all working-class toe-rags. A lot of them were toffs with plummy accents, professionals with top jobs, living in the smartest addresses. If they weren't into giving pain, they were into receiving it. Look at this note: 'Next meeting of Sadists and Masochists Disco. 24.1.92!'

Gary Jones got stuck into the research, too, but we had to be careful we didn't break the law ourselves. See, if ever I met any of these people, I would be seething with hatred. Thank God, I never found myself where a kid was present, because I'd have gone bang! I'd beat the pervert to shit or I'd shoot him. At the least, I'd make a citizen's arrest.

We were so thorough, and we piled up such a mass of hard evidence, that we decided to take everything to the Obscene Publications Squad (OPS) at Scotland Yard. As we had developed such a good relationship with the Regional Crime Squad on Stanfield, we felt we could safely do business with the OPS with this stuff. So I saw the governor there, and I told him, 'This is getting me down. When are you going to move on these guys, otherwise someone is going to have an accident? I promise you, something's got to be done.'

So the scheme was that the OPS would gather the additional evidence they needed to convict these beasts, but meantime we would run the exposé and get the credit we deserved. It would be a collaboration based on mutual trust. There was no actual agreement.

But blow me down! They took all our evidence, and then, all of a sudden, they hit it! It was on the news — BIGGEST PAEDOPHILE RING EVER BUSTED, ALL OVER ENGLAND — but the bastards never bothered to tell us. Gary and I were really pissed off. They had whacked us out — they did not say thanks to the *News of the World*. No, they had a fucking freebie — all my tape evidence. When that had been transcribed they had all the leads they needed. For them, that was a big, big catch. But they shat on us. Scotland Yard never even paid my phone bill. I was only asking them to pay for itemized calls to numbers we knew were perverts, but they bilked me!

After they'd done the arrests, I did get in to see the OPS guys and listen to tapes of interviews they'd done with these dreadful people. See, the perverts never blame themselves. They were all saying that the kids had led them on. The other sickening thing is that the courts look at paedophilia not as a crime but as an illness, and that's why they get parole straight away. But I don't agree, because these guys are organised. They are in rings, which pass victim kids from one batch of perverts to another.

Despite all our efforts, we were never told what happened to the individual perverts we had already identified. So I can't tell you exactly what happened to the magistrate, but I know it all turned out to be true, and he was convicted and jailed. At the end of it all, we were pretty depressed. I even felt I needed counselling, just from talking to these weirdos for so long. They really are sick. But because we had been shut out of the arrests, we never really picked up on the results. We felt snubbed. So my biggest ever investigation ended up with nothing at all in the paper.

Ron worked on other unpublished investigations. For every story that gets printed, half a dozen get scrapped. Then, by chance, he literally sniffed out a drugs exposé. It was in August 1992 that he jumped into a minicab with Gary Jones heading for the newspaper's Wapping headquarters when instantly he caught the unmistakable whiff of marijuana. Coming straight to the point, he said, 'Christ, mate, can you open the fucking window? You've been smoking some pretty good puff in here!'

The driver, equally direct, replied, 'Sorry, man. Do you fancy some — or something a bit stronger? I know a few people. If you want something, my boss will sort you out.' Ron looked across at Gary, who gave him a nudge, and Ron went for it. 'Yeah. I could do with a lot of whatever you've got.'

' "I can get you anything you like," he said. Silly bastard. And he said he would speak to his boss to set up a deal. And he gave me his boss's name, and his boss phoned me up next day, and that's how it started, just from me asking that little cab driver to open the window because hed been smoking a spliff. Boy! Was that controller friendly: "My man says you're all right, and I take his word for that." So just take care when you're driving round London. Half the minicabs are driven by space cadets!'

Ron was soon meeting the controller's supplier, a tall Afro-Caribbean in his mid-20s called Lennox Esprit. Ron told him to come round to his home to meet another guy who was a serious buyer. This, of course, was the *News of the World*'s Gary Jones in undercover mode. Lennox turned up and offered to supply two rocks of crack cocaine for £120, but he said he needed the cash in advance because he still had to get the stuff from his wholesaler. As security, he would leave his leather jacket in Ron's flat. Jones produced the money, and Lennox headed off. Half an hour later he was back with the crack. He handed it to Jones and retrieved his jacket. Congratulations all round.

Over the next few days Lennox popped round to see Ron several times. The relationship was building nicely into one of trust, and a further deal was set up for ecstasy, crack and cocaine itself. 'I can supply you with any amount of any drug,' boasted Lennox, though this proved premature as the deal fell through. He apologized for the hitch and told Ron and Gary, 'I shouldn't have messed you around. I trust you. You're cool. I'll arrange for you to meet the big man. I guarantee he'll get you a kilo of cocaine.'

The big man turned out to be not so big. He was Hugh McDonagh, an old schoolfriend of Lennox's, medium height, light build and slightly scarred on his upper cheeks. He was known as Junior, though he did not give any name when he first came to Ron's house with Lennox on Monday, 24 August 1992.

By now Lennox was dazzled by Ron's claim to hold high status in London's underworld. He had even told Junior a line that Ron had dropped into a previous conversation: he was Ronnie Knight's cousin. Both dealers were impressed when, they say, Ron produced a gun. 'You might be Old Bill,' Junior recalls Ron saying in what he now sees was a brilliant diversion. Thrown on the defensive, Junior said, 'No, mate, I've just come round to see some money. Look, I want to do business with you. I've been told you're sweet. But we'll want to see the money first.' Ron then produced what looked like £7000 or £8000 in £50 notes, though Junior would later reflect they might have been counterfeit.

Next evening he and Lennox visited Ron again and met a man whom Junior thinks must have been a plain-clothes policeman. A meet was set for the following night in the Metropole Hotel in Edgware Road, less than a mile away. At this point Lennox introduced Junior to the buyer, undercover reporter Gary Jones, but Ron had previously warned him, 'If the man seems a bit jumpy, take no notice. He's just a businessman.' This was a wise move on Ron's part because Junior noticed Jones had a strangely nervous, agitated air. The agitation made Junior nervous too. He told Jones the cocaine was in south London and asked him to come along to collect it. Jones refused to budge and told Junior to bring it back to the hotel. Two hours later Junior returned with Lennox and the cocaine, but, just as the transaction was about to take place, in the car park behind the hotel, Jones claims he was bundled on to some steps and threatened: 'Fuck us up, and you're in deep shit.'

Then a Ford Cortina drew up. Inside was a third conspirator, a Turk called Axelol Tahir. He pulled out a plastic bag containing a brown package and told Jones, 'This is the cocaine. Get the cash and make it quick.'

Suddenly the reason why Jones was nervous became clear. Junior says he saw Lennox getting a signal from someone to disappear, which he did. Then from nowhere came a swarm of plain-clothes cops. One moment they were just clusters of typical hotel guests, the next they were leaping on Junior and the Turk. The pair were taken to a police station and charged, but Lennox Esprit made a clean getaway, even though, physically as well as commercially, he was right in the middle of the scene.

Four days later Junior was locked up in Wormwood Scrubs, still trying to figure out what had happened, when he started reading a story in the *News of the World*. The headline ran, WE TAKE CAB RIDE TO SMASH DRUGS RACKET, but there was a confusing subtitle, 'How a Chance Chat Led to Vice Barons' and a picture of an attractive woman displaying a large slice of thigh. That side of the story related to the minicab controller arranging prostitutes at £200 a night, and a £1-million house near Harrods where call girls and drugs were on tap.

The rest of the story was all about a drug deal, involving a man called Lenny and an unnamed scarred man. Suddenly it dawned on Junior: 'That's me!' He had to be the scarred man for, now he had been charged, he could not be named directly in so graphic an exposé. He read on with increasing dismay as he saw that not only had he been grabbed by the cops, but he had also been set up by the newspaper known universally among the criminal fraternity as the *Screws*.

Junior had a very personal reason to spot the set-up, but any dedicated student of British investigative journalism, equipped with a carefully ordered cuttings system, would have noticed that once again, the Screws had got into bed with the South East (number 9) Regional Crime Squad; indeed with the very same unit within SERCS that had collaborated on Stanfield.

This alliance was turning into a lethal combination, producing big stories for the newspaper, prestigious arrests for the cops and excellent public relations for both sides. According to one detective quoted in Gary Jones's report, the cocaine was 'high quality stuff. It would have been cut up with other substances into a much greater quantity of drugs. This kilo is part of a large consignment that has been smuggled into Britain. We now have some good leads in discovering its source.'

The only officer named by Jones was the same detective inspector Des Cooke who had praised the paper over the capture of Malcolm Stanfield. This time he waxed, 'The *News of the World* did a marvellous job in leading us to these people. It's a tremendous result to take a kilo of cocaine off the streets.'

Confined to his cell, Junior was still perplexed. Why hadn't Lennox been arrested? Why had the reporter told him to flee? There was no way he could have escaped without police connivance. So was he a grass? Had he set up Junior and the Turk? Were they now going to jail for years while he walked free?

When the case eventually came to court, the prosecution would not need to mention Ron or even give the full name of the go-between. He would simply be called Lenny. Another boon for the prosecution was that this device would allow Gary Jones to be its main witness and bear the overall burden of the case. Jones's credibility was, of course, far greater than Ron's. And, of course, Ron did have one overriding principle: he would never show up as a witness in any court.

This scheme seemed perfect. Except that no-one had allowed for the possibility that Lennox had a sense of integrity. When Junior McDonagh and Axelol Tahir went on trial in June 1993, who should show up as a volunteer defence witness but Lennox Esprit! He told his version of the story, revealing Ron Farebrother's involvement, the run-up to the arrests and his own bizarre escape.

Through his intervention, the trial jury could not come to a verdict. The judge ordered a retrial. This was one situation Lennox had not allowed for. He was hoping that his co-conspirators would either be acquitted or the case would be dropped. But now the case was going to be heard all over again, the full vengeance of the law would fall on him. Already in jail serving two and a half years for burglary, he was charged with the cocaine job and stuck on trial alongside his co-conspirators when they reappeared in January 1994. This time they were all convicted. More rosettes for the Screws, the cops and Ron Farebrother.

From time to time Ron's own rotten problems with the law forced their way back into his life. He had successfully seen off the passport charge, but the Threshers matter refused to go away. Back on 2 January 1992 he had failed to appear at Harrow Crown Court over these offences. A warrant was issued for his arrest, but the court officers could not find him, even though he was in open and regular touch with other police in Barnet only five miles away, and with the CPS, over his passport offence. He was eventually caught on 27 October 1992 and sent to Wormwood Scrubs for contempt. He spent six weeks inside and was given a 75-hour Community Service Order when he was sentenced in February 1993.

Yet even in the Scrubs, Ron was able to work his magic for the *News of the World*, for he soon found he was sharing a cell with a man called James Daniels. When he learned that Daniels was on remand awaiting trial for a massive drugs operation, he became deeply suspicious.

'I thought he was deliberately put in my cell to entrap me, I thought he was a police spy, an informer, an agent provocateur. Why was I suspicious? Because as soon as he walks in the cell he's telling me he's just doing four weeks — out of six months suspended — for being captured over a ton of hash. Now that in anyone's language is a fucking wrong 'un. It's got to be that he's lying. He's either in jail for another offence, or he's bullshitting, or he's got one hell of a deal with the police himself. He's the informer at this point, not me.'

Ron figured that if Daniels was an informer, deliberately planted in that cell, he would either verbal Ron — claim he had admitted some serious unpunished offence — or entice him into a police trap as soon as they were both back on the streets. Ron's instinct may have been right. After all, it takes one to know one, and if anyone could spot the gambits of an informer, it was Ron. He decided the best form of defence was attack.

'That's why I had to defend myself: if I didn't get him, then sure as hell he was going to get me! So as we chatted in our cell I told him I was interested in getting hold of guns, especially an Uzi. Daniels bit on the suggestion straight away. He said he could supply any kind of weapon, anything I wanted — bazookas, machine-guns, even this Uzi. And at that time there had never been an Uzi taken off the streets in England. So I said to myself, that would make a great story for the *News of the World*. When we're both out, I'll call his bluff.'

First Daniels was released, as he had predicted. Then, two weeks later, it was Ron's turn. Sure enough, as soon as he came out of the Scrubs, he told reporter Gary Jones that Daniels was willing to supply an Uzi. Detective Sergeant Roger Hull was also informed, so the scene was set for yet another collaboration between SERCS, the *News of the World* and, of course, Ron Farebrother.

The scheme worked as if by magic. Daniels fell into the trap with suicidal ease. Later he would claim that Ron had offered him a flat in return for the Uzi: 'I didn't really want to do it. It was only because I was under a lot of pressure of somewhere to live, because I couldn't stay at my friend's place any more. I had no money.'

Daniels was so desperate to please that he came up with the gun faster than Ron or his collaborators wanted. On the morning of Saturday, 1 May he turned up at Ron's flat with the Uzi. Ron had to turn him away. He wasn't ready. He said he had people with him, so instead Daniels was to show up later that day at Camden Town tube station and wait for the mystery buyer to identify himself, then hand over the gun.

The reason Ron could not admit Daniels was that the people in his flat were Detective Sergeant Roger Hull and reporter Gary Jones, who, of course, would soon be performing as the mystery buyer. Once Daniels had cleared off — reduced to walking round north-west London with a machine-gun on his back —

Hull and Jones also departed, to liaise with their supporting cast of cops and photographers before heading for the showdown in north London's Camden Town, famous for its vast weekend market. And so it was that, among the swarm of tourists and shoppers who make the area around the tube station a potential disaster zone every weekend, James Daniels duly handed over this lethal weapon — which can fire almost 700 bullets a minute — to Gary Jones. As Daniels later recalled, 'Something was all wrong. Next thing, I looked up, and there was a photographer taking photos, and in seconds the police were there, and I was arrested.'

Of course, one reason the deal went down on the Saturday was the usual one: so all could be revealed in the next day's *News of the World*! And so it went. The headline ran, LETHAL WEAPON WAS SO UZI TO BUY, and Detective Sergeant Roger Hull paid the now traditional RCS tribute: 'The *News of the World* has done a brilliant job by taking the gun off the streets.'

Soon Ron was back in action with another tale of guns on the streets. For once the reporter was not Gary Jones but his colleague Mazher Mahmood, and this time the story did not go according to Ron's plan. He says he wanted to expose a place, not his old friend Vinnie Brown.

'It was just supposed to be a wine bar being exposed, where you could buy dodgy things. Not arrest Vinnie Brown. . . . That wasn't supposed to happen. He was a mate, a friend, I knew him since he was a schoolkid. I knew the whole family. There was no way he should have got arrested. I didn't know that was going to happen.'

Unsurprisingly, Vinnie did not believe Ron's blameless interpretation of his own conduct. Nor was he pleased by what appeared in the *News of the World* on 29 August 1993. Under the headline — GUN THUG SELLS US UZI AND SAWN-OFF — Mazher Mahmood described Brown as a 'lager-swilling crook' and a '23-stone slob, dubbed Mr Big because of his obesity', who was ready to hand over all sorts of guns to terrorists and armed robbers.

Mahmood wrote that the newspaper had contacted Brown through 'an underworld source in Spain, who introduced us to a villain known only as John.' Mahmood went on to describe this Cockney John as a well-built man in his early 40s, who 'claims to have just finished a prison term in America for his links with organised crime'.

If this character sounds familiar, then he is. For Cockney John and all the stuff about an introduction through an underworld source in Spain was baloney, a smokescreen to obscure the role of Mahmood's source: none other than Ron Farebrother! Not that this would have confused Vinnie Brown, for when this Cockney John was quoted as knowing him for more than 20 years, Brown knew only too well that Farebrother had also known him that long. They had been to school together!

Mahmood went on to describe meeting Brown at the wine bar in Hendon, north London, at 7.45 on the evening of Thursday, 26 August. While punters drank, played pool and watched TV, Brown used the bar's payphone to procure guns for crooked clients. Then he began his sales pitch to our reporter, who was posing as a drug-dealer with terrorist connections.

Brown told Mahmood he could supply 'a parcel of ten pieces by the weekend from a couple of sources'. He then took an order from Mahmood and made a phone call, after which he said he could supply three brand new handguns for £700 and pump-action machine-guns for £2400. First, however, to establish mutual good faith, he would supply a sawn-off shotgun that very night. After another call he told Mahmood, 'Your parcel's arrived', then took him outside, rummaged in a wheelie-bin and produced a bin liner containing the sawn-off. Mahmood produced £280, and Brown gave him the weapon and 12 rounds of ammunition.

The following afternoon Mahmood returned to the wine bar, where Brown and a sidekick entered a storeroom and plucked a carrier bag from the top of a stack of empty beer crates. Inside was a new Uzi sub-machine-gun, worth up to £3000 but sold to Mahmood for £2400. At this point something happened that was very surprising to Brown, though it was thoroughly predictable to regular readers of the *News of the World*.

As Brown brought it out to our man's car near the bar, officers from the South East Regional Crime Squad pounced. Last night they were hunting several other men believed to be involved in the gun ring.

Then came the familiar police seal of approval.

Detective Inspector Des Cooke praised the *News of the World* investigation. 'I'd like to thank your reporter for his professionalism and courage in tackling these dangerous people. We are grateful for any assistance in helping get these deadly weapons off the streets.'

But Ron still had a twinge of conscience.

'I would have made myself out to be a fucking liar — imagined the whole thing — rather than see Vinnie go to jail. Anyhow, that Uzi turned out to be a toy one, so I told the cops, "No, drop the fucking charge." Mind you, if you're reading this book, Vinnie, there's one reason you should be pleased — I got you arrested because you were well over weight, and I saved your life. You lost over two stone in prison in six weeks. Fat bastard!

Ah, such delicate sentiments. But for a fourth time Stanfield, Esprit and McDonagh, Daniels and now Brown the newspaper, the RCS and Ron Farebrother had pulled off a sensational story. And once again the timing seemed to suit the newspaper. But did it really? For Vinnie Brown had not only been arrested. He had also been charged at half-past noon on the Saturday, so the entire double-page spread including such phrases as 'lager-swilling crook', 'gun thug', '23-stone slob' and 'oaf' probably constituted contempt of court. Nobody seemed to care.

Indeed it seemed nothing could halt the triumphal progress of this unified team of public-service vigilantes — the cops, the hacks and the silent partner, Ron Farebrother. But something did.

THE FAREBROTHER FACTOR

As the remand wings of London's jails now teemed with the targets of the triumphant troika of cops, hacks and Ron Farebrother, some defence lawyers saw a window of opportunity for their clients. They felt they could discern a pattern of entrapment in these *News of the World* cases, which, though not illegal, might well render most of the evidence inadmissible.

The first reverse for the newspaper, the RCS and the Crown had come in June 1993 when Lennox Esprit made his self-sacrificing appearance at Junior McDonagh's cocaine trial. By voluntarily exposing the role played by the *News of the World*'s favourite vigilante, Esprit did himself no good — when the trial collapsed he was added to the indictment, and at the retrial he would be jailed for eight years — but his revelation of what might be called the Farebrother

Factor gave defendants in other trials some hope of walking free.

First up in October 1993 at Harrow Crown Court was James Daniels, Uzi supplier number one. His barrister, James Pavry QC, argued that the pressure exerted by Farebrother on Daniels was unfair. Daniels was claiming he had only supplied the gun because Farebrother had pestered him to the point of duress. The argument turned on Section 78 of the Police and Criminal Evidence Act, 1984, which states that a court may refuse to allow evidence relied on by the prosecution if it appears that its admission would have such an adverse effect on the fairness of the proceedings that the Court ought not to admit it. Whether it was fair or not could depend in part on the circumstances in which that evidence was gained.

A later Court of Appeal judgment had focused on how this section affected entrapment and the use of agents provocateurs. Their lordships felt it did not change the long-standing convention that entrapment did not in itself afford a defence to a criminal charge — it was not enough for a defendant to claim someone else had asked him or her to commit the crime — but now evidence gathered through entrapment could properly be excluded if it were unfair.

Fairness is in the eye of the beholder, and at Daniels's trial the beholder was her honour Judge Dawn Freedman. She concentrated on a specific factor raised by the Court of Appeal: Was the officer — in this case, Ron Farebrother — acting as an agent provocateur in the sense that he was enticing the defendant to commit an offence he would not otherwise have committed?

To resolve this issue, she closely examined the evidence of reporter Gary Jones who had said Farebrother had asked him whether he wanted to buy a gun. She recalled that Jones had also said: 'Farebrother was paid the sum of £2000 for providing information in relation to someone who would sell a gun and putting Jones in touch with that person.' In her view, Jones's evidence showed Daniels was being inveigled to supply the gun not to nail a gun-running gang — that is to say, a crime in being — but to sell a story that guns can be obtained on the streets of London. The crime was not a genuine crime but one created solely for the purpose of filling the pages of a newspaper. As James Pavry later put it: 'There was no suggestion that the police were dealing with a major drug dealer or major player in that field.'

Farebrother himself was not in court to justify his conduct. Even if he had been subpoenaed, he would have refused to testify. 'As I've told Old Bill, I've never stood up in court, and I never will because that is grassing, and that's one thing I won't do.'

In his absence Judge Freedman decided his behaviour in instigating the crime had so tainted the evidence that she could not be sure Daniels would have committed the crime if he had not been enticed. Her doubts were so serious, she felt compelled to exclude all the evidence gathered through entrapment. This meant that the entire case against Daniels collapsed, for there was no other evidence against him.

The following Sunday the *News of the World* was licking its wounds. In a report captioned UZI GUN DEALER IS LET OFF BY JUDGE, Gary

Jones wrote that Freedman's decision to free the villain caught red-handed by Scotland Yard's Regional Crime Squad has brought astonished protests from politicians. The newspaper itself had brought the case to the attention of two sound-bite kings to elicit these knee-jerk quotes: from Labour shadow minister Frank Dobson, 'The man shouldn't have had a gun in the first place, it must be an offence', and from Tory ex-minister Sir Teddy Taylor, 'I can only say I'm surprised at the decision.'

One man was even more surprised. That Sunday Ron Farebrother choked on his coffee when he opened the paper to see his name in print — twice: The bastards had even spelt it wrongly: 'Fairbrother'. Worse still for his long-term survival, Ron was identified as an underworld source who had told the paper he knew a man called Daniels who could supply an Uzi. The piece also quoted the judges scathing comment on Ron getting paid for his services.

Ron was not pleased. He had now been named as a police informer in the favourite Sunday reading of the criminal fraternity. Sure, he had been named there before, as the source for the Malcolm Stanfield story, but he could always justify his co-operation with the law that time as selfless humanitarianism. This time he had no such excuse to give his remaining underworld chums who, even if they had qualms about machine-guns, were unlikely to see why he needed to shop Daniels.

The day after this bombshell, who should be due to appear at Hendon magistrates court but Uzi supplier number two, Vinnie Brown, and his sidekick James Leonard. In 300 pages of prosecution evidence there was no mention of Ron, but, by the time their full trial began at Barnet in April 1994, Brown's defence knew just who had delivered him into the clutches of both press and police. He was represented by James Pavry, just the right advocate after his recent success representing Uzi Daniels. What happened next had a gripping inevitability about it. When Pavry made it plain that he would be seeking the informant's name, the case was dropped. He was sure this was because the prosecution could not afford to reveal that its evidence had been obtained by an agent provocateur who had initiated the process and solicited the crime. Of course, Pavry already knew the provocateur was Ron Farebrother.

The collapse of one Farebrother case after another coincided with the wholly honourable departure of Detective Sergeant Roger Hull from the Metropolitan Police. After 33 years in the job he had simply reached retirement age, but, from the tone of a valedictory in the *News of the World* (where else?), it was if he were resigning in protest. Interviewed by his partner-in-crime-fighting, Gary Jones, his onslaught on the problems of modern police work was withering.

Hull lamented that criminals are walking free because 'slick' defence barristers are unfairly using points of law to their advantage. Worst of all, they are insisting on police revealing their informants names. He cited Metropolitan Commissioner Paul Condon, who had said (in his first annual report) that 60 major cases had collapsed in Britain in the previous 18 months simply because the defence had insisted on seeing prosecution material that might have disclosed informant's identities.

Hull felt this was a huge underestimate and said, 'We live off informants. Most of our work comes from them. If we name them, they could be killed. It's as simple as that. You can't put them at risk. First and foremost, you must protect them.' He demanded a change in the law, saying he never thought the day would come when police could catch someone in the act of committing a crime, yet that person could escape conviction. He then asked lawyers themselves to step out of the shadows and help draft laws which are fair to the innocent, but don't protect the criminal. Lawyers should be leading the campaign for such reforms, but some are more worried about their fat wallets.

He talked of despairing detectives who say, 'What's the point?', after putting a lot of work into trials that collapse even before they reach a crown court. 'We recently nicked 11 blokes with their hands on two lorry loads of stolen televisions. As we cops like to say, they were bang to rights. But they all pleaded not guilty, and it was insisted that our informants be named. So we offered no evidence and the case was thrown out.' In another case four people were arrested with £200,000 worth of fake £20 notes, but the defence wanted the names of the undercover cops who had helped gather the evidence. The prosecution dropped the case, rather than name the undercover guys. 'So again, we just walked away. I can't believe anyone would think that's justice.'

Hull's theme was the increasing vulnerability of informants who would not now help the police because they're afraid. If criminals get their names, their lives will be hell. We have to do more to protect people brave enough to stand up against criminals.

Near the top of DS Hull's bravery roll was Ron Farebrother, who was thankful not to see his own name in print. But Ron had other worries. He could cope with any likely reprisals from gangsters. They were his people. He knew how they thought and felt he could predict their moves. Now another group of people were taking an interest in him, who in their own way posed as great a danger: journalists who had no enthusiasm for the way the *News of the World* worked with sources like Ron.

During 1993 a BBC *Panorama* team had caught a drugs officer based in the Surbiton offices of the South East Regional Crime Squad in acts of gross corruption. In a programme broadcast that September Detective Constable John Donald was seen on film and heard on tape doing deals with a suspected drug trafficker called Kevin Cressey, who had already paid Donald £18,000 for ensuring he remained on bail. Other fees were agreed for Donald passing Cressey his own police-intelligence file, losing surveillance logs and identifying an undercover informer. In all Donald's take would have reached £70,000 — if *Panorama* had not captured him in the act. In 1996 the programme and its makers would be wholly vindicated by the outcome of two Old Bailey trials, in which Donald ultimately admitted taking bribes, and Cressey was convicted of offering them. The men were jailed for eleven and seven years respectively. It was a brilliant piece of investigative journalism, though it won the BBC no friends in Scotland Yard.

Having investigated one branch of the RCS to such devastating effect, the *Panorama* team were understandably curious about the activities of another Surbiton-based unit whose triumphs had been trumpeted in so many issues of Britain's best-selling Sunday paper, but whose methods were being less than enthusiastically received in the courts. In these circumstances *Panorama* could scarcely refrain from probing the relationship between the RCS (officers Roger Hull and Des Cooke), the *News of the World* (reporters Gary Jones and Mazher Mahmood) and their sources, notably Ron Farebrother.

Both Cooke and Hull were above suspicion. Neither they nor any colleagues in their general crime squad were in any way associated with the Donald-Cressey affair or contaminated by it. Donald was in an entirely separate team dedicated to drugs cases alone. He had no contact with Cooke or Hull. But the highly publicized nature of their relationship with the *News of the World* meant they were in an exposed position when *Panorama* set about gathering material on the thorniest problem in all detective work: how to handle informants.

After months of inquiries an edition of *Panorama* was eventually broadcast on 8 August 1994. 'Grassed — The Changing Role of the Police Informant' explored the issue of whether informants were creating crimes in order to entrap police targets. After looking into the roles of two drugs informants (one in northern England, the other working for Customs in East Anglia), the programme switched its attentions to Richard Greene. This was, of course, the police pseudonym for Ledingham, the fraudster and conman who had ripped off hundreds of thousands of other people's money before setting up Joey Pyle. Some of his victims described the havoc he had wreaked on their finances, but the programme did not exonerate Pyle. It stressed that he had been convicted of a serious drug offence, and, anyway, entrapment is no defence under English law.

So far *Panorama* had raised issues fundamental to any cool examination of law enforcement's pursuit of crime: in particular, was its use of informers ethical, legal or indeed effective? It was also touching on a key question that detectives should always be asking themselves: are you running your informants, or are they running you?

But the mere fact that *Panorama* was asking these questions spread consternation throughout Britain's police establishment and caused leading forces, such as Scotland Yard, to press two buttons: one marked panic, the other pressure. This happens every time it leaks out that the role of informants is being explored by any branch of the media, and as this programme neared completion, the BBC was put under immense pressure by chief police officers. Rather than challenge the film's overall thesis, they stressed the outwardly reasonable point that the lives of any informers identified in the film could be endangered. The informer they deemed most at risk was Richard Greene.

His cause was also taken up by his Euro-MP James Moorhouse, who wrote to both the BBC's chairman and its director-general claiming that, because of his real fear of reprisals, the witness — who helped jail drug baron Joey Pyle for 14 years — now lives under an assumed name.

The combination of political and police pressure worked its usual magic. Insiders say it contributed to the programme being postponed twice and accounted for the BBC's craven decision to call the fraudster not by his real name but by his pseudonym. Even his picture was ordered out of the show. In the meantime, it was reported, a written promise to make these changes was sent to Ledingham's lawyers.

The logic of all this might escape neutral observers. The names and looks of Ledingham-Greene were already known to all his criminal victims. And any hapless straight citizen who might later meet him surely deserved to know who he really was. As a recidivist fraudster, he was a clear danger to the financial well-being of everyone with whom he might come into contact. Yet once again the innocent were being disadvantaged to protect the guilty.

When the show was at last broadcast, key faces were blurred or blacked out, Ledingham was wholly protected, and at times the commentary sounded as if it was written by lawyers. Even so, its makers did manage to preserve their editorial line. This was due largely to the one informant in the entire show whose identity was not protected, whose face was not blurred out and who answered any questions with remarkable candour. His courage, or foolhardiness, in appearing face-to-camera contrasted starkly with Ledingham sheltering behind his minders. As ever, the man out front was Ron Farebrother.

What on earth had possessed him to appear? Why would any fully paid-up member of the underworld publicly identify himself when surely straight criminals would immediately seek him out and give him a severe beating or worse? But somehow to Ron the idea of appearing on *Panorama* — cast in whatever light — tickled his fancy from the moment he heard about the show.

'It was the police who first told me that *Panorama* was on my tail. They said the producers were following me, so when I told my detective handlers I was game for it — I'd agree to be interviewed — they said, "You're mad!" Roger Hull had been talking to his boss, Des Cooke, and Des had said, "Just blank it." I said, "No, I ain't fucking blanking it. I've got to say what I feel about SO11. And it's about time it all came out about what they wanted me to do in LA." Then they said, "Well, you're cutting your own throat with us,"and I said, "Well, fuck you lot!" '

So once again Ron was ready to go against his handler's wishes. It was perverse but predictable, yet he had still had no contact with *Panorama*. When contact was later made, it came from an unexpected quarter: a law-abiding citizen called Den Phinbow, Joey Pyle's brother-in-law, who had known Ron for years.

Around April-May 1994 I'd had a couple of phone conversations with Den, about how Joe was doing in jail and whether there was any way we could help. Then Den asked me to meet him at Morden station, at the southern end of the Northern Line. He told me to be outside the café across the road.

When I turned up, he wasn't there, and I had to hang around for a while. That's how *Panorama* got those shots of me sitting on the steps waiting, with my coat over my shoulder. They'd obviously asked Den to leave me alone there for a while, like a sitting duck, so they could get some clear shots of me. I had no idea a *Panorama* crew was hiding up in a van opposite the café pooping away.

Then Den did turn up, and I got in his car. I must give him his due, he turned round straight away and said, 'You're right about your suspicion that you're being followed and that whisper you've heard about a *Panorama* programme. They're with me now. They want to interview you about some of the stories you've done with the *News of the World*. Now I've got a message from Joe. It's to tell you now: you can pull out. So, if you don't like this scene, we can stop the car, you can go, and that'll be the end of it.'

I was a bit queasy but I came out and said, 'No, fuck it. Go for it.'

Not that I was going to let *Panorama* off light, because when Den introduced me to the reporter, John Penycate — he's a little guy — I couldn't help noticing he had a big fucking bloke sitting beside him, a giant of a black man, built like a shithouse. I could tell he wasn't the cameraman because he didn't have a camera. So while we were having a first little chat, I said to this Penycate, 'Who the fuck's he?' 'He's my chauffeur,' said Penycate. I said, 'Don't take me for a cunt! He's your minder, so fuck him off out the room.'

So then everyone burst out, 'Oh, shit.' And I said, 'I'm serious. Fuck him off out! He's got nothing to do with this.' That was just my way of showing I don't fuck around.

Now what I didn't know then was that they'd been fed a load of crap by their witnesses about me packing a gun. So they were thinking I had a tool with me in my briefcase. Fuck em!

Up to this point *Panorama* was mainly trying to nail the RCS for those *News of the World* stories, but they mentioned a lot of nonsense cases I had nothing to do with, like one involving some Chinese people, where I'd been named as the grass. See, after my name had come out as the source in cases like Stanfield and Daniels, I was flavour of the month in jails all over England. Everybody on the prison grapevine had heard of this wonderful Wizard of Oz — me! — so they thought, 'Just say Farebrother's involved, and you've got a fucking re-trial!' That's what a lot of it was about. Suddenly everyone in jail was either innocent or they had been fitted up by Ron Farebrother. *Panorama* interviewed me three times. First I had to justify my role in those *News of the World* stories. It was nothing to do with Joe Pyle. They didn't have an inkling about America because I'd never dared tell Joe or anybody what had gone on in Los Angeles. Not even Den had any idea. Early on *Panorama* asked me, 'Have any RCS officers ever approached you about Joe?' I said no. As they knew nothing, they couldn't contradict me.

As I was talking with *Panorama*, I realized that, after exposing the bent cop John Donald, they were looking for more dirt on the RCS. I told them the squad I was working with was entirely separate from Donald's lot, and I couldn't give them any dirt because all my RCS guys were straight. So at the second interview I got them really excited. 'If you

257

want the real truth,' I volunteered, 'some detectives did ask me to go against Joe, but we'll talk about that another time.' That's what I did at a third interview. I told them what had gone on in Los Angeles and how I'd resisted the offer to bury Joe and his US connections. I gave *Panorama* the numbers of all the people involved. They rang them and satisfied themselves that what I said really did happen.

On the programme itself, Ron appeared to say that back in 1991 he had been questioned by two officers from Scotland Yard's SO11 (Criminal Intelligence) section who had American backing. 'They wanted me to bring back five kilos of cocaine (which is fact, not exaggerated or fabricated) through Customs (verification from US and English Customs) for me to deliver to a friend of mine called Joe Pyle.' The commentary then explained how Ron had been flown to Los Angeles accompanied by the Yard officers as part of their Pyle investigation.

Reporter John Penycate added: 'We don't know what they were planning or if guidelines were followed. But back in London, Farebrother claims other police officers put serious pressure on him to help them, and he yielded. Police would later acknowledge that Farebrother was a valuable informant, but he had also been a liability. Prosecutions have been dropped when his involvement was revealed. And he has exposed the police to accusations of breaking their own guidelines. His mercenary role shows how informants can undermine the criminal justice system.

The film then illustrated how Farebrother had worked with the RCS and the *News of the World*. Ron himself was quoted saying that once police had handed reporter Gary Jones £500 to give him: 'I didn't have to sign for it or anything.' As for the people he was setting up for arrest, according to Ron, they were just scumbags.

Panorama then examined the Daniels, Brown and Esprit-McDonagh cases in turn. Daniels and Brown made personal appearances to lay the burden of their actions on Ron, who himself denied using duress. He said Daniels was no angel and he did supply an Uzi. But reporter John Penycate said, 'You were a central figure in creating that crime.' Ron hesitated, then seemed to respond, 'I think you were right there. All right.'

When Ron saw the programme he claimed this was misrepresentation, for he had never coerced Daniels or put him under any duress.

'Now on *Panorama* he said I'd promised him a flat if he got me a gun. To which I say, how can that be called duress? Is it really an equal exchange of favours? Getting hold of a flat is legal, and he'd still have had to pay the rent. But getting hold of an Uzi isn't legal, and how do you do it anyway? Where do you go and find one? I don't know, so how did he? Do you just walk into a corner shop or a supermarket and say, "Can I have an Uzi?" He must have had connections in place. He was already "at it". That's the only way he was able to turn up with an Uzi in its case, brand spanking new, ammunition, the whole lot, at Camden Town. So what provocation did I commit? What have I done wrong? No way did I make him do it.

'Yes, Daniels did turn up at my flat when Gary

Jones and Roger Hull were there, but there was nothing odd about us sending him away. This had to be done because at that point Gary did not have the money to buy the fucking thing. This guy turns up hours early, so Gary steps outside the flat to talk to him. Gary says, "I'll meet you wherever you want," and it's Daniels who says, "I'll meet you outside Camden tube station". And when Gary turns up, Daniels is standing there holding a big fucking balloon — to identify himself — in one hand, and the Uzi in the other! Can you believe it? Right there outside the station with thousands of people around! That's how crazy the guy is. Isn't he a danger to society? How can any judge then disallow all this evidence and say he has no case to answer?'

Ron expressed no such robust defence on *Panorama*, but he was allowed a fairer share of the argument on the Vinnie Brown case, even though the programme claimed this was a classic example of a crime created by Farebrother that tied up valuable police resources and made a sensational story in a Sunday newspaper. Brown claimed that not only had Ron instigated the crime but that, when Brown spent two weeks failing to get a sawn-off shotgun, Ron himself had also rung to tell Brown he would find a sawn-off in the wheelie-bin behind a wine bar on the very night Khan (the *News of the World*'s Mahzer Mahmood) was pressing to collect one from him.

In other words, Ron himself had provided the sawn-off for Brown to sell Mahmood. The implication was that Brown could have gone to prison for a crime that was entirely the circular creation of an unholy alliance between the informer and the newspaperman. If true, this would have escalated their offence from mere entrapment to criminal conspiracy.

Ron now appeared on *Panorama* to deny supplying the sawn-off (a claim he maintains today). He was followed by Brown who accepted that, after selling the sawn-off, he had searched out an Uzi. This turned out to be a toy, which was why the Uzi charge was later dropped.

So what did Ron think of his old school mate whom he had well and truly kippered: 'I quite like Vinnie Brown. I've known him since I was a kid. There's no way I'd have got him involved in anything.' And Vinnie's views on Ron? 'He's a dirty, no-good slag. He's a waste of time, an animal.'

Then up came the defence version of the cocaine case: not only had Esprit, McDonagh and Tahir been entrapped but Ron had arranged the cocaine pick-up as well. As Esprit's girlfriend, Leeanda Brinkley, explained, 'Lennox told me he was going to collect something for this Ron Farebrother. He went and picked it up, and, next thing he knew, there's police swarming everywhere.' At his trial Esprit had also claimed Ron paid him to collect the cocaine.

Ron himself did not appear on the programme to give his side of this case, but, when he saw the *Panorama* version of events, he felt that again it was all wrong.

'My only real involvement in the Esprit and McDonagh case was right at the start — just like it said in the News of the World article — when Gary and I jumped in the minicab that smelt of puff. We then met the owner of the cab firm, a white man with gold teeth, with Gary posing as a punter. It was this guy who later offered Gary prostitutes and dope, but we met him first when he came to my flat to introduce us to Lennie Esprit. Then Gary bought a bit of crack off Lennie for £120 to establish a bit of credibility. This was a "controlled buy". In other words, to keep things legal, Gary had already got police clearance to do it.

'It was only then that the meet was set up to buy a kilo of cocaine, and that's when Junior McDonagh got involved. The odd thing is that, although 22 officers ambushed that car that night at the Metropole and caught the cab driver, Junior and the other guy who supplied the kilo, Lennie just got out of the car and walked. Nobody grabbed hold of him. And he made his way straight to my flat. The ease with which he walked away made me wonder if he was an informer too.'

On *Panorama* Leeanda claimed that, after Esprit's escape from the Metropole, she had gone with him to confront Ron at his flat: 'As he sat down, I saw him slide a hand-gun down the side of the chair.' Ron did not appear on the show to give his side of this story, but McDonagh's wife, Cathy, popped up saying that, after the bust, Ron had left a message on her answerphone. When the police paid a visit, they took the tape containing that message. She later applied to get it back, but, *Panorama* said, the police admitted taking it on another enquiry, and it was now lost. Again the programme contained no response from Ron.

'*Panorama* put these cases as if I were the provocateur. That's how they portrayed me, but it wasn't true. My so-called victims weren't innocent "lambs to the slaughter". They were thorough villains, like I used to be.'

Reaching for conclusions, *Panorama* posed the rhetorical question: had Ron Farebrother, in orchestrating the cocaine deal, 'hindered the fight against drug-trafficking?' And then: if reporter Gary Jones had told the RCS that Esprit was going to south London to buy the cocaine, why hadn't they followed him to identify the real source? In court Esprit's barrister had asked the same question and was told the RCS was under-resourced. In his view the big fish had been allowed to get away: 'Esprit is a prolific burglar, but he has no previous convictions for dealing drugs in any quantity. Not even a small amount to friends, family, neighbours or the pet cat. He was led into it, pressured into committing the crime and offered inducement to do it.'

Once more Ron himself felt *Panorama* was totally taken in by this line of argument. After seeing the show he remarked, 'These kind of guys couldn't wait to supply whatever commodity came up in conversation drugs, guns, even girls. If I'd mentioned the Empire State Building it would probably have been delivered to my door the next day. But, oh, no. *Panorama* said my victims were far from willing, they were shrinking violets.'

Panorama reporter John Penycate did quote Ron just one more time, saying he believed in independently overstepping police guidelines on entrapment 'out of a perverse sense of public duty.' On camera Ron himself said, 'The police have a guideline to how far they can step. The reporter has the same sort of guidelines, and he cannot go and break the law. People like me step over that line.'

Closing the show, barrister James Pavry said that the use of informers is a necessary part of the police armoury, but this could be undermined by any alliance between the police and newspapers who 'simply want to sell more papers.' Under the guise of investigative journalism newspapers pay substantial sums to informers, the risk being that these individuals then find it profitable to act as agents provocateurs, 'soliciting, generating crime.'

The heart of *Panorama*'s argument was that informers are no longer mere sources of genuine crimes, planned and executed by bigger fish. Now informers stimulate crimes that would not otherwise happen. In this sense, the programme seemed to say, Ron Farebrother was a one-man crime-creation industry.

Now, for Ron himself, exposure had come not on a Sunday morning but on a Monday night as *Panorama* — not traditionally watched by the criminal classes — served him up for ritual slaughter by the people he had been betraying. The fate awaiting him looked far bleaker than anything his victims had ever suffered. He had watched the programme alone in his north London flat.

'Sure I was upset by the way I came over. And I couldn't work out why I was the only "informer" (as they put it) whose face was shown, especially after all the fuss beforehand. But life's full of hard knocks and surprises, and I'm not going to spend my time looking behind me or sitting facing the door watching out for the hitman who's come to kill me. Fuck 'em all, I say.

Don't let the bastards grind you down!'

Most people in this squeeze would have gone to ground, changed names, emigrated or committed suicide. But not Ron. Not only did he stand his ground. He went on the aggressive, calling up his remaining underworld chums to deny almost every detail of the *Panorama* version.

At Scotland Yard the film had gone down as badly as all its prior pressure on the BBC had augured. But no new undercover methods had been exposed, and Ledingham had been protected. No other informants were endangered except, of course, Ron, for whom no-one at the Yard had much sympathy. If he had been shot dead that night few detectives would have grieved, for surely he was the author of his own misfortunes. Though *Panorama* had first tricked him into being filmed, he had then collaborated, giving three interviews and failing adequately to defend his activities or those of his RCS handlers. Worse still, he had slagged off several detectives (by implication, if not by name), even singling out those who had taken him to Los Angeles.

The Yard now held an inquest, when it was decided that the mutual admiration pact between the RCS and the *News of the World* must be ended. Close co-operation with the newspaper was to be curtailed, for the time being at least, and on no account was Ron Farebrother ever again to be used as a source of intelligence. He was deemed a dangerous informant. In future no information he might offer, directly or through newspapers, was to be acted on. The order went right down the RCS chain of command: stay away from this man.

Ron did his best to backpedal. He went into the Yard itself, saw one of the chief detectives and claimed that almost everything he had told *Panorama* was lies. He volunteered to make a statement reneging on all his interviews — except for what he had said about LA. His offer was immediately taken up. He was given a new handler, Detective Inspector Dick Leach. The pair went straight to Kent, where Ron gave a senior constabulary officer a statement about the entire circumstances surrounding his *Panorama* appearance. He duly withdrew everything he told the programme — with the continuing exception of his American tale.

It now occurred to Dick Leach (and other observers) that, if Ron's new version were anywhere near true, then just as *Panorama* was claiming that Ron had used duress on petty criminals, had not *Panorama* used duress on Ron? Once the programme makers had secretly trapped him on film, it was clear they intended to brand him an informer and show his face. This effectively forced him to go for it — he had to take part to limit the damage the programme would surely inflict on his reputation as a staunch member of the underworld.

Despite his recantation, Ron was not restored to the Yard's high priesthood of informants. Like a bishop caught on the wrong side of the Reformation divide, no matter how much he forswore his dalliance with the anti-Christ, he would still be burnt at the stake — or, in this case, be put in the index marked 'Informants, dangerous — unsafe, no matter what their information.'

Once more, it seemed all up for Ron. Not for the

first time in his life, The Vigilante was on his own professionally, at least. Even the Lone Ranger used to have Tonto by his side.

It was time for Ron to move on again, and not just because his landlady wanted him out. Surely this time he had burnt all his boats. . . .

Or had he?

FEAR AND LOATHING IN HAMPSTEAD GARDEN SUBURB

Positive thinkers have an irritating habit of saying, 'Today is the first day of the rest of your life.' For Ron, in his current predicament, each today felt like the last day of his entire life. He had reached a dead end almost literally. Detectives were banned from running him, the *News of the World* was shunning him, and dozens of criminals were gunning for him.

Occasionally I would drop in to see how he was getting on. He was not in good shape. He was smoking and drinking far too much, paranoia was taking charge, and as he popped out to the off-licence for another carton of cigarettes and just one more bottle of booze, he could swear that even dogs were turning their backs on him.

There were a few tiny bright spots. He had moved to a smarter part of north London. Hampstead Garden Suburb was the height of respectability (no scumbags, he thought), and his new flat was clean and warm. And he had been in even tighter spots that this. But there were other problems.

I had only just moved into this flat, above some shops, when my mother passed away. That hit me hard. I thought back to how she had shaped me, during all my early tempestuous years. I must have been a bloody pain throughout her life, but, instead of beating the rebellion out of me, she harnessed my fury. She could see I was never going to go straight, but she tried to channel my anger into constructive trouble-making. She'd always be coming out with words of wisdom.

She'd say, 'Never show fear. No good being poor and looking poor. Those who expect never get. Don't count unearned money unless you've got it in your hand. Whatever you do in life, take caution. Cover your back.' Plant the seed, she definitely did.

Anyway, with one of my brothers, I had to organize Mum's funeral, and when it was over, I spent too much time on my own. I was getting depressed and morose, and I was sinking a bottle of vodka a day. Silly bastard. Then, of course, there was *Panorama*, which drove me to nearer two bottles. Maybe I was trying to kill myself before someone else did.

Right beneath me was a video shop — what else could I do but watch videos? — and I went in there so often I got friendly with the young lady who ran it. Then I noticed another customer who was in there as often as I was. He was trying to be friendly and seemed to want to talk to me, so I spoke to him. He said his name was Stephen Yarrow, and he lived about five doors away, but it became clear that he wasn't interested in renting videos. He was trying to see if the lady was interested in buying hot pirate videos. He was offering brand-new material: mint copies straight off the masters out of Sky TV, and even features only just on general release.

'Any sort of films,' he kept saying, 'I can get you any sort of films.' But the lady wasn't that way inclined. She didn't trade in pirate material — she's strictly legitimate — and she was not a bit interested in any sort of films, by which he meant hard porn.

Now there was a restaurant next door to the video shop, which had been closed for a year. One night there was to be a grand reopening. I was invited and so was Brenda, the young lady from the video shop. She asked me to go with her, so I did, and this guy Steve Yarrow was on the table next to us. We chatted with him while we had a nice meal, and afterwards we said, 'Come over to our table.' We chatted some more, and then he said, 'I have to tell you what I told Brenda about you: "He's either a right villain or he's Old Bill!". And I said, 'Well, you're wrong on both fucking counts.'

I just thought he was being nosey. Then he said, 'Look. I've got some business you might be interested in talking about.' So I said, 'Well, give us your number, and I'll phone you,' and I just left it alone. But over the next few days he made a pest of himself and said, 'Can I have a chat with you? Business!' I said, 'What business?' He said, 'I can get you anything. Tapes!'

Then it hit me like a ton of bricks. I realized what he was talking about. Sure enough, a few minutes later he came out with, 'Even kiddie porn, if you've got any friends who might be interested.'

Now that's a fucking no-no to me. That is a no-no

no-no! So I said, 'What do you mean?', and he said, 'Well, I'll get you any films. Young kids.'

How I didn't hit him then I do not know, because I'd just had enough of all these fucking arseholes round me. It just hits you after a while — all this crime, perverts, paedophiles — and you just want to get away from everybody. So I rang him and said, 'I'll see if I can get someone who'd be interested in this stuff. I'll make a call.'

And I did make a call — but not the kind he thought I meant. I went back to the flat and rang one of my old mates at the RCS! I said, 'This geezer's offering kiddie-porn videotapes.'

Then a few hours later I went back and got talking to him, and he said, 'You look like you can handle yourself. Now I know you a bit, I know you'll be all right. You're a bit of a villain!' And I'm still looking at him, and I'm debating whether to say to him, 'Haven't you watched fucking *Panorama*, you silly cunt? You must know who I am.'

You would have thought the same. This is only a couple of months after *Panorama* had been watched by goodness knows how many million people, and this Yarrow actually works in the TV business. He's some kind of transmission engineer. That was how he could get access to video-copying machines for his crooked sidelines. So naturally I thought he must have seen the programme, and he was sending me up. But I managed to keep my mouth shut.

Then a day or two later I'm on the phone to him, and he said, 'My mother wants a job done.' So I asked him what it was. But, remember! I'm taping this conversation because straight away I'm thinking this guy is the front for a set-up — cops, crims, TV reporters, no matter who. And when I'm thinking this way, I'll tape every conversation with these cunts. Especially if it's people I don't know. Even if it's Old Bill, I tape them bastards as well.

Then he tells me he wants his stepfather — this is what he said — murdered. His mother wants him tortured first, his balls cut off — he told me this all in one breath — and then murdered.

So I said, kind of disinterestedly, 'Oh. And also you're supplying tapes?'

'Yeah, yeah, yeah, I'll introduce you to a man.'

Now as soon as he said, 'I'll introduce you to someone,' it's in the back of my mind that it's a fucking UC — an undercover man — he's putting me into, the cunt. Because that's exactly what I would have done.

So I said, 'What have I got to meet anyone for? I can deal with you, can't I?' He said, 'No, this man, you've got to deal with him direct.' So I say, 'Oh. All right mate,' but straight away, I'm thinking it's a fucking set-up, a definite set-up. Why else would he want to introduce somebody?

So I contacted old Dick Leach, the last Yard cop who was handling me before they shut me down. And Dick came over, and I said, 'In my opinion, it's a set-up. It has to be, especially as this Yarrow works in TV. Maybe it's *Panorama*. They've fucked me once. I'm not having it fucking twice! Or it could be Roger Cook you don't fucking know, do you?'

So Dick set the ball rolling. He said, 'Right, I'll put it to the Yard.' And the Yard came back. Someone right at the top of the CID had weighed up the dangers of using me again — breaking their own prohibition —

against the chances that, if they didn't, some middle-class guy would be laid out stiffed on the streets of Hampstead, dead as a post, because Yard bosses ignored my warning. So down the chain of command came this decision:

'We'll have to act on this information but, as it's that rogue Farebrother again, we can't give it to the RCS! We'll give it to some other squad.'

And then they brought in a guy I never thought I would see again. It was the same guy who went undercover on the Stanfield case. Then he was known as George. Now we had to call him Billy.

See, although the Stanfield job was done by the RCS, these undercover boys are floaters. They can work with any squad and with any force. You might get a Welsh copper still formally serving in a Welsh force, but he's working with the Met, or a Met guy up in Yorkshire. These guys are full-time undercover. They go from one assignment to another. God knows what it does to their home life. They must wake up some days and forget who they really are!

So Billy gets briefed by Dick Leach and me. Then he turns round, and, reading between the lines, he says, 'Right, if this is a set-up, it's a fucking good one.' Then he said, 'Have you led him on?' and I said, 'Have I fuck!' So I got out my little tapes, and I played them, and he said, 'I'll take them, I've got to use them.' And I said, 'You won't! They're for my benefit, not yours. I'll keep them, to cover my arse. Cos we might still find this Yarrow's working for some other bunch of cops even Customs — and then where will I be? Back in Brixton nick on a murder rap!' So they agreed. It was to be done entirely by the book. The timings had to be perfect. And Billy said, 'Whenever this guy rings you, page me on my bleeper. Then it's recorded, timed, minuted by me.'

Shortly after this conversation, Steve Yarrow did ring again. It was now time for Ron to spring his usual trap by introducing the target to the undercover operator. He had performed this routine so often, with undercover cops and undercover newsmen, that he was beginning to sound like those characters in Automobile Association advertisements: 'No, I don't do murders, but I know a man who can.'

And so it was agreed that, over a drink in the restaurant next to the video shop, Ron would duly bring Billy and Steve together. From that point on Ron was to stay out of Steve's way, for Scotland Yard was adamant that, if the case ever did get to court, the Farebrother name had to be kept out of proceedings. If not, Ron would again be branded an agent provocateur, the defence would bamboozle the judge or jury, and the case would be lost. But if Billy alone now worked on Steve and his mother, his incontestable evidence could be so overwhelming that the defence would not dare plead entrapment by duress à la Ron.

On 17 October 1994 at 7.01 in the evening, Undercover Billy switched on his hidden tape recorder and entered an Italian restaurant in north-west London. Ron was already there. Seconds later in came Steve Yarrow, apologising for being late because the bloody phone wouldnt stop ringing. Ron introduced him to Billy, then said, 'I'll leave you two here. I'm gonna do something, right!' Steve was nonplussed, 'I thought you were gonna stay', but Ron said, 'Don't get drunk' and promptly disappeared.

Thoroughly bemused, Steve now had to conduct negotiations with a complete stranger, whom, he thought, was a stone killer — without even a friendly go-between to smooth the deal. No wonder, when Billy pressed him to sit down and have a drink, Steve gulped down a glass of the house red and started jabbering in a manner both braggadocio and self-destructive. After several minutes' small-talk about their respective holidays in Cuba, the conversation turned to the business that had brought them together. Later Ron found out what the two men said.

Steve explained that his mother had been divorced from his father long before meeting the guy who became her second husband: Stanley Redwood. Then it all went wrong. For 15 years this Redwood character had been knocking her about: blacking her eyes, smashing teeth, breaking her arm, splitting her head open. He even banned her from talking to Steve. He wasn't allowed to phone his mum, and she wasn't allowed to phone or even see him.

They could meet only in secret, when all Steve could see was her bruises. But now, Steve told Billy, she's finally had the sense to come out of it. Enough's enough. She's got fed up with the beatings.

So now Billy needed Steve on tape spelling out exactly what he wanted doing to Redwood. Steve came straight out with it: 'I want him to disappear, basically.' Billy could allow no room for misinterpretation so immediately he picked up on Steve's remark: 'You want him to disappear, permanently.' 'Mm. Go, for fucking good,' said Steve, 'he's no fucking good at all.'

'Yeah,' said Billy, but there was always a way of

making the killing look like a robbery gone wrong: 'I'm in there with a sawn-off, right? We can make it look like we was in there to take the dough off him, and, like, the shooter's gone off and just blown his chest away.' But Billy was crafty: he also agreed with Steve that the easiest thing was for him to take Redwood's body away, put him in the dirt and 'that's the end of it.'

It was clear from the continued conversation that Steve wanted his stepfather murdered — no room for any doubt — but at this point he borrowed Billy's mobile phone to ask his mother, Mrs Anne Redwood, to join them in the restaurant to continue negotiations. While they waited for her to arrive, they discussed how Billy was to be paid. Steve pointed out that he and his mother believed Stanley Redwood kept £30,000 in cash in his house, so Billy could take his hitman's wages out of that. Billy explained that normally the going-rate was between five and ten grand but, in this case, he proposed taking two-thirds of whatever was in the house.

Steve replied that Billy could take whatever he liked, but if he found the entire £30,000 he might give some back to Steve and his mum. Billy agreed but he was insisting on a small deposit beforehand. He explained that if he was expected to come up with some sneaky photographs of the target — so that Steve could say, yeah, that's definitely him, that's where he is, that's his movements — he would expect to be paid a monkey [£500].

Billy explained all his needs. He wanted the target's phone number, address and everything about his likely movements. Steve explained that he worked in the minicab firm that his mother had set up but that Stanley Redwood now ran, with his own son by another marriage. So it's a doddle, then, said Billy, meaning it would be very easy to identify the target and follow him home.

A few minutes later Steve spotted his mother on her way in. After the introductions, Billy insisted on leaving the restaurant for a more discreet place (he needed a clear recording of Anne talking about the contract she wanted to take out on her husband). Leaving Steve behind, they went to Anne's car where she discussed her ex-husband's finances and then alleged this guy had split her head open right across her dome, knocked her teeth out, scarred her for life, kicked her shins and disfigured all her legs. The last time she went to hospital, she said, she had multiple injuries.

But what about paying Billy in advance for his services? She confessed she had no money at all but, if Billy could find the cash in her ex-husband's house, he could have what he liked, she didn't care.

So what exactly did Anne want doing to Redwood? Billy asked if she wanted him 'topped', like Steve wanted, which wouldn't worry Billy one little bit. He said, 'If you want the geezer put in the ground, he'll be put in the ground.'

Only now did it come out that Anne did not really want him killed, as this would let him off far too lightly. She was just trying to economise. She was certainly looking to save money on the contract. 'What would it be to just have him crippled?' she asked. So Billy replied, 'You're looking at four grand. And five grand for a proper job.'

Anne moaned that she did not know how to get hold of that kind of money, but Billy was insisting on a deposit. Anyhow, they drove to her home so she could collect a photo of the target, his phone number and his various addresses. When they arrived, Billy heard a bark. Anne had a big boxer. Its name? Bullet!

She then told Billy that whenever she had gone to hospital with all the injuries caused by the beatings, she pretended wardrobes had fallen on her or car boots had accidentally closed on her. She was so frightened of her husband she dared not tell the truth, 'but I'm not scared any more.' She certainly wasn't, because she gave Billy photos, addresses, phone and car-registration numbers to ensure he got the right man.

But Billy still needed to know what the couple really wanted. Was it four grand to do Redwood a right mischief and make him a cripple for the rest of his life? Did they just want a GBH — to put him in hospital for a long time — or did they want a proper job done on him? So Anne says she was figuring that if he's put in hospital, he's really going to suffer. If he's injured and he's hurt, he's gonna be in pain, like she'd been in pain for over 20 years. So Billy asks how good a job she wants doing on him? 'You're sure you want him a cripple?' 'Yeah, why not?'

Now Billy and Anne went back to the restaurant to find Steve, and they all arranged to meet again the next Friday, so Billy could report his findings, they could finalize the bits and pieces and sort out the money. Then, as Anne went off, leaving the men together in the restaurant, she said to Billy, 'Nice meeting you. You've got a gentle touch.'

Gentle touch! Christ! Imagine what Anne

thought of Billy's 'gentle touch' when she discovered what he was really up to? At the time Billy — and the detectives monitoring these conversations — were still trying to find out what the couple really wanted doing to Redwood. But whenever Billy tried to remind Steve, he would spin off into recollections of his miserable adolescence. He said that when he was 18, Redwood 'made her give him a blow job in front of me. What do you think of the mentality?'

But for Billy, this was no time for psychoanalysis, social work or sentimentality. He had to get on with the job. He sympathised, but explained that for him it was business.

Besides, Billy and his bosses had another problem to sort out. Right at the start Steve had told me that, before asking me to kill his stepfather, he'd asked a man called Ray to do the job. He had even given this Ray a photo of the target. Now the detectives running this case feared that while Billy was still negotiating with Steve and mum, Ray might go ahead and kill Redwood anyway. So Billy had to ensure Ray was off the case. Ideally, he would find out who Ray was and check out if he really was a hitman. Steve said he was a builder but no problem.

Steve then explained how Ray was trying to find a friend of his to do it. He was supposed to be a championship kick-boxer, but no one had seen him. This was not good enough for Billy: he had to know who else knew about the plot. Well, of course, one man knew a lot about it: me! So Billy says, 'Ronnie Farebrother. I'll have to talk to him about that, keep his mouth shut.'

Steve — poor fool — had every faith in me. He

told Billy, 'He'll keep his mouth shut, won't he? He's a professional.' 'Oh, yeah,' said Billy, 'he's a professional'.

Yes, I was a professional. But not in the sense that Steve meant. Billy was a professional too — and he still had to sort out what this pair really wanted him to do. So on the evening of Friday, 21 October, he taped himself up again and went to Anne's home in Beaufort Lodge Drive. After struggling past Bullet the boxer and listening to her story of Stanley's latest efforts to recover some of his belongings from the flat, Billy tried to get Anne to do some straight talking.

This time she said she still wanted the job doing, but her finances were very sticky. So again Billy asked, what did she want doing. 'Well, I don't think bumping him off's gonna do the trick,' she said, 'I'd rather him suffer. Wouldn't you, Steve?'

But Steve was still arguing that Billy should go all the way:

'No, the thing is, you make him suffer, then you bump him off.'

Steve and his mother were having a row over this, and poor Billy was stuck in the middle, trying to mediate. Then they seemed to settle on giving Redwood a good hiding, but what did even that really mean? 'You mean, put him in hospital proper?' asked Billy. 'Oh, yeah,' said Anne, 'I don't just mean give him a black eye or knock a tooth out. Intensive-care routine,' added Steve.

Billy then built up his own logic for this solution. He would demand money from Redwood, 'if he's got 30 grand round his drum, and he don't tell me where it is, I can put him in intensive care without any problems at all, and he'll never walk again.'

Then Anne — the ex-wife from hell — told Billy, 'Good.' 'That'll teach him a lesson,' added Steve.

'But,' explained, Billy, 'If it goes wrong, and he bleeds to death, there's nothing I can do about that.' This did not seem to worry Anne: 'No, I don't care. Billy, can you see any tears there?' 'None at all, babe.' 'Can you see a smile?' 'A big 'un!'

By now Anne had become so fond of Billy, she didn't think of him as a cold killer. He was more a friend, a shoulder to cry on, than a professional assassin. When he told her their next meeting would be in two weeks time, Anne invited him to come for dinner. Imagine! Inviting the man youre paying to cripple your ex-husband to dinner!

Just 12 days later Billy was back at Anne's, introducing Dave as his trusty partner on this contract (but, in reality, another undercover cop). Billy reported on his progress, staggering Anne by saying he had been right in the target's cab office, but he needed more photos of Redwood and his relatives.

Anne handed him £150 expenses in cash (there was a further £50 to come), and a deal was fixed that Billy would give her and Steve one-third of whatever he found in the house. Imagine! This is a contract killing where the hitman pays his hirers!

'Anne kept lapsing into lurid descriptions of her brutal marriage, but her trust in Billy was so total, I don't know how he could keep up the act. Then came the final confirmation from Anne's own mouth. First Billy said, if she wanted to say to him, "Billy, Davey Boy, knock it on the head—", but Anne interrupted him, "No way, no. I don't want to walk away. I'm not backing out. I want it to go ahead. I want to go full steam ahead."

So Billy picked up her turn of phrase and said, "That's it. Well, it's going, full steam ahead." "Full, full steam ahead," she emphasized. He understood, and so would everyone else who ever heard the tape.

Over the next three weeks, in phone calls, the fine detail of the hit was confirmed, with not the slightest wavering from either Anne or Steve. On the evening of 23 November Billy and Dave visited her to say how close their surveillance had taken them to Stanley Redwood. Ron recalls what he was later told.

'So Billy tells her that at one point his car was just two feet away from Redwood's. He could have shot him there and then, in the car, and driven away. "Fucking hell," was all Anne could say. "Yeah," added Dave, "we could have done him this morning."

'Well, now Billy has to go into the fine detail to make sure Anne knows exactly what's going to happen to Redwood. The dry run that morning had been a doddle, so Billy says, "We'll take him as he gets out the motor in the car park. He'll get a .38 straight into him, straight in the motor, 'Sit in the motor! You're taking us home!'" Then Billy and Davey would take him back home, cripple or torture him, exactly as Anne tells them she wants done: "We'll take the dough off him, and we will hurt him the way you want him hurt."

'Anne was over the moon: "Lovely. . . . He will have it in one hit. I've had it over 20 years." Billy said there was no doubt that by the time he'd finished, Redwood would give him the money but "If he snuffs it, there's nothing I can do about that. You understand what I'm saying?" "Yeah," said Anne.

'Billy then explained that he and Dave would be doing "this bit of work" the following Wednesday, and he set about arranging how to bring Anne and Steve the news and deliver them their share. They, in turn, had to sort out hiding the money. Billy told Anne, stick it in the freezer, in a freezer bag within a box of ice cream. He explained that he did not want her to have all the money in her house, so he would send Dave to give half to Steve at his current place of work, TV3, the Swedish satellite station based near Heathrow Airport.'

A little before eight that night the conspirators all said their goodbyes. Billy signed off by telling his recorder how pleased Steve and Anne were, now that the deal had finally been settled. 'He's smiling and very, very happy. She was smiling, very, very happy, and a very firm handshake to say thank you.'

The thank you should have been earned on the morning of Wednesday, 30 November, six weeks after Ron had introduced Billy to Steve. At 6.15 a.m. Billy drove to Woodside Park station and awaited the target's arrival in the car park.

At 8.02 a.m. up drove Stanley Redwood. Billy got out of his car and walked towards him. He did not shoot him. Instead he pointed him out to a police inspector who approached Redwood and told him they were acting to protect him. Billy then headed off to Anne's flat to tell her the operation had been successful. With him, but at a discreet distance, was an arrest squad. After greeting Bullet the boxer, he went through the motions with Anne, telling her there were no problems at all. That it went like clockwork.

At this point his recorder did not function

properly, for the first time in hours of talk with the conspirators. This was unfortunate because, to guarantee a conviction, Billy needed a truly positive reaction from Anne. Yet even the comments that could be heard were damning.

'Billy told her she looked really, really pleased and asked if she was happy now. "Billy, look in my eyes. Do you see . . ." The missing word might have been "tears" or "happiness". Either way, it meant satisfaction. Ron recalls what he heard later.

'Billy was brilliant. As he handed Anne her first thousand pounds of loot, he told her Redwood would never worry her again. She replied that he was never going to have another holiday. Billy agreed and really hammered it up in a final flourish, telling her he was bleeding pretty badly when they left him, that they might have got him in a big artery.'

Billy counted out another £3000, making Anne's share £4000 in all. According to his subsequent statement, he said that she was very happy and excited and gave him a kiss. She was really pleased. She handed him an ice-cream box, and they hid the £4000 in it. He wrapped it in cling film and covered it with ice cream as she watched and placed it in the freezer.

Anne had just made Billy a cup of tea when he said he had to pop out for a couple of minutes. He'd be back. He then left the flat, on the pretext of getting the diamond ring he had allegedly stolen from the victim. In fact he was seeing his police colleagues. He led them up to the flat, went back in alone, leaving the door open, and made friendly remarks to Anne. Suddenly she heard a knock at the door and other people coming in. 'Who is it? Who is it? Pardon!' were her last words before she was arrested for conspiracy to murder.

At the same time 20 miles away, on an industrial estate near Heathrow, Dave — also wired up — was parked outside TV3s studios. He made a call to Steve Yarrow who was working in the building, and told him he was right outside his place and had something for him. Steve quickly emerged. From the car Dave told him to jump in. Without a trace of irony, Steve replied, 'I can't. I'm gonna get shot. I can't disappear for too long.'

Dave gave him the news he had been waiting for. Steve did not want to be involved in any details. He took his £4000 share and with a cheery goodbye headed back into the studios. At this point four detectives waiting in unmarked cars, swung into action. They had seen Yarrow push a white package containing the money into his rear right-trouser pocket. Two challenged him, they produced their warrant cards, and there was a struggle. He was brought to the ground and arrested for conspiracy to murder. 'This is a joke,' he replied, as he was handcuffed. He was taken home while a search was made and afterwards to Belgravia Police Station.

For Billy and his bosses the operation had, so far, proved an outstanding success, but for Ron Farebrother it was akin to the Resurrection.

'Of course, now I'm back on track, with the police. Who would have believed it? One minute I was as dangerous as a nuclear fuel rod, not safe to go near for a thousand years, the next I've stopped a guy getting killed. Whatever they thought of me, they had to accept I'd done a good job. That must have hurt bad, but cops can't be hard-and-fast moralisers. In the end there aren't any rules to this game — at least not the ones set by *Panorama*.

Arresting Anne Redwood and Steve Yarrow for conspiracy to murder may have been more for melodramatic or intimidatory effect than an accurate reflection of what was on Billy's tapes. While Steve clearly wanted Redwood dead, it was equally clear that Anne wanted him crippled but alive, so his suffering would be all the greater. By the end Anne had won the argument, although even she had accepted that if Billy did shoot only to wound, Redwood might die anyway. A .38 fired at close quarters in what might have become a struggle could have killed him. Indeed death was as likely as wounding, so Anne and Steve's premeditated contract to shoot Stanley could reasonably be parlayed up to conspiracy to murder — or so the police thought.

But eight months later, in July 1995, when the pair appeared at the Old Bailey, the charge had been plea-bargained down to conspiracy to cause grievous bodily harm. They pleaded guilty, and the judge was impressed by their lawyer's tales of the target's violence against them.

'I am quite satisfied that in the background to this plot there was a long history of serious and sustained violence, especially of you, Mrs Redwood, but also in a different way of your son.'

The court heard of her broken arm and knocked-out teeth and of her being forced to perform sex acts on her husband while young Stephen was forced to watch. Redwood wasn't there to defend himself against these claims, but it was on the record that in December 1993 (after 19 years of marriage) Anne had obtained a court order banning him from their home and then been granted a divorce.

Yet the judge could not overlook the crude financial angle to the plot. There was no doubt that Redwood's coveted £30,000 in cash had heightened her sense of humiliation and powered her hunt for a hitman in October 1994. The judge said that, however much she had been abused, 'you wanted Mr Redwood to be quite simply crippled, which is a terrible plan for anyone.' As for Steve, his relentless expressions of murderous intent on Billy's tapes left little room for clemency. Nor did his satisfaction when told his stepfather had been shot. The prosecutor said his response was not one of horror or surprise but of pleasure in receiving his cut.

Three years in prison was the sentence they both received. It could have been a lot worse for them, but, far from being relieved, Anne and Steve were horrified. Very soon a spate of sympathetic articles appeared in local papers, portraying them as victims of crime, not perpetrators. One story featured a group called Justice for Women, which was backing Anne Redwood on the grounds that she was driven to act after suffering 20 years of sexual and physical abuse. Her offence was clearly premeditated, so she could not claim 'impulse', but she did tell the *Hampstead and Highgate Express* that she was appealing against her sentence on the grounds that she was suffering from post-traumatic stress disorder.

Said Harriet Wistrich of Justice for Women, 'We have been arguing that when a woman kills, she doesn't always do so in immediate response. There are reasons for a time lapse, not all of them simple. When a woman's level of self-confidence and self-esteem has been bruised and undermined for so long, any response to violence is very difficult. It is only after she realizes the horror of what has happened that there is a kind of ongoing rage within her that needs to be taken account of.'

One remedy might be to define the defence of provocation more clearly in law, but which provocation did Ms Wistrich mean? Redwood's alleged violence or the Billy-and-Dave double act? According to Ms Wistrich, what was appalling in this case was the way the undercover police agents exploited that distress and rage.

Two weeks later the *Ham and High* returned to the case with a second article in which Anne told reporter Paul Waugh of her ex-husband's enormities. If she served tea at the wrong temperature he would spit it out and toss the rest of the cup over her. If he disliked her food, he would chuck it on the carpet, grind it in and make her scrub the carpet clean. If she were late home, he would give her a beating. Between these regular assaults, he clouted her with a phone and split her head open, forced her to clean the balcony with a toothbrush and once ordered her to stand in the corner and repeat, 'My son is a homosexual,' 500 times. She also claimed he had threatened to kill her if ever she left him. Often badly bruised and battered, and in hospital several times after suicide attempts, she should have involved the police, but whenever they were called, she refused to press charges. It seems she was psyched out with fear, until finally driven to seek help from the Golders Green police domestic-violence unit.

Only when she was away from him, she claimed,

did her self-esteem rise to the point where she wanted him punished for all the pain he had inflicted on her. 'It was only after I had been away from him that it really hit me what he had been doing all those years.' And only then did she come up with the idea of hiring a hitman. Enter Ron Farebrother and Billy Undercover.

By this point in the story, if not before, Anne was playing with the truth. She was claiming that at first she and her son had told Billy they only wanted Stanley's knee caps broken, and it was Billy who had come up with the idea of killing him. The article stated: 'What really upsets her is the way the undercover police egged her on to conspire against her ex-husband. "Haven't they got better things to do than waste money trying to trap me? All I was doing, in a stupid way, was talking about it. I know I was naive, but I wasnt thinking straight. He wasn't even hurt."

That he wasn't hurt was no thanks to Anne, and certainly not to her son Stephen — who had wanted Redwood killed all along. Indeed, long before he got talking to Ron and Billy, Steve had approached Ray the builder to do the job. It was only because Ray was a 'wanker' (as Steve himself put it) that Redwood had not been murdered before Ron and Billy had even come on the scene.

'Now Yarrow may claim he was set up, but as soon as the police got involved I was told not to speak to him, and I only spoke to him twice. Once when he was getting a lottery ticket, I said, "All right? I don't want to talk to you, cos it's best that I don't, cos I don't want to know what's going on" because that was between him and Billy. But then he calls by and said, "Do you want to go for a drink?" and I said, "No, I've packed up drinking. I don't want to go drinking. I don't want to be seen with you." He said, "Oh, I'm going to let Billy know, I've got someone else, a builder." I said, "Oh, yeah. Don't even tell me that, you cunt."' So I walked into the video shop and told the police, "This guy's just made contact. You better get hold of him, he's approached a builder."

'But Yarrow had not only approached "Ray" the builder. He'd also asked a greengrocer guy. The bloke told me about it afterwards. Yarrow had told him he wanted his father taken care of. He said he had already approached a couple of villains, but they were too long-winded about it. Well, this greengrocer didnt want to do it either, but it all shows just how bad Yarrow wanted the man killed. Imagine, with all that shit hitting the paper, I'm the bad bastard!'

Two weeks later the *Ham and High* dedicated another entire page to Yarrow's self-defence, as vouchsafed from the visits room at Brixton prison. His special pleading was even more breathtaking than his mothers:

'I must admit, the whole thing was exciting. Billy offered to kill him, but my mother said that was over the top. I said that I just wanted him to disappear. I meant disappear from my mother's life.'

Yarrow went on to complain about anti-Semitism in the prison: not just from prisoners but also from screws (prison officers) who were calling him offensive names. He did not see the irony of his being in jail only because he had schemed to kill another Jew. Or perhaps he did, for the last line of the article quoted him saying: 'My main regret is that a wife-beater isn't in here and I am.'

Yarrow's ferocious self-defence is perhaps explicable in terms of his tortured upbringing and his need to justify scheming to plot the death of his and his mother's alleged torturer. But it is ridiculous for either to claim that Billy Undercover had spontaneously offered to kill Redwood or egged them on. The tapes prove conclusively that they originated the idea, and Billy gave them many opportunities to express a change of heart, so they were lucky to get off with three years. They served just half that time. Immediately they were released, another local paper ran an interview with them both. Headlined WE ARE THE VICTIMS, it included this quote from Yarrow; 'The policeman who said he was a hitman played on us both. We were as gullible as hell.' Gullible? Not according to Ron Farebrother.

'Rubbish. What Steve said on those tapes shows that topping his stepfather was only a starter. There was the time Billy came to his flat and saw him working his computer. Straightaway Steve offered to commit a fraud, by getting inside a bank computer. He even put a robbery up to Billy. He told him that he knew someone who had loads of cash, all the time. It was a shop, like a warehouse, with tens of thousands of pounds. It was a very big place in Enfield with hardly any credit-card transactions, nearly all cash. "It's the perfect place," he assured Billy.

'Not content with getting Redwood killed, he wanted Billy to damage some other bloke who had given him a slap in a pub. He told Billy he wanted him to teach the man a lesson. He said shooting Redwood was serious work, but this other job was just to make him feel better. Oh, yeah, Steve, we believe you. Sure, you are a victim! A victim of your own criminal inclination!'

So beatings, robbery and computer crime: all imprisonable schemes put up to Billy by poor, wronged Yarrow without prompting. But Yarrow was also the crucial link to another racket exposed by Ron Farebrother. Remember that, even before asking Ron to do the contract killing, he had offered to introduce him to a man who sold obscene videos. Even worse, as it turned out, many of the videos on offer portrayed sex with young children: paedophile material of the worst order.

Yarrow felt Ron might be receptive when they had first met in the video shop run by the woman who would become Ron's girlfriend. In fact he had no such interest. Indeed he had a deep hatred of paedophiles, as he had proved in 1992 when he penetrated vast paedophile rings before delivering the hard evidence to the Obscene Publications Squad (OPS) with devastatingly successful results. So when Yarrow talked of a neighbourhood chum offering really strong stuff, Ron found it difficult to suppress both his contempt and his glee as yet another victim was being delivered into his clutches. Somehow he showed sufficient controlled interest to lead Yarrow to believe he would be receptive and left it at that. A few hours later Yarrow rang him up.

'I taped the conversation, and this time it wasn't about killing his stepfather, it was about the kiddie-porn videos. He said he'd given the supplier my number. Then the supplier rang, told me his name was Andy and said he wanted to meet. So I said, "Right," we fixed a time for him to come to my place, and I gave him the address. Remember, at this time we were right at the start of the murder-plot sting, so I got straight on to Billy's boss for this job — Detective Inspector Dick Leach of the Flying Squad — and we arranged for a team of surveillance cops to be around the door to my block of flats when this Andy arrived.

'At the agreed time up he came, we had a chat, and then he left. He was a huge great brute, smooth-talking and obviously well educated but well over six foot and at least 18 stone. So when he came out, the surveillance boys waiting outside couldn't miss him. They followed him off in his car and housed him — found out where he lived — only a couple of miles away in Edgware.

'Then I met him again, and I agreed to buy two kiddie-porn videos, at £30 each. Two days later he rang me to arrange to bring them round. I said, "Not tonight, I'm busy. Tomorrow night." That was to give me time to contact the police, so they could set up a full operation. They said, "Right. Now we've got to get into him, you've got to step aside," so I said, "Well, that's fine by me. The whole business revolts me. You take care of it all from now on." That's when we agreed to introduce Billy Undercover into this job, too, because we were still weeks off busting Yarrow and his mum for the murder plot, so Billy was still totally credible.

'The scheme was for me to tell Andy that I would introduce him to a really big buyer of this kind of stuff. So we set up a joint meeting, only this time Andy arrived early. Fortunately, the surveillance guys were already outside so they phoned me as he was coming up the stairs saying, "The bastard's here so, as soon as he comes in your door, get rid of him. Tell him he's got to meet Billy downstairs, cos he's the buyer now." And that's what I did. He was in my flat for no more than a minute or two, I gave him Billy's mobile number, and they agreed to meet outside the off-licence a few doors away.'

The point of insinuating Billy into the role of buyer, in lieu of Ron, was the same as insinuating him as the hitman: to keep Ron wholly out of the main evidence so none of the targets could squeal agent provocateur in court. There was still huge anxiety in Scotland Yard about acting on any tip-off from Ron, but, yet again, he had come up with information that could not be ignored.

One undercover job is complex enough, but here were two operations that had to run side by side, in perfect synchronicity. The problem was that the kiddie-porn story was moving far faster than the murder-plot sting. Just on the strength of the videos that Ron had bought from Andy, the police were already sure they were on to a major paedophile ring, but the speed with which Andy now let Billy into his confidence would test their operation-management skills. He quickly sold half a dozen videos to Billy, then the pair discussed a drugs deal. On this evidence alone he could already be busted for two very serious crimes, but he could not be touched until the Redwood conspiracy had matured. The police feared that Steve Yarrow was so close to Andy, he would hear of Andy's arrest as soon as it happened. He would immediately realize he was the target of a police sting and promptly backpedal over killing his stepfather. He would cut all contact with Ron and Billy, or tell them the whole idea was a joke. So now Billy had so slow things right down with Andy until there was incontrovertible evidence against Yarrow and his mother. Then all three arrests could be carried out simultaneously.

Early on 30 November, at the very moment Billy was leading an arrest team to Anne Redwood, and his undercover colleague was doing the same to her son, the Obscene Publications Squad raided Andy's home in Edgware. They seized a staggering 603 paedophile videos. Andy was promptly arrested for possessing and publishing obscene material containing indecent photos of children, and for incitement to supply dangerous drugs. He was then taken to Harrow Police Station, where he was fingerprinted, photographed, interrogated and charged.

Andy's world had suddenly fallen apart. Two days after his arrest he was still struggling to work out who had informed on him. In a daze he rang Ron and poured out all his troubles to the very man who had brought those troubles upon him. As ever, Ron had the tape recorder going. Their conversation was rich in irony, especially when Ron could barely suppress his satisfaction at the paedophile's downfall or his outrage that the man was still at liberty.

Andy: I got arrested last Wednesday, and I've been charged with supplying child pornography. At Harrow.

Ron: Oh, good God! At Harrow?

Andy: So Billy has obviously turned us all in. They have the tapes he had off me. What have you heard about Stephen?

Ron: Stephen's been arrested. But for conspiracy

to murder.

Andy: You're joking.

Ron: No. And his mother. Well, that's the rumour going around.

Andy: The police had all the numbers of all the notes that Billy paid me with. The £20 and £10 notes. I just wondered if you'd heard anything. Have you heard from Billy?

Ron: No, I haven't heard from Billy for a week and a half.

Andy: He's either been arrested or he's an undercover police officer. You've not had a visit yet?

Ron: No, I haven't. You got me worried now.

Andy: After I got home tonight, there were photographers here and everything. They've been ringing me on the mobile number, which Billy and you had. I've had the papers ringing me, hounding me. I've just been hanging up on them.

Ron: Bloody hell. . . . Thank God, you're out anyway. How did you get out?

Andy: I'm out on bail.

Ron: What! On child pornography?

Andy: And they're also trying to get me on drugs, which would be a bit stupid anyway. Billy was mentioning drugs — serious. That's how it is anyway. It has to be Billy. It has to be.

Ron: Good God.

Andy: If you've got any tapes there, erase them and smash them up afterwards. Get rid of them. They found some other tapes here. I had some other tapes here. Children's ones.

Ron: So Billy could be arrested too?

Andy: Yes. He's obviously spilled his guts. Told them about me, and you. That's how it stands....I'm not staying home anyway. Photographers were here, but they've left.

Ron: Do you want me to move anything?

Andy: Not really. I don't want anyone to follow me. Not the police or the press.

Ron: Well, you know I'll help you as much as I can, if there's anything you want me to do for you.

Andy: Yes.

It is clear from the tape that Andy had been introduced to Ron by Stephen Yarrow. Indeed, as Andy tries to work out who has betrayed him, he keeps returning to the riddle of how Billy had ever come into his life. Sure, Ron had introduced him to Billy, but the man who had introduced him to Ron was Yarrow.

Andy: A couple of weeks ago Steve told me he had some business with Billy anyway. I didn't ask him what it was. . . . Get hold of Billy anyway.

Ron: Yeah, I've got to ring him and tell him about Steve. And you! Now I've got to see him about you.

Andy: If I were you, I'd be careful about what I'd say. I'm using the name Andy. I was always a little bit iffy about him anyway, I'd decided. . . . Perhaps Billy's been banged up, as well as Steve and his mother. Perhaps he was involved. Perhaps he's spilled his guts about everything ....

Ron: Thanks for marking my card, anyway.

Andy: If you have anything at all — books, magazines, tapes — get rid of it, if I was you.

Don't stick anything in a dustbin.

Ron: I'm pleased you phoned me because — bloody hell — it's serious.

Andy: Have you got Billy's mobile number? I've only the pager number.

Ron: I'll see if I can get hold of him. He's got a girlfriend, I think. Phone me back in half an hour.

Half an hour later Andy duly called back, still trying to puzzle out the source of the treachery.

Ron: Hallo, mate. Yeah, I've got hold of his wife cos he's out on a bit of business since last night. She is expecting him back. She sounds all right.

Andy: It's weird. I got arrested on Wednesday. Who gave him the money if not the Bill? That's how I look at it. They had the tapes, which I gave him. They actually showed me those. So it's weird.... If Billy's told them about me, he's obviously told them about you.... He may be involved with Steve on this murder conspiracy

Ron: Bloody hell. When you phoned up tonight, I thought you were ringing up about Steve.

Andy: It must be well over 20 years I've known Steve.

Ron: Well, I'm gobsmacked, I don't know what to say really.

Andy: How do you think I feel?

Ron: Bloody terrible, I suppose.

Andy then introduced a bizarre sub-plot: about a

senior police officer (now dead) who had viewed paedophile video tapes at Andy's home.

Ron: They must have asked who you got [the tapes] from. Did you give them any help that way?

Andy: Well, I got them off another man called Ian originally. . . . He had them all, he gave me copies of them to look after. Years and years ago. There was a police officer who used to be with Ian. He used to come into my flat if Ian wasn't in he used to go into the bedroom and watch them. He was a commander. I had to tell them. He actually died a couple of years ago. He had a heart attack.

Ron: While watching the films probably . . . [laughs] I shouldn't joke about things like that.

Andy: He was in the Special Branch at the time anyway. They almost caught up with him, but, because he had the heart attack, obviously they couldn't do anything about it.

So what about the tapes that Andy had given Undercover Billy?

Andy: These were all the old ones I had. . . . I've had these knocking around at home for ten years or more. So when Steve asked me to get you some, it was a good excuse to get them out of the house, really. They took away loads.

Again Andy returned to the conundrum of who had betrayed him.

Andy: When it starts appearing in the tabloids,

obviously the neighbours are going to get ugly.

Ron: The Old Bill must have told them where you live, then.

Andy: The press had the number of the mobile phone. They've been ringing me virtually non-stop. And the address must have been leaked too.

Ron: It doesn't sound too well for you, does it?

Andy: No, that's right. That's very true. No. The cameras were flashing away.

Ron: Fucking hell . . .

Andy: Speak to anyone else who's involved, obviously, put the word around. Because if he shopped me, they could be watching you. And he may have shopped anyone else that you're acquainted with.

Ron: Bloody hell. You can't trust no bastard, can you!

Andy: Why does he set me up? That's what I want to know. Why did Billy do me? It's a sting operation, or Billy is one of the filth.

Ron: Well, I know he's not that.

The next day, Saturday, 3 December, Andy again called Ron.

Ron: Hallo. Well, I've got all the papers today, nothing in there.

Andy: I'm wondering about tomorrow's, because they're still hounding me, still ringing up on the mobile. I'm just hanging up on them, though.

But who was this Andy? Ron did not yet know his real name, but he did know he had connections in high places, for he had already told Ron he worked in the

House of Commons as a consultant to an MP. It later turned out that this really was true. Under his real name of Michael Lewis, the paedophile worked for Andrew Hargreaves, the Conservative MP for Birmingham, Hall Green. Even now, with Lewis a.k.a. Andy well and truly snared, Ron was still digging for information, though he had difficulty controlling his natural wit and maintaining fake sincerity, especially when Andy told him the press had been on to the MP.

Andy: They told him what it's all about, and, it being the Ministry involved, it will be the gutter press that will be interested in it. Tomorrow's papers.

Ron: Bloody hell.

Andy: *News of the World. People.*

Ron: So what did the minister say then?

Andy: He was obviously worried.

Ron: So who is he? If the press know I might as well know.

Andy: Andrew Hargreaves.

Ron: That's fucking bad news. So he wasn't very happy about it?

Andy: No, that's very, very true, very true indeed.

Ron: So what's happening? You'll still go to work, though, won't you?

Andy: Well, no.

Ron: What, he's told you not to?

Andy: Well, the police still have my ID. I can't enter the House without it. He doesn't want me on his staff there any longer, obviously. So, I'm screwed.

Ron: Fucking hell. . . . Did the police ask you anything about Billy? Did you mention me at all?

Andy: No, no. No mention at all. They asked me how I knew Billy. I said through Steve and through another person, but I wouldn't mention the other person's name, obviously.

Ron: Well, I've done fuck all wrong — fucking hell. Well, how do the press know about Hargreaves or whatever his name is . . .? Cos nobody knew about Hargreaves. Well, I didn't know about Hargreaves until you just told me.

Andy: It's the police. They're doing it all.

Ron could not resist a dig about Andy's luck running out.

Ron: You bought your lottery ticket today? [laughing]

Andy: Excuse me?

Ron: Have you bought your lotto ticket?

Andy: No, I haven't been out at all yet . . .hardly slept at all, with the worry of everything. If only we hadn't started all this.

Ron: Well, Steve was the one who got you in touch, wasn't he?

Andy: Yeah, that's right. Yeah, Steve put me on to you, and you put me on to Billy.

Ron: So what did he have to say, the old MP? Did he give you any advice or what?

Andy: Hah, a lot of verbal diarrhoea. Obviously he's not very happy because it goes against him because I was on his staff. Yeah?

Ron: What sort of job did you do for him then?

Andy: Computers. So yesterday afternoon after the press spoke to him, he contacted the security officer at the House and had my pass withdrawn. So that's over. So all in all it's bad news. Really bad news.

Ron: That's when you find out who your friends are now.

Andy: True enough.

Ron: Anyway I better shoot off.

Andy: OK. Look after yourself. Be good, be careful. If you get anything —

Ron: Yeah, give me a tinkle tomorrow.

Andy: Bye.

The call ended at 1.39 that Saturday afternoon. Andy never phoned again. Someone must have tipped him off. Nothing appeared in the Sunday papers, either that weekend or the next. But on Sunday, 18 December, the story finally broke in the *News of the World*. In an article headlined AIDE OF MP ON PORNO CHARGE, the piece described how 'posh-talking Michael Lewis' was a 'top computer expert' working at the House of Commons. Since being charged over the distribution of kiddie porn, however, 'hulking 18-stone Lewis has had his Commons security pass withdrawn by Tory MP Andrew Hargreaves, for whom he worked. Although Mr Hargreaves has no connection with the police investigation, he will be routinely questioned.'

The article revealed that Lewis 'claims he is known in government circles as a specialist in computer technology . . . and he says he has had tea at 11 Downing Street, home of Chancellor Kenneth Clarke. He claims he has worked for a number of other Tories.' An 'insider' was then quoted as saying, 'Many people will be shocked by the news of charges against him. He has many contacts in the security services and in politics.'

The case against Michael Lewis was finally dealt with at Harrow on 22 March 1995, when he pleaded guilty to the pornography charges. The drugs charges were shelved. He was given a four-month sentence, but this was suspended, so he never spent a day in jail. Ron was appalled: 'He had 603 videos in his home. You can't claim, as he did, that he was just looking after them for somebody. And they could hardly have been all for his personal use. So the truth is obviously far worse: he was in the wholesale distribution business. How could he have got off so light? He was even doing charity work with handicapped kids.'

And where does the case of Lewis a.k.a. Andy leave Stephen Yarrow's claims of put-upon innocence? After seeking out a hitman to kill his stepfather and then proposing acts of computer crime, robbery and grievous bodily harm, what credibility does he have to continue to squeal, on television programmes such as *Kilroy*, that he is a 'victim'? According to Ron, no credibility at all.

'Stephen Yarrow gave me a blinding reference to this paedophile. He's lucky he wasn't charged with aiding and abetting the paedophile, because he introduced him.'

And just how close was Yarrow to Lewis? What was it that bonded them so closely together?

'Yarrow was very good friends with the paedophile. They were members of the same Masonic lodge. Yarrow was a Senior Warden, and this parliamentary aide was in the same little club. This friendship between Yarrow and Lewis gives Masonic back-scratching a new meaning. Who else was involved in this circle of friends, and how high did it go?'

OUR UNDERCOVER REPORTER

Ron's 'win double' — bagging up Yarrow and his mother for conspiracy, and capturing the parliamentary pervert — not only restored him to the ranks of Scotland Yard's most valued (if most dangerous) informants. It also convinced the *News of the World* it could not do without his services either. The embarrassment and disruption caused by the *Panorama* exposé had led the newspaper to steer clear of Ron for a while. He had become too hot to handle. However, when he delivered the hitman-sex-and-brutality conspiracy and the kiddie-porn-merchant tale straight to the police without directly involving the *News of the World*, it was clear that he had to be put back on the strength.

Now Ron, rehabilitated and off the booze, was about to enter his most productive period yet for Britain's favourite Sunday read. On 4 June 1995 the

News of the World ran a double-page story based almost entirely on Ron's information. SOCCER ACE MERSON IN DEATH QUIZ ran the headline. The name of Paul Merson, the cocaine-snorting Arsenal forward whose manic beer-swilling, goal-scoring gestures had helped make him a Highbury hero, was enough to attract millions of readers. But the death in the headline referred to Bill Goodman: best man at Ron's highly irreverent wedding to Pat Sherman. Now it had to be Ron who vowed to bring everyone to public account for his friend's murder.

'See, Bill had gone to seed since he was my best man. At that time he was a slim fellow, but now he was 17 stone, a dangerous weight when you're 45. Then suddenly I found out he had been stabbed to death at his girlfriend's house. They discovered him in a pool of blood, with an ounce of cocaine and a fat wad of notes. This was enough to show he wasn't killed for either drugs or money, so his girlfriend became the obvious suspect. But when the police showed up, they weren't only interested in her. They also took a good look at his little black address book stuffed with the names of his rich customers.

'One used to be Paul Merson. When he wasn't playing for Arsenal or England, he often popped into the Mousetrap in Borehamwood where Bill could always be found downing vodkas and selling cocaine at £50 a line. As the pub was near Elstree Studios, you could often see *EastEnders* stars in there. Then Arsenal players started hanging round. The landlord, Tony Giner, knew all about Bill because Bill was in there right from nine in the morning. He was always good for a laugh, and he brought in a lot of general custom for the pub itself. People like Merson were an attraction — strange and sad though that may seem!

In the *News of the World*, landlord Tony Giner reeled off a long list of footballers and actors who dropped in, but (in a line reeking of legal caution), 'I know for sure none of the TV stars or other footballers got involved with drugs. They were only here for the beer — nothing else.' Yet Paul Merson was fingered. Giner claimed that, after Merson had snorted cocaine with Goodman, his character would change completely: 'His eyes would start bulging, he'd grind his teeth and gibber like an excited young kid.' But even Giner had to take action when Merson was coming in three times a week to pick up cocaine from Goodman: rolling up after midnight, wearing just shorts and a T-shirt, and blabbering, 'Give me some Charlie!'

Soon after this article appeared, Merson went on a very public, cocaine-kicking course of treatment. But what had brought Bill Goodman to his miserable end? He had only just finished a two-month sentence for pinching a female traffic-warden's bottom. On his release, he had left his wife and three children and moved into the home of a girlfriend, which is where he had now died from a stab wound in his left thigh.

Giner described this bankrupt carpet fitter as a 'half-decent fool who played up to his hangers-on and a huge drinker who could knock back a litre and a half of vodka a day.' Despite this backhanded testimonial, Bill's friends could not forgive Giner for letting him deal in drugs not only to stars but also, more damagingly, to himself. They were threatening to beat Giner up when, just before the article appeared, he shut down the pub and fled Borehamwood. Hot on his trail was an avenging Ron Farebrother, who was the first person to tell the police that Bill Goodman had been slain. His fury about pub and publican was uncontainable.

'It was a known fact that the Mousetrap was openly dealing drugs. All they were missing was to put an advert in the local Borehamwood Post stating their prices. You could go in there and blatantly get it across the counter.

'It was when they found Bill bleeding to death after a massive row with his girlfriend went badly wrong that the police found a book on him with phone numbers of 'who owes what' in code. Paul Merson was among the names, and I knew it was true because Bill had told me all about it. He and I used to have bets on whether Merson would score or not. Of course, Bill had the advantage because he knew if Paul was high on cocaine or not on any particular match day. My only indicator was whether he was going for the man or the ball. If it was the man, he had to be playing with a nose full of Charlie.

'I don't think any of this would have happened if I'd still been living in Borehamwood. I would have kept Bill well away from cocaine. When he died, I decided to open up on all these activities through the *News of the World*. And by making sure the pub was closed down, I stopped all that shit being supplied to *EastEnders*. There was one exception, a particular young lady who got sacked from the show because she was a heroin addict. For her benefit I found out who was supplying her in Borehamwood, and that got stopped.'

The week after that report appeared, Ron was serving up yet another classic *News of the World* scoop. It had fallen into his clutches without prompting or manipulation on his part. He had merely been ordering a takeaway from his neighbourhood pizza parlour when the proprietor, an Iranian named Suwn Zadeh, volunteered, 'What do you want on it — weed? Whatever you want on it, I will put it on. My people are in south London. I'll call them tonight. An eighth will be nice. I'll bring it down.'

Ron was staggered. To think that in outwardly respectable Top Pizza in little old East Finchley, cannabis was being mixed in with the tomato sauce. Ron promptly contacted Gary Jones, who would dress the story with a series of gastronomic puns. PIZZA'S POT TOPPING — PIE GETS YOU HIGH ran the headline. 'Junkie Food' ran a photo caption, while 'Wheeler Dealer' underscored a covert shot of Zadeb using his Cadillac to deliver an order to Ron — our undercover reporter — who had asked for a meal for six. When Ron opened the door, Zadeh produced two large pizzas in return for a relatively modest £20. 'I hope you have a good party with them.' Clearly dedicated to customer satisfaction, he rang up a little later and asked, 'Are your pals out of their heads yet? Let me know what they think of it.'

Another Iranian working at the parlour was quoted as saying, 'We often mix hash in food in our country. You can't get stoned, but you get a nice mellow feeling.' He offered only one warning, and it wasn't about eating the food, 'I don't want any fucking cops here. We've got to be careful.' Alas!

Neither Gary nor Ron could be trusted in that direction. Indeed, Gary ended the piece with his paper's traditional pay-off: The *News of the World* is passing its dossier on the pizza shop to the police.

Three months later Ron was back in print with an investigation into one of the tabloid's all-time favourite subjects: bogus marriages. This story had just come his way. He had done no prior research, and no one at the paper had told him to discover a professional serial bride. He was just in the habit of hanging around a north London junk shop when he got to know a woman customer who did the most dangerous thing anyone can do with Ron: she confided in him!

Theresa Booth, an Irish-born blonde, had a vivaciousness that belied her 51 years. Recognizing in Ron a fellow ducker-and-diver, she poured out tales of her various villainies: her multiple false passports, her connections with the IRA and her prize speciality of marrying immigrants, legal and illegal. For them it meant securing a right of residence and, in time, a British passport. For her it meant easy money: 'I've been married so often that wedding bells sound like a cash register.'

Ron had a word with Gary Jones, and they decided that Ron should tell Theresa that he had a Nigerian friend who needed a British bride. Ron then arranged a meeting in a smart café on his home territory in Hendon for the blushing bigamist, Jones (posing as a British businessman) and fellow reporter Kizzi Nkwocha (his Nigerian partner). Ron was there too. To maintain his cover when the *News of the*

World published the exposé, he would be described as Theresa's 'burly bodyguard'.

Theresa was a muck-raker's dream. She poured out the details of her bigamy business system as if she were making a presentation of Avon cosmetics or Ann Summers sex aids to a bunch of housewives at a hen party. It was this reckless enthusiasm that had first drawn Ron to her.

'Theresa was extraordinary a bit like Sylvia for sheer nerve. I had only just met her when she started telling me how she charged £7000 to £10,000 for a wedding. I told her that was a fortune, but she explained she provided a level of "aftercare" that other bogus brides never did. She would rehearse her grooms for all the Immigration interviews they would have to go through. She would tell them exactly what to say and how to con officials into believing their marriages were genuine. She told me she had been married four times so nothing was ever likely to come up in the interviews which she could not predict. But she had also seen guys come out after a grilling, knowing they'd blown it and would be on the next plane back to Ongobongoland.

'Well, when I introduced her to this reporter, Kizzi Nkwocha, she gazed at him, then really turned on the charm. She said, as he was so good looking, she would charge him a mere £5000, but that would have to be in cash and handed over before the ceremony at the Register Office. After that, she would look after all the official documentation, which was to be sent to her address. The idea was for her home to look as if it was genuinely lived in by Nkwocha so, even if the Immigration guys made a surprise visit, it would look a really cosy inter-racial domestic scene.'

In a master-stroke, the undercover *News of the World* reporters asked Theresa if she had married anyone recently. 'Yes,' she smiled, 'a lovely Algerian boy. He paid me twice what you're paying.' She then explained how he was practically living with her at the moment, so they could study each other's habits before the big Immigration interview. 'I don't just take your money and leave you stranded. I'll stay in touch and make sure you don't have any problems. *After all, bigamy is a crime, and I don't intend to get caught. That's never going to happen* [*News of the World* italics].

Another meeting was set up when Theresa told her Nigerian 'fiancé' that she was trying to get an emergency booking at the Register Office — taking up a cancelled spot — so the officials would have no time to check up on her.

At one more meeting Theresa handed the bogus groom a British driving licence to help him over his citizenship hurdles — in return for £100 in cash. When she caught sight of his gold ring, she exclaimed, 'That's lovely. You can bonk me all night if you give me that ring, and I'll still be able to teach you a thing or two.'

Come the big day, Theresa was driven to Harrow Register Office by her burly bodyguard, Ron Farebrother. She still had no idea that she was the target of a tabloid sting that was elaborate, yet at the same time beautifully simple. It was even the blushing bride who pressed the groom to pose for wedding snaps before the ceremony, to help convince Immigration officials that they had really got married.

Unbeknown to her, the snapper was from the *News of the World*.

Now it was crunch time. She pulled her black groom close and whispered, 'You better get the money now.' Instead he said, 'I don't actually have £5000, but I do have this.' It was his press card. Theresa cursed him. 'You're dead,' she said, before jumping into a getaway car.

It was a perfect *News of the World* sting, complete with before-and-after photos of the bride, first flushed with joy, then puce with rage. But who had fended off the photographers and driven her from her persecutors? None other than her good friend, Ron Farebrother, staunch to the last — or at least until she had poured out her shocked reactions to the ultimate confidence-trickster's nightmare: your photo in the *News of the World*, your nice little earner destroyed, a knock on your door at dawn and the hand of the law on your shoulder. The last prospect must have felt very real when Theresa read all about herself on 10 September 1995. Jones and Nkwocha's final words read, '*We are sending our file on Booth to the Immigration Department*' [*News of the World* italics].

In January 1996 the *News of the World* broke another Ron Farebrother scoop, wholly in the public interest but utterly repellent in its content. At the same north London junk shop where he had met the serial bride, Ron was tipped off about a man who often came in offering artefacts of death. The shop owner, Noel Lynch, had mentioned a man called Tony O'Dwyer.

He's sold me some rings. . . . He's into the

occult, crystal balls and things like that. He likes skulls. The way he's talking, he's well into witchcraft . . . .I've been offered skulls three or four times but I didn't buy them because I thought they must be bent. . . . I told him, 'This isn't right.' I was offered a coffin, too, almost as new. He wanted £100 for it, but it was too big for my shop. . . . The world is full of weird people and I seem to get most of them in my shop.

At this point O'Dwyer himself walked in. He was wearing elaborate rings on every finger. Ron, fighting his revulsion, started talking to him and found he was only too keen to explain the source of the items he was offering to sell. It was the St Pancras and Islington Cemetery, just south of the North Circular Road, close by the junk shop and O'Dwyer's own home. Ron immediately realized that here was a grave-robber whose interest in the cemetery went far beyond mere commerce.

This became overwhelmingly clear when he took Ron on an after-dark trip round the graveyard. The wet and windy weather that night made Ron think he had been thrust into a horror movie and was about to be sacrificed to Count Dracula. O'Dwyer tried to comfort him: 'I've been in here hundreds of times. I know my way around. There's not a lot I don't know about what goes on here.' He boasted of knowing the precise movements of the security guards and their dogs, and then explained how he removed coffins and pillaged their contents. In short, he body-snatched to order. 'The thing is, it is the same as anything. It's the same as if someone wants a Mercedes. Say, it's an order for the 16th, it has to be there.'

In one part of the cemetery there are elaborate vaults, which O'Dwyer was finding particularly productive. According to Ron, he became very excited as he pointed to a tomb that could be entered through an unlocked door.

'That was when this O'Dwyer character offered me the body of a baby and pointed to a tiny little white marble coffin. I was practically vomiting, but I had to keep reasonably cool or we'd never get the story, so I asked, "How am I meant to get this thing out of the place?" He just said, matter of fact, I should stick it in the back of a car. Then he told me not to do any speeding. On no account was I to get pulled by the cops. "This is serious, worse than robbing a bank. If you come in front of a judge, he could throw away the key," so he knew exactly how criminal it all was.' O'Dwyer told a distinctly squeamish Ron that the coffin, with the tiny body inside, was his for a mere £500. A baby is better for black magic, it's so pure and innocent. Ron wasn't all that keen. His reluctance communicated itself to this creepy reincarnation of Burke and Hare.

'I really felt sick at this point, but O'Dwyer was revelling in it. He really was one sick son of a bitch. "Its only a baby coffin. There's nothing to be frightened of," he was saying, but I couldn't go through with it that night, because I didn't have anyone with me from the *News of the World*. I told him I would come back for the body, when it was light (we needed light so we could get some good pictures). So I arranged to meet this beast at ten next morning, when we went back to the poor child's tomb. Now O'Dwyer was almost foaming for the £500. That was when I told him I was doing this for a paper. His knees buckled, and I thought he'd had a heart attack. Mind you, if he'd died, we wouldn't have had to pay for a hearse. He was already at the cemetery!'

Then, as Gary Jones and a photographer sprang from behind vaults and tombstones, Ron told O'Dwyer he had taped him boasting of his traffic in corpses and their adornments. All the palpitating grave-robber could do was claim he had made up the entire story, but this failed to explain his £500 proposition for the baby in the coffin, the cluster of Victorian rings on his fingers or his many funereal offerings to the junk shop. With so much dirt sticking to the body-snatcher, Jones naturally ended the story by saying the newspaper was sending its dossier to the police.

Yet nothing ever happened to O'Dwyer, as Camden Council issued a quick denial that there had been any body-snatching from the cemetery for which it was partly responsible. An official stated: 'We would like to reassure our residents that we have found no evidence of any interference with any of the graves at the cemetery.' When Ron heard of the denial, he headed straight back to the cemetery and took photographs of the tombs that O'Dwyer claimed he had broken into. It was obvious that they had only recently been desecrated, yet Camden was claiming to have noticed nothing. This was, as Ron himself observed, 'a matter of grave concern.'

By now Ron was now widening his field of operations.

Dissatisfied with shopping mere criminals, in March 1996 he delivered an amusing little tale about his old minders, the Regional Crime Squad, having their phones cut off. This crack force is meant to spearhead the police fight against professional criminals, a task made impossible for the unit in Slough when it failed to pay its £1344 phone bill. British Telecom (BT) makes no exceptions: 'I found out about it one day when I was just giving those cops a call. I couldn't get through. It was lucky for them I wasn't tipping them off about some serious crime.'

In April it was BT's turn to suffer the slings and arrows of the ever vigilant Ron. He had found out that one of its engineers was running his own phone-sale business: flogging offsets stolen from BT itself, from the back of his BT van. Gary Jones faithfully chronicled his trusty undercover reporter's taped evidence. Outside Brent Cross tube station the engineer, Tithat Nazir, showed Ron a series of brand-new phones and offered them up at less than half price. When Ron asked about mobiles, Nazir was equally willing to oblige. He was even ready to provide illegal phone lines, which cannot be traced to the customer and never result in any bills: 'If you have some good mates who are discreet, we can get them a line put on. There'll be no bills — if the money's right. Gary Jones added a final swipe: *Perhaps his BT bosses will now take steps permanently to disconnect him* [*News of the World* italics].

Diverse though Ron's exposés had been in the 18 months since his triumphs against Steve Yarrow and his mother for conspiracy and Michael Lewis for kiddie-porn, they all had one thing in common. None was carried out in league with the police. Gone was the intimate collaboration between the *News of the World* and the South East Regional Crime Squad that had brought such remarkable results, from Malcolm Stanfield's wife-killing plot on. That had all been ended by the Panorama story in July 1994 and had never been resumed. Sure, Ron was back in good odour with Scotland Yard, and his relationship with the *News of the World* was flourishing. The big obstacle was a disastrous breakdown in the relationship between the cops and the hacks. The newspaper had fallen out with the Metropolitan Police over a crime-busting story, published in September 1994, when an attempt at collaboration had collapsed with rancour on both sides.

The story had nothing to do with Ron. It was the word of the newspapers chief investigative reporter, Mazher Mahmood, who had gone undercover for two months, posing as a buyer of £500,000 worth of counterfeit Spanish pesetas. When his efforts were nearing completion, the News of the World approached the South East Regional Crime Squad to clear what would obviously be an illegal purchase if not sanctioned by the police as a controlled buy. Agreement was reached, the police monitored the buy, and three conspirators were arrested as they delivered the notes. WE SMASH £100 M FAKE CASH RING — COPS SWOOP ON GANG OF FORGERS ran the headline, as master-forgers Tony Hassan, Anthony Caldori and a confederate were exposed in four and half million copies of the newspaper.

But in July 1995 that triumph turned sour as the trio were acquitted at Isleworth Crown Court because, in the *News of the World*'s own words, the judge refused to allow their trial to go ahead and blamed us. The problem, as Judge Samuel Colgan saw it, was that the original article might prejudice the mind of any jury member, even though it had been published ten months before. He ruled that the *News of the World* was guilty of an abuse of the process of the court.

Both the paper and the police were distraught. One detective was quoted as saying, 'We couldn't believe it when the judge called it off. Your evidence was so damning that no way could these men have escaped prison.' There certainly seems no room for doubt that they were all guilty as charged, for they were caught on sound tape and video discussing their production process in detail and handing over fake notes worth many thousands of pounds. They were also videoed carrying bin-bags of the stuff and offering to supply £500,000 worth of forged pesetas in return for £80,000 in genuine money. With its tail up, the *News of the World* published an editorial headlined JUDGES PRESS GAG IS A CRIME, which claimed it was nonsense to believe that anyone would have retained anything but a superficial impression of the facts unless they had a special interest. Through this decision the judge was effectively saying, 'we must not write about criminal activities, for fear of influencing a possible jury some time in the future. And that is a gross interference with the duty of a free press. It is also an insult to the intelligence of those citizens who take on the responsibility of jury service.'

That might have been the end of the spat, except

that now Scotland Yard officers were asked to look into the affair and decide what contempt, if any, the *News of the World* really had committed. One detective gave me this background interpretation: 'It would have been all right if they'd just taken their medicine and shut up, but instead they slagged the judge off! So he said, "Well, let's look properly at the contempt aspect," and the Attorney-General got involved. He decided it had to be investigated, so statements were taken with a view to the newspaper being done for contempt of court.'

A little unwisely, perhaps, one detective mentioned this inquiry during a phone conversation with Ron. Later he suspected that Ron had pressed the record button on his tape machine and had then played the tape to a chum on the *News of the World*. In July 1996 a tape's existence formed the lead story on the front page of British journalism's trade paper, the *UK Press Gazette*. The magazine also quoted Gary Jones:

> We are under scrutiny. I don't know why . . . We talk very directly to the police and give them co-operation. This officer [on the tape] goes on to complain about the *News of the World* and criticises the paper for acting in what he considers is an unethical way. The *News of the World* is an investigative paper. We don't understand why we are being targeted. Are they saying to us, 'Well, don't bother coming to us in the first place?' One would have thought we were roughly in the same business. They can't expect newspapers to co-operate with them and

at the same time make their life doubly difficult.

What had begun as a run-of-the-mill inquiry into a judge's assertion of a *prima facie* contempt of court was now gaining a distinct edge. Even at the time of the original counterfeiting story, there had been bad feeling, because Scotland Yard had wanted to let the counterfeiters run for a while, in order to bag up the rest of the gang and get to the printing press itself. As one detective explained it to me:

It was on the Friday when the top brass, including Assistant Commissioner Dave Veness, decided to pursue the conspiracy to a higher level and to pull the plug on the planned joint operation with the paper that weekend. So they went to the editors and asked them to delay publication, but they refused to co-operate, saying, 'We've got a deadline and we're going to print the story anyway'. Well, this forced our hand. Obviously we had to arrest the front men for the gang, otherwise they'd run as soon as they read the paper. So we arrested and charged them on the Saturday, and on Sunday the paper did its full-page story, printing the three guys' names, photos and previous convictions (which were wrong anyway). So, inevitably, when they went to court, the defence made an application saying this was an abuse of process, it's in contempt of court. Of course it was, but the *News of the World* has been doing it this way for years and getting away with it.

Matters now seemed to be getting personal. On

26 May 1996 the newspaper ran a story by Mazher Mahmood headlined TOP COPS EVIL SON SELLS DRUGS AND VICE. It concerned Steven Veness, a son of the Assistant Commissioner. A month later this was reproduced on the front page of the *UK Press Gazette* beneath the headline *News of the World* SAYS POLICE ARE INVESTIGATING ITS STAFF.

Ron Farebrother watched this bitter break-up of a special relationship with interest. It extended to two later *News of the World* revelations of low-level corruption in the Metropolitan Police. In August 1996 the newspaper caught a detective constable in the act of taking a bribe from the madam of a brothel in Lewisham. A week later it revealed that two uniformed officers, serving in central London, were selling Ecstasy tablets. All this was a far cry from the days when the *News of the World* and the Regional Crime Squad were bonded like blood brothers, preventing murders and busting one gang of villains after another — all on information from Ron.

So what do the police think of Ron now? I asked one serving detective who has worked with him a lot.

After the mother-and-son murder plot and the kiddie-porn jobs, which were excellent, everything was hunky-dory. He was back on board. And then we get this saga. He's cut himself adrift yet again. We can't be expected to work with him now. It's sad in a way, because these days he seems to be motivated very much by money. As for the *News of the World*, I've had my own run-in with them. They asked for help on a job. I said, 'I'll put it on paper, for clearance from above.' I got clearance. They agreed to do it with us, and then what did they do? They went out next day, did it their own way, and then blew the story out with photographs. You think, well, they're just taking us for mugs.

And what does Ron think?

'I've gone back to my old opinion. When we were working with the RCS, with Roger Hull and Des Cooke, I used to think, "Well, at least some coppers are OK. I can work with these people." But now Roger's retired, and Des has moved on, I'm back to thinking, all coppers are bastards. You just can't work with these guys. You risk your life delivering murderers, drug-traffickers, gun-dealers and pederasts, all tied, bound and ready for jail; you remove them from the streets; and when you do it all over again with a new generation of villains, they try and arrest you instead. Well, I've had enough.

'Some cops have told me that, when this book comes out, "You're dead." They don't mean they'll kill me themselves. They just mean they won't work with me again, and I can't expect any protection. Well, I don't need their protection. I can look after myself — and I'll go on exposing villains and perverts, whatever their game. The newspapers want this stuff, the readers love it, and the public need it. If it wasn't for the scandal sheets — the *News of the Screws* and the rest of the 'gutter press' there'd be a lot more crime about. We've put some pretty big operators out of action, taken a lot of guns off the streets, saved a few lives and locked up a load of perverts. What have most coppers done? Sat on their arses until they got their pensions. There aren't many real thief takers left. And most of them aren't cops. They are thieves like me.

In November 1996 Ron proved his point with two more stories. On the 10th he was the source for yet another tale of guns on the streets. Back in his undercover-reporter role, he had been tipped off that deadly weapons were in store on an East Finchley council estate, Strawberry Vale. Pretending to be a bank robber (well, he hadn't tried to rob a bank for some years!), Ron strode on to the estate and trapped the local heavies into showing him a high-powered MP40 sub-machine-gun, firing at 500 rounds a minute and 'capable of ripping a man in two', as the *News of the World*s Neville Thurlbeck put it. This German army World War II weapon is so dangerous only 30 gun-dealers in Britain are licensed to hold them.

Ron went back a day later and bought the gun for just £100, doing the deal in the same graveyard where he had ensnared the body-snatcher (the St Pancras and Islington Cemetery backs on to the twilight-zone estate). The 20-year-old vendor told Ron: 'It's capable of doing a lot of damage. If you carry this you have no competition.' When he was given the money, he told Ron the gun was hidden behind a row of tombstones. When Ron asked him from where it came, the thug replied, 'You have your gun, now get lost before you get hurt. Don't hang around here. I don't want to see you again.'

Ron brushed the threat aside and took the

weapon over to the photographer who had been secretly snapping the gun-merchant. Thurlbeck was then pictured holding the gun, which the photographer took straight round to Golders Green Police Station. The detective inspector told the *News of the World* boys: 'This was a highly dangerous operation. If these people had sussed you, your lives would have been in great danger.' Even going on the estate was dangerous enough, thought Ron.

The following week Ron was back in the newspaper with a story headlined WE SMASH BANK SCAM PLOT. Through following up small computer advertisements in *Loot*, Ron had tracked down a boffin, known (in the words of crime correspondent Thurlbeck) as 'the Black Professor'. A disgruntled former London University adviser, Melvin Taylor told Ron of a scanner that he had invented that could read bank customers' Personal Identification Numbers (PIN) as they punched them in at cash machines. All you had to do was sit in a van 20 yards from the bank and pick up the PIN signal on a receiver, which then translates back the figures.

Taylor described how these numbers could then be imprinted on fake cash cards and used to empty accounts. For such a device he wanted Ron to cough up £15,000. Ron, who was 'posing as a crook', pretended to be very interested and drew Taylor on to discuss his other breakthrough gismos, including a decoder to pick up satellite television without paying for it, and a sonar stun-gun to knock out horses during races and thereby beat the bookies. It had already worked years ago at Royal Ascot, though only the user of the device was caught, not its inventor Taylor.

GREEDY BOFFIN CALLED TO ACCOUNT
screamed the newspaper, alongside a picture of this
flawed genius.

And what of Ron, the *News of the World*
reporter who was now only posing as a crook?

'Another day, another dollar. But as we tucked
Taylor up, we were all saying, "Why don't we forget
about the story and go into business with this guy?"

'I'm joking of course.'

Of course . . .

In the year 2000 Ron Farebrother is still pumping out
exclusives and front-page leads, not just for the *News
of the World* but also for the *Mirror* and *Sunday
People*. His most distressing exposé came in July
1999. It was about a man who had walked into a
London police station claiming total loss of memory.
Thirty-one-year-old Erez Tivoni was faking a
convincing air of having no idea who he was, when a
BBC documentary team deduced from his mental
droppings that he came from Israel. Sensing a
powerful programme about 'a man coming to terms
with his loss of memory', the BBC then spent many
TV licence fees on flying him and the would-be film-
makers to Tel Aviv. There the good news emerged
that Tivoni had a wife called Etti and two infant
children. The bad news was that they had all gone
into hiding in a hostel for battered wives to escape
from his extreme violence. The BBC crew filmed him
going to court to gain access to his children and then
flew back to London.

Three weeks later Tivoni took advantage of a

reunion with his children to douse them in petrol and set them alight. The daughter died instantly, the son survived for three weeks before he too expired. Tivoni had also been carrying a knife to stab Etti to death but she had not attended the reunion.

Ron first heard about this tragedy from a source within the BBC, close to the documentary team itself. He made some initial checks and then handed his information to the *Sunday People* which ran the story as a front-page lead, with smiling photos of the two tiny tots and quoting Etti in massive headlines: 'BBC KILLED MY BABIES'. Inside she said, 'I thought we were safe but these TV people were taken in by him. I can't understand why they would help a man like this'. The BBC responded by claiming that psychologists and psychiatrists had diagnosed that Tivoni really was suffering from amnesia and 'at no time was the question of Tivoni committing violence raised by these professionals'. What then of the violence which had driven the family to take refuge from him? The road to Hell is paved with good intentions and illuminated by the bletherings of gullible mind-doctors.

Sunday People reporter Mike Jarvis had put together three pages of outstanding investigative journalism but if Ron Farebrother had not acted on a leak from a conscience-stricken whistle-blower, the BBC's role in this tragedy would never have become public. The BBC told the newspaper that it will not be showing its documentary. Since the exposé Tivoni has been given two life sentences in jail.

On 29 November 1998 a picture of Ron himself appeared in the *News of the World* alongside a story about his bigamous wife, Sylvia Barnes. It seemed she had resurfaced. Or had she? It was all very mysterious.

'I was watching a TV show called *The World's Most Wanted* when up came a picture of a woman who looked very much like Sylvia — or as she might look almost ten years since I last set eyes on her. If you allow for the distortion you get from a surveillance camera, it could have been her spitting image, but the programme said the woman was Elaine Parent, wanted in Miami for questioning about the murder of her former flatmate back in July 1990. The victim, Beverley Ann McGowan, had been found in a canal with her head and hands hacked off, and all tattoos cut out from her skin to prevent her being identified.

'I didn't think Sylvia was capable of anything as vicious as that but then it came out that this Elaine Parent was believed to be British and had used a lot of aliases: Elaine Haviland, Antonia Russell, Victoria Dark and Alexis Hart. All those sounded as if they had been drawn from a hat filled with the names of Hollywood stars and soap opera characters, but another one seemed to give the game away: Sylvia Hodgkinson. It wasn't just the Sylvia bit. The surname sounded like some of the identities on those fake passports she had when she was with me, like Rollingson and Atkinson.

'What's more, the dead woman's credit card had been used to buy all sorts of goods in the smartest stores in Miami — just my Sylvia's kind of scam. To cap it all, as Sylvia Hodgkinson, the suspect had flown to Britain and tried to rent a car on the same card. This all sounded too much like the rotten confidence trick that Sylvia Barnes had pulled on the parents of her son's best friend a year before this murder.

'This may all be just a dreadful set of coincidences, as Sylvia spent most of 1990 living with me in what she called "this shit-hole town, Borehamwood", until we flew into Los Angeles in September as Mr and Mrs Atkinson. But she could have slipped off to Miami for a few weeks in the summer, when I thought she'd gone to visit her mother. Who knows? I may be the only alibi she can come up with. How's that for a twist of fate! Me saving her from the electric chair!

'I've told Scotland Yard and the FBI about the close similarity between Sylvia and the murder suspect. I even appeared in the States on *America's Most Wanted*, talking about Sylvia. The interview was done in London and shown coast-to-coast but, despite this massive publicity, Sylvia hasn't come forward and no-one else has turned her in. The last time Miami police had the woman called Elaine Parent in their clutches was May 1991, since when she's also vanished without trace. When reporter Ian Edmondson was writing the *News of the World* story, a Florida detective summed up the fugitive like this: "I imagine she is conning someone right now, perhaps in England. She has a magnetic personality. She is brilliant at what she does".

'That sounds just like Sylvia. The *News of the World* gave the story the headline, MY WIFE IS THE WORLD'S MOST WANTED WOMAN, as if we are still married, but legally we never were. Thank God

Vigilante!

I'm nothing to do with Sylvia any more, but I'd still like to turn her in, dead or alive. I've got a reputation to keep up. After all, I am the Vigilante.

'I'll be in touch soon. Take care.

'Ron.'

ALREADY AVAILABLE FROM

BLAKE'S TRUE CRIME LIBRARY

DEADLIER THAN THE MALE
Ten true stories of women who kill
Wensley Clarkson

NATURAL BORN KILLERS
Britain's eight deadliest murderers tell their own true stories
Kate Kray

IN THE COMPANY OF KILLERS
True-life stories from a two-time murderer
Norman Parker

THE SPANISH CONNECTION
How I smashed an international drugs cartel
John Lightfoot

DOCTORS WHO KILL
Terrifying true stories of the world's most sinister doctors
Wensley Clarkson

DEADLY AFFAIR
The electrifying true story of a deadly love triangle
Nicholas Davies

COMING SOON FROM — BLAKE'S TRUE CRIME LIBRARY

THE FEMALE OF THE SPECIES
True stories of women who kill
Wensley Clarkson

WOMEN IN CHAINS
True stories of women trapped in lives of genuine slavery
Wensley Clarkson

THE MURDER OF RACHEL NICKELL
The truth about the tragic murder on Wimbledon Common
Mike Fielder

CAGED HEAT
What really goes on behinds the bars of women's prisons
Wensley Clarkson

YOU COULD WIN THE AMAZING
SLEUTH'S SILVER DAGGER!

The first twelve titles in Blake's True Crime Library series each contain a question relating to the book. Collect the numbered editions of Blake's True Crime Library, and when you have the answers to all the questions, fill in the form which you will find at the back of the twelfth book and send it to Blake Publishing to be entered into a prize draw.

HERE IS THE SEVENTH QUESTION
What was the name of the pub where Martin first met Ron Farebrother?
The winner will receive the exclusive sleuth's silver dagger and five runners-up will receive three free copies of Blake's True Crime Library titles.

How To Enter
Fill in the answer form contained in the twelfth book in the series and post it to us. If you have won, we will notify you. Whether you are a winner or not, you will still be eligible for a *FREE* True Crime newsletter!

Competition Rules
1.   The 'How to Enter' instructions form part of the rules.
2.   These competitions are not open to any members of Blake Publishing or their families, or Blake Publishing's advertising agents, printers or distributors.
3.   The prizes will be awarded in order of their value, to the senders of the first winning entries after the closing date.
4.   Entries must be on the entry coupon supplied and will not be accepted after the closing date.
5.   No claim is necessary, winners will be notified.
6.   In cases where a manufacturer discontinues a product which has been specified as a prize, Blake Publishing Ltd will substitute the nearest equivalent model of similar or higher value.
7.   The Editor's decision is final, and no correspondence can be entered into.